REEDS
MARINE
DECK

CRAMMER
FOR DECK OFFICER
ORAL EXAMS

REEDS
MARINE
DECK

CRAMMER
FOR DECK OFFICER
ORAL EXAMS

SIMON JINKS

REEDS
LONDON · OXFORD · NEW YORK · NEW DELHI · SYDNEY

REEDS
Bloomsbury Publishing Plc
50 Bedford Square, London, WC1B 3DP, UK
29 Earlsfort Terrace, Dublin 2, Ireland

BLOOMSBURY, REEDS, and the Reeds logo are trademarks of Bloomsbury Publishing Plc

First published in Great Britain 2023
Copyright © Simon Jinks, 2023
Illustrations © Dave Saunders, 2023

Images pp9, 28, 29, 31, 35, 37, 39, 40, 45, 58, 60, 64, 77, 119, 135, 145, 153, 162, 190 © Getty; p25 © Kerri Cuthbert; pp51, 104 © Jinks; p91 © Wikimedia/United States Navy; pp100, 111, 140 © Ocean Safety; pp148, 196 © Adobe Stock

Simon Jinks has asserted his right under the Copyright, Designs and Patents Act, 1988, to be identified as Author of this work

Contains public sector information licensed under the Open Government Licence v3.0

All rights reserved. No part of this publication may be reproduced or transmitted in any form or by any means, electronic or mechanical, including photocopying, recording, or any information storage or retrieval system, without prior permission in writing from the publishers

Bloomsbury Publishing Plc does not have any control over, or responsibility for, any third-party websites referred to or in this book. All internet addresses given in this book were correct at the time of going to press. The author and publisher regret any inconvenience caused if addresses have changed or sites have ceased to exist, but can accept no responsibility for any such changes

This product has been derived in part from material obtained from the UK Hydrographic Office with the permission of the UK Hydrographic Office, His Majesty's Stationery Office.
Pages 166, 167, 187 © British Crown Copyright, 2023. All rights reserved.

THIS PRODUCT IS NOT TO BE USED FOR NAVIGATION
NOTICE: The UK Hydrographic Office (UKHO) and its licensors make no warranties or representations, express or implied, with respect to this product. The UKHO and its licensors have not verified the information within this product or quality assured it.

While all reasonable care has been taken in the publication of this book, the publisher takes no responsibility for the use of the methods or products described in the book

A catalogue record for this book is available from the British Library
Library of Congress Cataloguing-in-Publication data has been applied for

ISBN: PB: 978-1-4729-9108-9; ePub: 978-1-4729-9105-8; ePDF: 978-1-4729-9107-2

10 9 8 7 6 5 4 3 2 1

Typeset in Roboto by Rod Teasdale
Printed and bound in India by Replika Press Pvt Ltd

To find out more about our authors and books visit www.bloomsbury.com and sign up for our newsletters

Excerpts from selected IMO publications are reproduced with the permission of the International Maritime Organization (IMO), which does not accept responsibility for the correctness of the material as reproduced: in case of doubt, IMO's authentic text shall prevail. Readers should check with their national maritime administration for any further amendments or latest advice. International Maritime Organization, 4 Albert Embankment, London, SE1 7SR, United Kingdom

Statement

This book discusses and includes hundreds of laws and regulations and is meant to give the general principles of how they work. Laws and regulations get changed and adapted every day – please ensure you double-check any information in this book for technical accuracy.

This book will get updated from time to time, but even by the time it is updated a change may have occurred. Marine notices and regulatory information and best practice are constantly changing so – whenever a reference is given – don't be surprised if there is a newer version. Please use wisely.

Contents

Introduction   **8**

1 Business and law   9
- UNCLOS   10
- IMO   12
- Shipping legislation   13
- Main conventions   15

2 Vessels and legislation   25
- Guide to UK vessels   26
- Inland waters   27
- Small commercial vessels   29
- Large yachts   31
- Larger shipping   33
- Ship classification   33
- Ship certification   34
- High-speed craft   37

3 General responsibilities of the Master   39
- Considerations prior to arrival   40
- First impressions   40
- Handover   41
- The Master's responsibilities   42

4 Safe working   45
- Responsibilities   46
- Code of Safe Working Practices   47
- Safety Management Systems   48
- Risk assessment   50
- Permit to work   52
- Dangerous spaces   53
- Lifting and work equipment   55
- Hours of work and rest   56
- The 'human element'   57
- Near miss, accident and incident reporting   58

5 Records and logbooks   60
- Official logbook   61
- Other records and logbooks   62
- Continuous synopsis record   63

6 Seaworthiness and seamanship   64
- Safe access and movement   65
- Stability   68

7 Pollution prevention   77
- Oil   80
- Garbage   81
- MARPOL certificates, plans and records   82

8 Emergencies   91
- Drills   92
- Muster list   95
- Life-saving appliances   96
- Fire   97
- Digital distress alerting   99
- MAYDAY   101
- Pyrotechnics   102
- Liferafts   103
- Distress signals   105
- Emergency actions   106
- Man overboard   110
- Piracy   112
- Search and rescue   114

- Emergency preparedness teams 117
- Towage and salvage 118

9 Manoeuvring 119

- Steering 120
- Propellers and rudders 120
- Effects of water pressure 122
- Handling characteristics 124
- Anchoring 129
- Emergency stop 132
- Manoeuvring information regulations 133
- Towing 134

10 Bridge equipment 135

- SOLAS V R19 bridge equipment 136
- Small vessel bridge equipment 138
- Compass requirement 138
- Voyage data recorder 141
- Automatic Identification System (AIS) 142

11 Watchkeeping 145

- Watchkeeping and Master's authority 146
- Bridge induction checklist 147
- Watchkeeping responsibilities 147
- Code flags 151

12 Meteorology 153

- Weather instruments 154
- Scales and terminology 154
- Tropical revolving storms 158
- Fog 159
- Low-pressure systems 160

13 Navigation 162

- Charts and nautical publications 163
- Passage planning 173
- Ships' routeing 175
- Maritime safety information 176
- Lights 176
- IALA buoyage 180
- Terminology 184
- Compass 185
- Techniques 187
- GNSS systems 188
- ECDIS 190
- Radar 190
- Navtex 195
- Sextant 196

Useful measurements 197

Questions and answers 198

Index 220

Sources 223

Endnotes 224

Introduction

This book does not hope to replace the main source data such as the Conventions, Codes, Circulars, M Notices or industry best practice documents as these are where we get the underpinning knowledge in the first place. These documents give the whole picture and not just words in isolation.

What this book hopes to achieve is to give a well-read student or qualified Officer, Mate, Master or Superintendent an aid to remember the key points of major regulation and this, of course, covers the major examination points. This book contains extracts of a lot of the key information from major regulations, put together as a reference or study aid.

Revising for Officer of the Watch (OOW), Mates and Masters exams is hard work. This is especially true when there are just so many reference publications containing the different regulations of SOLAS, STCW and MARPOL and good practice such as Code of Safe Working Practices and Bridge Procedures Guide, that you need to become familiar with.

I have tried to make the remit of this book wide, because there are many safety elements that are the same whether you are going deep sea or staying within a harbour. It therefore contains information on vessels that do not go to sea, small commercial vessels, passenger ships and large tankers. If you are looking for information on large vessels, I suggest you do not concern yourself with the small vessel information. Similarly, if you do not go to sea then you can concentrate on the other elements.

I have decided to use a table format so that the key information is easy to get to and extract. I strongly recommend you use a highlighter pen and make your own notes as this is when the book truly becomes yours.

The exam syllabus for various Mate and Master's exams is printed in M Notices. Cross-referencing your exam syllabus with the tables in this book is a good start to know what subject areas to look at.

When revising for examinations, it is worth working through sections and getting a good understanding of each section. If possible, try to put into practice any of the theoretical parts of the text on your own ship, so that you have something practical to relate it to rather than simply words.

Section 1
Business and law

Business and law is often a candidate's thorn in their side. Often people go to sea to get away from paperwork – unfortunately, running a vessel is full of processes, legislation and regulation. Getting to grips with how the maritime environment is regulated is a real benefit to 'how the system works'.

Importantly, regulation also identifies legal responsibilities of the Owner, Operator, Master, OOW and Seafarer. This business and law section gives an insight into who makes the laws, who enforces them and why.

UNCLOS

UNCLOS seems an unlikely place to start with maritime legislation and it is probably a piece of legislation that most people have never come across. However, it sets out the overarching framework about how our seas are divided up for control by countries (states) and the responsibility of the state to take ownership of these waters and the safety of its vessels and seafarers.

UNCLOS – United Nations Convention on the Law of the Sea	
What is it?	The United Nations is not known for maritime policies and laws. However, UNCLOS is the overarching legal framework of the seas and how those seas are managed. Its aim is 'maintenance of peace, justice and progress for all people of the world'. It establishes the sovereignty and 'legal order of the seas'.
Sample articles	It consists of 320 'Articles' in 17 'Parts' and 9 supporting Annexes, and covers areas such as: • Explanations of juridical sea areas such as territorial sea and contiguous zone • Definition of 'baseline' from where the territorial sea is measured • Rights of innocent and transit passage • Rules applicable to merchant vessels and warships • Jurisdiction within navigational straits and Traffic Separation Schemes • Legal regime in the Exclusive Economic Zone • Legal status of ships on the high seas • Duties imposed on the flag state.
UNCLOS designates the legal juridical sea areas and rights a state has within them. The terms are:	
Baseline	Approximated as the low-water line along a coast. Straight baselines are used to cut across a harbour mouth or river entrance and are usually joined at the seaward extent of the low-water line.
Internal waters	These are waters to landward of the baseline. Often consisting of rivers, estuaries, ports, canals and lakes. A state can apply and enforce all of its laws in internal waters.
Territorial sea	This is 12 nautical miles (NM) measured 'to sea' from the baseline. When two states are opposite each other and territorial waters overlap, they will be equidistant or conform to whatever legal treaty those states already have in place. A state has all rights of sovereignty and can exercise its law within its territorial sea. However, vessels have a right of innocent passage through a state's territorial sea.
Contiguous zone	This extends up to 24NM from the baseline. A coastal state may exercise the control necessary to prevent infringement of its customs, fiscal, immigration or sanitary laws and regulations within its territory or territorial sea. Often a country will only use their territorial waters and Exclusive Economic Zone.
Exclusive Economic Zone	This extends 200NM from the baseline and the coastal state has sovereign rights for the purpose of exploring and exploiting, conserving and managing the natural resources. It can also exploit resources such as oil, wind and water power.
List	A list of juridical sea areas is published annually in the *Annual Summary of Admiralty Notices to Mariners Part 1* (NP247)(1).

SECTION 1

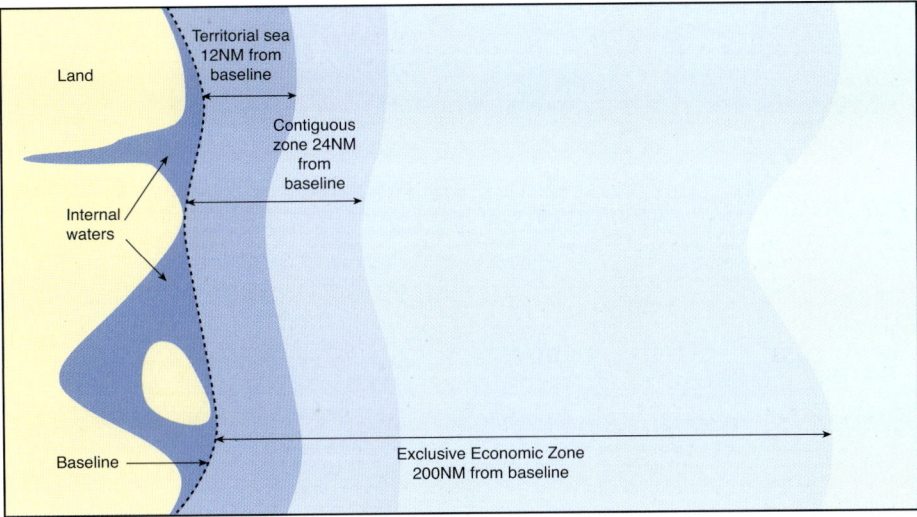

▲ Juridical sea areas measured from the baseline

Because UNCLOS identifies the juridical sea areas, it imposes a responsibility on the state to manage those areas effectively, this includes regulating ships flying the flag of the state and how to act when vessels of other flag states enter these waters.

Flag state

UNCLOS states: 'The sovereignty of a coastal State extends beyond its land territory and internal waters to an adjacent belt of sea, described as the territorial sea.' It goes on to say: 'Every State shall effectively exercise its jurisdiction and control in administrative, technical and social matters over ships flying its flag.' This therefore gives definition to the term 'flag state'. A flag state has responsibilities, in particular every state shall:

Flag state responsibilities	Maintain a register of ships flying its flag, except those excluded from international regulations on account of their small size. Assume law over each ship flying its flag and its Master, officers and crew in respect of the ship.
The flag state will ensure safety at sea with regard to:	(a) the construction, equipment and seaworthiness of ships; (b) manning of ships; (c) the use of signals, communications and prevention of collisions; (d) ensuring inspected vessels have on board charts, nautical publications and navigational equipment and instruments as appropriate; (e) ensuring the Master, officers and the crew are conversant with international regulations concerning the safety of life at sea, prevention of collisions, prevention, reduction and control of marine pollution, and the maintenance of communications by radio; (f) ensuring vessels visiting its ports conform to international regulation; (Port State Control) (g) Ensuring an enquiry is held on marine incidents or casualties.
Maritime and Coastguard Agency (MCA) and Department for Transport (DfT)	Laws, either national or international, go through Parliament and, when passed, are then implemented by various UK government departments. For most maritime applications this is via the Maritime and Coastguard Agency (MCA) as it is an Executive Agency of the Department for Transport (DfT). The MCA therefore takes the role as the UK Flag State Administration.

11

IMO

IMO regulation applies to ships differently, depending on their size, whether they are travelling internationally and what type of operation they are doing. For instance, the Collision Regulations (ColRegs) apply to all vessels, whereas parts of MARPOL only apply to vessels over 400GT and SOLAS states only vessels over 300GT need to carry an AIS. However, IMO regulation provides the overriding principles of maritime safety.

International Maritime Organization (IMO)	
Remit	The IMO is a specialised agency of the United Nations. Its remit is safety and security of international shipping and the prevention of pollution by ships. It does this through representation of its 'member states', of which there are approximately 170, who form the IMO's 'Assembly'.
Committees	The main technical work is carried out by committees covering Maritime Safety, Marine Environment Protection, Legal, Technical Co-operation and Facilitation, to name but a few. Decisions made by the Assembly and the Committees form regulation and are ratified by member states. The main regulations come in the form of 'conventions', which have been adopted by the member states.
Conventions covering all ships (there are others)	**SOLAS** – Safety Of Life At Sea **IRPCS** – International Regulations for the Prevention of Collisions at Sea **ILLC** – International Load Line Convention **STCW** – Standards of Training, Certification and Watchkeeping **MARPOL** – International Convention for the Prevention of Pollution from Ships **TONNAGE** – International Convention on Tonnage Measurement of Ships **FAL** – Convention on Facilitation of International Maritime Traffic **SALVAGE** – International Convention on Salvage **SAR** – International Convention on Search and Rescue **AFS** – International Convention on the Control of Harmful Anti-fouling Systems on Ships.
Other specialist agencies	The **IMO** is just one of many specialist agencies that work with the UN. Others that have a direct relationship to the maritime sector are: **ILO** (International Labour Organization) **ITU** (International Telecommunications Union) **WHO** (World Health Organization) **WMO** (World Meteorological Organization) **IMF** (International Monetary Fund).

It is not just the International Maritime Organization that has a say in maritime regulation, there are many other legislators. Importantly for the mariner, it really comes down to ensuring that we know what rules apply to us. The MCA's way of communicating is through M Notices, which are downloadable off the internet (see page 14).

Shipping legislation

Maritime Law Structure

United Nations Convention on the Law of the Sea (UNCLOS)

International Maritime Organization (IMO)
International Labour Organization (ILO)
Regulation by 'CONVENTIONS'
SOLAS MARPOL STCW IRPCS ILLC MLC
Or UK Domestic law or retained EU legislation

GOVERNMENT and FLAG STATE
UK Flag – MCA
Regulations and guidance by
Merchant Shipping Act 1995
Statutory Instruments, M Notices (MSN – MGN – MIN)

Owner
Seafarer

LOCAL or PORT AUTHORITY
Acts, byelaws or best practice

▲ Overview of a simplified maritime law structure

Legislation	
Overview	Legislation is influenced by various organisations, some global some local. Legislation differs between vessel sectors such as: vessels of a certain size, those that are travelling to other states, those that are working inland or carrying particular cargoes.
Legislators	International Maritime Organization (IMO) International Labour Organization (ILO) European Union directives, which have been integrated into UK law National (UK) legislation such as Maritime and Coastguard Agency (MCA) Harbours through Acts and byelaws.
UK	The MCA is responsible for implementing the UK government's maritime safety policy on behalf of the Department for Transport (DfT). Other countries have similar arrangements. The overarching legislation is the Merchant Shipping Act (MSA)(1995), which covers many general areas. Under the MSA there are many Merchant Shipping Regulations that detail requirements on particular subjects.
Statutory Instruments	UK legislation is made up of Acts of Parliament (primary legislation) and Statutory Instruments (secondary legislation). Acts of Parliament are the highest level of law and often grant power to government ministers to create more detailed regulations called Statutory Instruments (SIs). Most UK legislation is in the form of SIs. Many maritime SIs have supporting documentation in the form of Marine Notices and 'Codes of Practice' and the MCA uses these to provide shipping and fishing industries with details of regulation, guidance and information.

M Notice Type

Merchant Shipping Notice (MSN)
- mandatory guidance on legislation
- to be complied with when enforced by an SI

Marine Guidance Notes (MGN)
- guidance and interpretation of law
- best practice
- general safety advice

Marine Information Notes (MIN)
- targeted to a specific audience/small group
- give time-limited information and expiry date

Codes of Practice
- Some codes give best practice
- Others are a code based on an MSN and underpinned by an SI

Example

MSN 1893: Carriage of dangerous goods, packaged marine pollutants

MSN 545 Transportation of dangerous goods (marine)

MIN 516 Amendment: International Maritime Solid Bulk Cargoes Code

Code of Safe Working Practices (COSWP)

The Workboat Code Edition 2 (MSN 1892)

▲ Examples of types of Marine Notices (M Notices) and Codes, as distributed by the MCA

Marine Notices (M Notices)	In the UK, M Notices are the method that the MCA communicates with shipowners, operators, surveyors, Masters, engineers and seafarers. They publicise to the shipping industry important safety, pollution prevention and other relevant information.
Merchant Shipping Notices (MSN)	Contain details of UK law, regulation and are legally enforceable when referred to by a Statutory Instrument.
Marine Guidance Notes (MGN)	Give guidance, recommendations, and best practice to industry on the interpretation of law and regulation.
Marine Information Notes (MIN)	Provide less important time-limited information, often to specific sectors. They have an expiry date.
M, F or MF	M Notices have either an (M) (F) or (M+F) after the number to indicate their reference to a particular industry sector: M = Merchant, F = Fishing, M+F = Merchant and Fishing
Local regulation	Local harbour authorities and councils also issue laws, acts and guidance, which need to be complied with when inside their port jurisdiction. These often give useful information such as speed limits, where a narrow channel starts, or modifications to ColRegs/IRPCS when in that area.

SECTION 1

Main conventions

There are many conventions and codes from the IMO, some generic and some very specific. We have concentrated on the generic ones here, so if you are operating in polar regions there is a book for you.

SOLAS: International Convention for the Safety of Life at Sea 1974, as amended

The first version was adopted in 1914 in response to the sinking of the RMS *Titanic*. It has 14 chapters on specific subjects. Often the scope of a chapter requires an accompanying 'code' to be produced to provide greater depth. These 'codes' are mandated under the SOLAS convention. For example, SOLAS Chapter III Life-Saving Appliances is supplemented by the Life-Saving Appliance Code.

Application does not apply to:	• Ships of war and troopships • Cargo ships of less than 500GT • Ships not propelled by mechanical means • Wooden ships of primitive build • Pleasure yachts not engaged in trade • Fishing vessels, unless expressly stated otherwise. Therefore, while it is mainly for larger shipping, there are some chapters that can apply to all vessels by national prescription – such as Chapter V.

Chapter	Accompanying code
I – General provisions	International Code for the Investigation of Marine Casualties.
II-1 – Construction – Subdivision and stability, machinery and electrical installations	International Intact Stability Code (IS Code 2008).
II-2 – Fire prevention, fire detection and fire extinction	International Code for Application of Fire Test Procedures (FTP Code). International Code for Fire Safety Systems (FSS Code).
III – Life-saving appliances and arrangements	International Life-saving Appliance Code (LSA Code).
IV – Radio communications	Radio Regulations of the International Telecommunication Union.
V – Safety of Navigation	
VI – Carriage of Cargoes	International Maritime Code for Solid Bulk Cargoes (IMSBC Code). International Code of Safe Practice for Cargo Stowage and Securing Code of Safe Practice for Ships Carrying Timber Deck Cargoes. International Code for the Safe Carriage of Grain in Bulk.
VII – Carriage of dangerous goods	International Maritime Dangerous Goods Code (IMDG Code). International Code for the Construction and Equipment of Ships Carrying Liquefied Gases in Bulk (IGC Code). International Code for the Construction and Equipment of Ships Carrying Dangerous Chemicals in Bulk (IBC Code).

VIII – Nuclear ships	Code for the Safe Carriage of Irradiated Nuclear Fuel, Plutonium and High-Level Radioactive Wastes in Flasks on board Ships (INF Code).
IX – Management for the Safe Operation of Ships	International Safety Management Code (ISM Code).
X – Safety measures for high-speed craft	International Code for the Safety of High-Speed Craft (HSC Code 1994 or 2000).
XI-1 – Special measures to enhance maritime safety	
XI-2 – Special measures to strengthen shipping security	International Ship and Port Facility Security Code (ISPS Code).
XII – Additional security measures for bulk carriers	
XIII – Verification of compliance	
XIV – Safety measures for ships operating in polar waters	International Code for Ships Operating in Polar Waters (Polar Code).
Note: While the codes above have been matched to a particular SOLAS chapter, there are crossovers throughout the chapters and codes. For example, the ISM code will in effect cover all chapters in some way.	

SOLAS Chapter V has specific relevance to deck and bridge areas as it covers safety of navigation. It could be argued that the first 18 sections are of more relevance to administrations (flag) rather than the vessel. From 19 onwards, this has more bearing on the vessel's equipment, checks to be made and the actions of the seafarers, especially the Master.

SOLAS V (included specifically as it mainly applies to all ships on all voyages)

Reg	Regulations within SOLAS Chapter V
1	Application
2	Definitions
3	Exemptions and equivalents
4	Navigational warnings
5	Meteorological services and warnings
6	Ice patrol service

SECTION 1

BUSINESS AND LAW

7	Search and rescue services
8	Life-saving signals
9	Hydrographic services
10	Ships' routeing
11	Ship Reporting Systems
12	Vessel Traffic Services
13	Establishment and operation of aids to navigation
14	Ships' manning
15	Principles relating to bridge design, design and arrangement of navigational systems and equipment and bridge procedures
16	Maintenance of equipment
17	Electromagnetic compatibility
18	Approval, surveys and performance standards of navigational systems and equipment and voyage data recorder
19	Carriage requirements for shipborne navigational systems and equipment
19/1	Long range identification and tracking of ships
20	Voyage data recorders
21	International Code of Signals and IAMSAR Manual
22	Navigation bridge visibility
23	Pilot transfer arrangements
24	Use of heading and/or track control systems
25	Operation of main source of electrical power and steering gear
26	Steering gear: testing and drills
27	Nautical charts and nautical publications
28	Records of navigational activities and daily reporting
29	Life-saving signals to be used by ships, aircraft or persons in distress
30	Operational limitations
31	Danger messages
32	Information required in danger messages
33	Distress situations: obligations and procedures
34	Safe navigation and avoidance of dangerous situations
34/1	Master's discretion
35	Misuse of distress signals

STCW

The STCW Convention & Code establishes international requirements on training, certification and watchkeeping for seafarers on an international level. It includes the syllabi for STCW courses and Chapter VIII contains important information on watchkeeping arrangements for the bridge, engine room and deck.

STCW: International Convention on Standards of Training, Certification and Watchkeeping for Seafarers	
STCW Code is in 2 parts	Part A (mandatory requirements) Part B (guidance on Part A)
STCW Convention & Code chapters	
Chapter I	General provisions
Chapter II	Master and deck department
Chapter III	Engine department
Chapter IV	Radiocommunication and radio operators
Chapter V	Special training requirements for personnel on certain types of ships
Chapter VI	Emergency, occupational safety, security, medical care and survival functions
Chapter VII	Alternative certification
Chapter VIII	Watchkeeping
Chapter VIII contains information about how a bridge and engine room is manned, run and operated.	
Part 1	Certification
Part 2	Voyage planning
Part 3	Watchkeeping at sea
3-1	Principles to be observed in keeping a navigational watch
3-2	Principles to be observed in keeping an engineering watch
3-3	Principles to be observed in keeping a radio watch
Part 4	Watchkeeping in port
4-1	Taking over the deck watch
4-2	Taking over the engineering watch
4-3	Performing the deck watch
4-4	Performing the engineering watch
4-5	Watch in port on ships carrying hazardous cargo

Prevention of marine pollution

MARPOL: International Convention for the Prevention of Pollution from Ships	
Prevention of pollution of the marine environment by ships from operational or accidental causes.	
Annex I	Regulations for the prevention of pollution by oil
Annex II	Regulations for the control of pollution by noxious liquid substances in bulk
Annex III	Regulations for the prevention of pollution by harmful substances carried by sea in packaged form
Annex IV	Regulations for the prevention of pollution by sewage from ships
Annex V	Regulations for the prevention of pollution by garbage from ships
Annex VI	Regulations for the prevention of air pollution from ships

Other conventions relating to prevention of marine pollution (non-MARPOL)	
Dumping of wastes and other matter	Convention on the Prevention of Marine Pollution by Dumping of Wastes and Other Matter, 1972
Pollution from bunkers	International Convention on Civil Liability for Bunker Oil Pollution Damage, 2001
OPRC	International Convention on Oil Pollution Preparedness, Response and Co-operation (OPRC), 1990
OPRC-HNS Protocol	Protocol on Preparedness, Response and Co-operation to pollution Incidents by Hazardous and Noxious Substances, 2000
Anti-fouling Systems	International Convention on the Control of Harmful Anti-fouling Systems on Ships (AFS), 2001
Ships' Ballast Water and Sediments	International Convention for the Control and Management of Ships' Ballast Water and Sediments, 2004
Recycling of Ships	The Hong Kong International Convention for the Safe and Environmentally Sound Recycling of Ships, 2009
INTERVENTION	International Convention Relating to Intervention on the High Seas in Cases of Oil Pollution Casualties (INTERVENTION), 1969

Maritime Labour Convention

The Maritime Labour Convention (MLC) is a relative newcomer to maritime regulation. In fact, many items covered in the MLC were already regulated. However, the MLC neatly wraps many labour regulations into one rule book.

Maritime Labour Convention, 2006

The MLC consolidates and updates 60 international maritime labour regulations into one convention.

Title 1	**Minimum requirements for seafarers to work on a ship**
Regulation 1.1	Minimum age
Regulation 1.2	Medical certificate
Regulation 1.3	Training and qualifications
Regulation 1.4	Recruitment and placement
Title 2	**Conditions of employment**
Regulation 2.1	Seafarers' employment agreements
Regulation 2.2	Wages
Regulation 2.3	Hours of work and hours of rest
Regulation 2.4	Entitlement to leave
Regulation 2.5	Repatriation
Regulation 2.6	Seafarer compensation for the ship's loss or foundering
Regulation 2.7	Manning levels
Regulation 2.8	Career and skill development and opportunities for seafarers' employment
Title 3	**Accommodation, recreational facilities, food and catering**
Regulation 3.1	Accommodation and recreational facilities
Regulation 3.2	Food and catering
Title 4	**Health protection, medical care, welfare and social security protection**
Regulation 4.1	Medical care on board ship and ashore
Regulation 4.2	Shipowners' liability
Regulation 4.3	Health and safety protection and accident prevention
Regulation 4.4	Access to shore-based welfare facilities
Regulation 4.5	Social security
Title 5	**Compliance and enforcement**
Regulation 5.1	Flag State responsibilities
Regulation 5.1.1	General principles
Regulation 5.1.2	Authorisation of recognised organizations
Regulation 5.1.3	Maritime labour certificate and declaration of maritime labour compliance
Regulation 5.1.4	Inspection and enforcement

Regulation 5.1.5	On-board complaint procedures
Regulation 5.1.6	Marine casualties
Regulation 5.2	Port State responsibilities
Regulation 5.2.1	Inspections in port
Regulation 5.2.2	Onshore seafarer complaint-handling procedures
Regulation 5.3	Labour-supplying responsibilities
Scope of Inspections	<ul><li>Minimum age</li><li>Medical certification</li><li>Qualification of seafarers</li><li>Seafarers' employment agreements</li><li>Use of any licensed or certified or regulated private recruitment and placement service</li><li>Hours of work and rest</li><li>Manning levels for the ship</li><li>Accommodation</li><li>On-board recreational facilities</li><li>Food and catering</li><li>Health and safety and accident prevention</li><li>On-board medical care</li><li>On-board complaint procedures</li><li>Payment of wages</li><li>Financial security for repatriation</li><li>Financial security relating to shipowners' liability</li></ul>
Certification	Ships over 500GT and operating internationally require certification: MLC Certificate, DMLC Parts 1 & 2 Certificates. Commercial vessels under 500GT may require inspection.
Validity	Initial, intermediate between 2nd and 3rd years and renewal at 5 years.

Provision is made in the MLC for 'substantial equivalence' where it is not practical to comply with the full MLC standards set out in part A of the MLC Code – this is true when looking at applying the MLC to small vessels.

Application of MLC inspection on small vessels (MGN 600)

	Pleasure vessel	Small vessel (coded)	Small vessel (non-coded)	Large workboat less than 500GT	Registered fishing vessel	Ship of traditional build	Warship	Naval auxiliary
UK inland waters	✗	✗	✗	✗	✗	✗	✗	✗
UK vessel on domestic voyage no more than 60NM from a UK safe haven	✗	✗	✗	✗	✗	✗	✗	✗
UK vessel on a domestic voyage operating more than 60NM from a UK safe haven	✗	✓	✓	✓	✗	✗	✗	✗
UK vessel on international voyage	✗	✓	✓	✓	✗	✗	✗	✗
Non-UK vessel operating in the UK	✗	✓	✓	✓	✗	✗	✗	✗

Seafarer Employment Agreement (SEA) is a requirement under MLC (MGN 477) as amended

	PART 1 – Provisions to be included in all agreements
1	The full name, birthplace and date of birth (or age) of the seafarer.
2	The name and address of the shipowner.
3	The place where the agreement is entered into.
4	The date on which the agreement is entered into.
5	The capacity in which the seafarer is to work.
6	If the agreement has been made for a definite period, the termination date.
7	If the agreement has been made for an indefinite period, the period of notice of termination required and the circumstances in which such notice may be given.
8	If the agreement has been made for a particular voyage, the destination port and the period following arrival after which the agreement terminates.
9	The health and social security benefits provided to the seafarer by the shipowner.
10	The maximum period of service on board following which the seafarer is entitled to repatriation.
11	The seafarer's entitlement to repatriation (including the mode of transport and destination of repatriation) and the circumstances in which the seafarer is required to meet or reimburse the shipowner for the costs of repatriation.
12	The maximum compensation the shipowner will pay the seafarer in respect of any loss of personal property arising from the loss or foundering of the ship.
13	Details of any collective bargaining agreement which is incorporated (in whole or part) into the agreement or is otherwise relevant to it.
	PART 2 – Provisions to be included where seafarer is an employee
1	The wages (either the amount or the formula to be used in determining them).
2	The manner in which wages must be paid, including payment dates and the circumstances (if any) in which wages may or must be paid in a different currency.
3	The hours of work.
4	The paid leave (either the amount or the formula to be used in determining it).
5	Any pension benefits to be provided to the seafarer, including any entitlement to participate in a pension scheme.
6	The grievance and disciplinary procedures.
	PART 3 – Provision to be included where seafarer is not an employee
1	The remuneration (either the amount or the formula to be used in determining it).
2	The manner in which the remuneration must be paid, including payment dates.

SECTION 1

Seafarers Employment Agreements and Lists of Crew

Duty of Master to produce SEA when asked by	- The Secretary of State - The Registrar General of Shipping and Seamen - The Commissioners for Her Majesty's Revenue and Customs - Any person authorised by or acting on behalf of the above - Flag state or port state inspectors.
Copies	The shipowner and crewmember must have copies. The Master must have a copy on board to satisfy the above.
Signed by	The seafarer and the shipowner (or authorised signatory).
Record of employment	The shipowner must provide the seafarer with a record of their employment on board the ship. This could be in the Seafarers Discharge book or a Certificate of Discharge. It should include: i. name of the ship, port of registry, gross or registered tonnage and official number, ii. description of the voyage, iii. capacity in which the seaman has been employed on the ship, iv. date on which the seafarer began to be so employed, v. date and place of the seafarer's discharge.
List of crew	Still a requirement for 'a list of crew' to be maintained and kept up to date showing all seafarers on board a vessel at any time.
Registry of shipping	There is no requirement to send SEAs to the registry of shipping, however, lists of crew and official logbooks should be sent to them at the specified intervals (often 12 months).

Retention of Crew Agreements for vessels not subject to MLC & SEAs (MGN 474) as amended

Applicable on vessels not subject to MLC; e.g. fishing vessels, ships of traditional build, naval auxiliaries, pleasure vessels and vessels which are not ordinarily engaged in commercial activities.

Legislation	The provisions of the Merchant Shipping (Crew Agreements, Lists of Crew and Discharge of Seamen) Regulations 1991 (SI 1991/2144) continue to remain in force.
Specific example	Pleasure vessel where Owners employ their Master & Crew privately. They may wish to use SEAs or could use a Crew Agreement.
Required documentation (examples in MGN 474)	ALC 1(a) – List of Crew and Signatures of Seamen Who Are Parties to the Crew Agreement. ALC 1(b) – List of Crew Relating to Seamen Exempted Under Section 25(5) of the Merchant Shipping Act, 1995, from the Requirement to Sign a Crew Agreement. ALC 1(c) – List of Young Persons. ALC 1(d) – Contractual Clauses. ALC 6 – Copy of the Crew Agreement (posted on Notice Board).

BUSINESS AND LAW

When the MLC was introduced, this led to the adoption of the so-called four pillars of maritime safety: SOLAS, MARPOL, STCW and MLC.

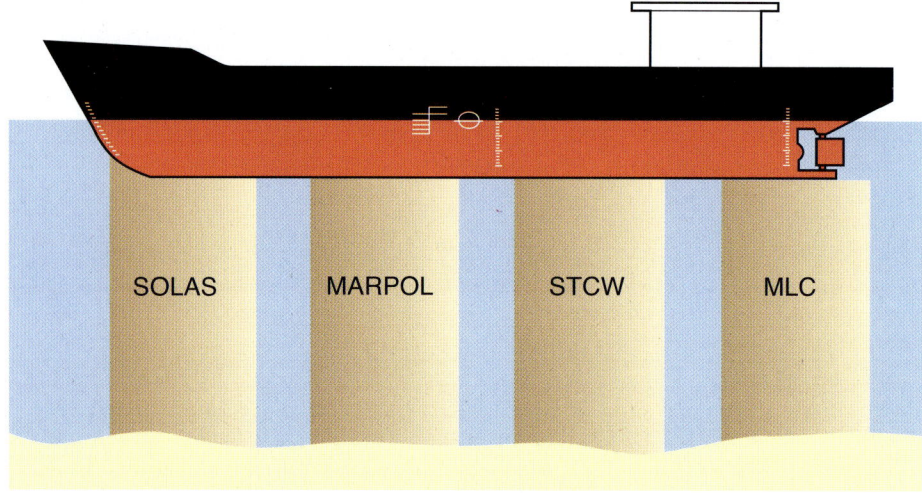

▲ The key elements underpinning safety in the maritime world. However, it is the Master, implementing a good safety culture on board, who should have the greatest influence implementing these regulations and others.

Section 2
Vessels and legislation

There are a multitude of vessel types operating on the water. Each type of vessel will be governed by similar, but often slightly differing, regulation and best practice.

To both the initiated and the uninitiated it is a confusing bundle of legislation, especially between large vessels operating under class rules and small vessels operating under code.

The best advice is to know the types and classes of vessels that you operate and their regulation. Then look at one or two other classes that are close to your type of vessel.

Guide to UK vessels

There are different regulations that influence the build and equipment specifications of vessels:
- Size
- Operating nationally or internationally
- Operating at sea or in inland waters
- Whether they are passenger vessels – taking more than 12 passengers.

Rough guide to UK vessels

Size	Examples	Legislation	Levels	Legislator
Under 24m recreational (no more than 12 passengers)	Yachts, motorboats, RIBs	Recreational Craft Directive Class XII (over 13.7m)	Built for: A ocean B offshore C inshore D sheltered waters	EU Directive MCA
Under 24m commercial that go to sea (no more than 12 passengers)	Dive and fishing charter. Workboats, tugs, sail training charter and multicats	Small commercial vessel codes blue, yellow, brown, red. MGN 280, Workboat Code Ed 2/3	Categories: 0 – unlimited 1 – up to 150NM 2 – up to 60NM 3 – up to 20NM 4 – 20NM by day 5 – 3NM by night 6 – 3NM by day	Certifying Authority MCA/Flag
Inland commercial 'do not go to sea' (no more than 12 passengers)	Workboats, tugs, tankers, small passenger boats (less than 12 passengers)	MGN 469 Inland Waters Small Passenger Boat Code Class IX(A) & IX(A)(T) Local harbour rules	Cannot go to sea Category of inland water: A – canal – depth less than 1.5m B – river – depth more than 1.5m/ wave no more than 0.6m C – tidal river/ estuary. Wave no more than 1.2m. D – tidal river/ estuary greater wave height. Wave no more than 2m	Local Authority MCA/Flag
Inland commercial passenger (over 12 passengers) 'do not go to sea'	River and port passenger boats, harbour or river cruises and ferries	MSN 1823 Built under Class rules to international convention (SOLAS/ MARPOL) Class IV or V		Classification society MCA/Flag
Large yacht over 24m	Super yachts mega yachts, large charter boats	Built under Class rules to large yacht codes. Large Yacht code LY2/3 Red Ensign Group (REG) Code	Short range (up to 60NM) or normal (worldwide). Normally up to 12 passengers. REG code allows more passengers	Classification society MCA/Flag
Seagoing merchant vessels over 24m	Tankers, freight, car carriers, seagoing large tugs, support vessels	Built under Class rules to international convention (SOLAS/ MARPOL) Class VII, VIII, IX	Inshore/domestic Short international voyage Long international voyage	Classification society MCA/Flag

SECTION 2

Seagoing passenger vessels	Ferries, cruise liners, RoRo, seagoing passenger boats	Built under Class rules to international convention (SOLAS/MARPOL). Class I, II, III and VI Small Seagoing Passenger Ships Code, <24m <250 passengers, 5/15 PoRefuge	Inshore/domestic Short international voyage Long international voyage	Classification society MCA/Flag

Inland waters

Inland waters in the UK are commonly canals, lakes, lochs, rivers and harbours up to the harbour mouth. They also cover large bodies of protected water such as the Solent and the Clyde. As these areas are sheltered it allows a considered level of safety to be applied in these areas.

UK inland waters

Many regulations start when a vessel goes 'to sea'. However, there are 'Categories' of waters inland of the 'at sea' line (see MSN 1837, as amended). These are categorised as 'inland waters' and affect vessels that do not go 'to sea', such as inland waters passenger boats, including harbour ferries and cruisers, harbour tugs and workboats.
They can carry certification to only operate in inland categorised waters and this affects the construction, stability, safety, manning and certification of the vessel.
These inland waters categories do not affect seagoing vessels, which can ply their trade at sea and visit inland waters and ports.

Definitions of the four types of categorised waters. In the UK these are categorised alphabetically, in the EU they are categorised numerically by zone.

UK inland water categories	Description	EU inland water zone
Category A	Narrow rivers and canals where the depth of water is generally less than 1.5 metres.	Zone 4 uncategorised
Category B	Wider rivers and canals where the depth of water is generally 1.5 metres or more and where the significant wave height could not be expected to exceed 0.6m at any time.	Zone 3 Wave height of up to 0.6m
Category C	Tidal rivers and estuaries and large, deep lakes and lochs where the significant wave height could not be expected to exceed 1.2 metres at any time.	Zone 2 Wave height of up to 1.2m
Category D	Tidal rivers and estuaries where the significant wave height could not be expected to exceed 2.0m at any time.	Zone 1 Wave height of up to 2m
The UK categorisations apply all times of the year unless indicated summer or winter		
Summer	April to October, inclusive	
Winter	November to March, inclusive	

VESSELS AND LEGISLATION

Example: from MSN 1837 Categorisation of waters		
Location	Category A, B or C	Category D
River Mersey	Category B The docks (excluding Seaforth Dock) Category C Within a line between the Rock Lighthouse and the North West Seaforth Dock	None in winter In the summer within a line from Formby Point to Point of Air

Inland waters vessels are often harbour tugs and workboats, or inland waters passenger boats and ferries operating within that area of inland water. Importantly, they are limited to those waters and cannot go 'to sea'.

Types of inland waters vessels

Class IX (A) or (T)	Workboats
Local licence boats	Workboats and small passenger boats (up to 12 passengers) ▶ Class IX(A) vessels such as small workboats that do not go to sea
Certification and inspection	Inland waters workboats and Class IX(A) vessels come under different certification and inspection regimes, depending on the local authority and byelaws. Section 94 of the Public Health Acts Amendment Act 1907 gives power to local authorities to license these vessels. It can range from yearly inspections and certification, for instance the Thames Freight Standard and South West Regional Ports Association requires annual survey, to purely owner-led inspections and little certification.
Class IV	**Passenger boats operating in A, B, C, D waters**
Class V	Passenger boats operating in A, B, C waters ▶ Class V passenger vessel – restricted to Category C inland waters and a max wave height of 1.2m.
Certification and inspection	
Classification societies	It is normal for classification societies to oversee the build and to issue the initial sign off to show the vessel complies with minimum safety construction standards.
UK authorised classification societies	• American Bureau of Shipping • Bureau Veritas • Det Norske Veritas • Germanischer Lloyd • Lloyd's Register of Shipping • Nippon Kaiji Kyokai • Registro Italiano Navale
Partial declaration of survey	Issued by the classification society under which the vessel is built, this verifies the hull construction, machinery, control systems, electrical arrangements and bilge pumping systems are in accordance with recognised class standards.
Declaration of survey	Provided by the MCA surveyor when they are content that the ship complies with all relevant requirements. Allows a Passenger Ship Safety Certificate (PSSC) to be issued.

SECTION 2

Passenger Ship Safety Certificate (PSSC or PC)	Records the vessels details, its operating area, maximum passengers and minimum crew, validity and endorsement for annual surveys.
Supplementary record	Comes attached to the Passenger Ship Safety Certificate and records all details of the vessel, including freeboard markings, where passengers can be located (on deck and in cabins), required qualifications of Master and crew, lists of LSA and FFA, navigation equipment and machinery.
Domestic Safety Management Certificate (DSMC)	The DSMC is a required certificate to ensure safe management of the vessel. The DSMC would be inspected before the vessel was put in use to ensure that systems were in place to ensure safe operation, management, maintenance, and standard and emergency procedures were in place. If the vessel is under ISM for any reason, it would need DOC and SMS certification.
Passenger Counting Certificate (PCC)	This certificate is required to ensure that the company and vessel have an adequate way of recording and updating the numbers of persons on board at any one time for search and rescue. It must be approved by the MCA/Flag.

Small commercial vessels

Small commercial vessels that go 'to sea' are a very large part of the UK commercial fleet. They incorporate workboats, tugs, charter fishing and diving, sail training and small fast craft (RIBs). Because they are under 24m, much of the IMO type regulation does not fit well with them, therefore the MCA has introduced small vessel 'coded', which are based on a range and risk basis and apply levels of safety and manning dependent on how far the craft travels.

▶ Small commercial vessels include crew transfer, sail training, dive charter, tugs and workboats.

Small Code vessels

Small commercial vessels under 24m and carrying no more than 12 passengers operating under a Small Commercial Vessel (SCV) or Small Work Boat (SWB) certificate have their own operating area criteria.

The distance a vessel can operate depends upon:	Vessel stability	Level of equipment fitted
	Manning	Certificate granted
Area Category 6	Within 3NM of land and not more than 3NM radius from either the point of departure to sea or the seaward boundary of protected waters in favourable weather and daylight.	

Area Category 5	Within 3NM of land and not more than 3NM radius from either the point of departure to sea or the seaward boundary of protected waters (see definition of 'protected waters') in favourable weather.
Area Category 4	Up to 20NM from a safe haven, in favourable weather and in daylight.
Area Category 3	Up to 20NM from a safe haven.
Area Category 2	Up to 60NM from a safe haven.
Area Category 1	Up to 150NM from a safe haven.
Area Category 0	Unrestricted service.
Safe haven	Means a harbour or shelter of any kind that affords entry, subject to prudence in the weather conditions prevailing, and protection from the force of the weather.
Protected waters	Are not 'categorised waters' but the location of which are explicitly defined and accepted as 'protected' by the Administration, having regard for the safety of the small vessels that operate in those waters.
Nominated Departure Point	The designated point(s) of departure of the vessel, as specified on the vessel's certificate. Where this point lies within Category C or Category D waters, it is to be taken as the seaward boundary of these waters.
Yellow Code	The Safety of Small Commercial Motor Vessels – A Code of Practice.
Blue Code	The Safety of Small Commercial Sailing Vessels – A Code of Practice.
Brown Code	The Code of Practice for the Safety of Small Workboats and Pilot Boats.
Red Code	The Code of Practice for the Safety of Small Vessels in Commercial Use for Sport or Pleasure. Operating from a Nominated Departure Point (NDP).
MGN 280	The harmonised code: Small Vessels in Commercial Use for Sport or Pleasure, Workboats and Pilot Boats – Alternative Construction Standards.
Workboat code edition 2	The Code of Practice for the Safety of Small Workboats and Pilot Boats (Brown code revision).
Code certificates required on board	
SCV or SWB Certificate	Certificate that shows the vessel is in 'code' issued annually. Certificate posted or kept on board.
SCV or SWB disk	Coffee cup-sized disk that is shown in the vessel's window to show it is 'in code'. Has on it name and category of operation.
SCV or SWB 2 document	15–30-page document listing all the vessels equipment and detailing how it complies with the 'code'. Useful for checking.
Inspection and survey	
Who (MIN 538)	Authorised Certifying Authorities (CA) delegated by the MCA e.g. MECAL, RYA, YDSA, IIMS, Lloyd's, SCMS, BV, Burness Corlett, DNV, RINA.
5 year	Initial out-of-water survey – or renewal by CA.
2–3 year	Mid-term/intermediate survey – code will specify whether in or out of the water by CA.

SECTION **2**

1 year	Annual check by owner or surveyor (CA) – code will specify whether in or out of the water.
Other certification that may be required	• Certificate of Registry • Load line certificate or SCV/SWB Certificate • International Sewage Pollution Prevention Certificate (if on international voyages and certified for over 15 persons) • Gas Safe certificate • LSA and FFA certificates • LOLER Certificates • Insurance.

Large yachts

The large yacht codes are similar to the small vessel codes and are applied to super and mega yachts.

They incorporate both an agreed code standard to which they apply and have adaptations to allow a more reasoned approach to the fit-out of a super/mega yacht. They have been known as the large yacht codes, but the new version is the REG code – which also allows an uplift in the amount of passengers that the super yacht can carry.

▲ Large yacht codes cover super yachts over 24m.

Large Yacht Code or REG Red Ensign Group Code	
Large Yacht codes – vessels operating under previous large yacht codes can do so. However, some elements do need bringing into line with new codes.	
Large Yacht Code 1 & Large Yacht Code 2 (MSN 1792)	Over 24m – less than 3000GT. Not more than 12 passengers. Does not carry cargo.
Large Yacht Code 3 (MSN 1851)	Over 24m – no upper size limit. Not more than 12 passengers. Does not carry cargo.
Passenger Yacht Code	Large Yachts carrying 13–36 passengers operate using the Passenger Yacht Code. Does not carry cargo.
REG Code	Part A – over 24m – no upper size limit. • Not more than 12 passengers • Does not carry cargo. Part B – Updated Passenger Yacht Code. • 13–36 passengers and does not carry cargo.
Short Range Yacht, a vessel under 500GT, constructed prior to 01/08/05, or 300GT if constructed after.	Restricted to operating in forecast or actual wind of a maximum Beaufort Force 4, for a motor yacht, and Force 6 for a sailing yacht. Within 60NM of a safe haven. (The Administration may permit operation on specified routes up to 90NM from a safe haven as appropriate.)
'Unrestricted'	Geographical operation outside polar regions. Yachts that intend to operate in polar regions must meet 'polar' requirements of one of the recognised classification societies and stability conditions should include icing.

Certification	
Certificates issued to all vessels:	Certificate of British Registry. International Tonnage Certificate. REG Yacht Code Certificate. Certificate of Classification. International Load Line Certificate. Load Line Conditions of Assignment. Certificate or Statement of Sewage Pollution Prevention (when more than 15 persons are carried on board on international voyages). Minimum Safe Manning Document. Antifouling Systems, Owners Declaration (<400GT). EIAPP Cert./NOx Tech. Files (for each engine >130KW built after 1 January 2000). Ship Station Radio Licence. International Ballast Water Management Certificate/Statement (if applicable).
Additional certificates to be issued to vessels of 300GT and over	Safety Radio Certificate and Form R (Part A vessels only). Wreck Removal Convention Certificate (Nairobi Convention).
Additional certificates to be issued to vessels of 400GT and over	International Oil Pollution Prevention Certificate and Record. International Air Pollution Prevention Certificate/Statement and Record. International Energy Efficiency Certificate/Statement. Antifouling Systems Certificate/Statement (Class Declaration) (>400GT).
Additional certificates to be issued to vessels of 500GT and over	Safety Construction Certificate (REG code Part A vessels only). Safety Equipment Certificate (REG Code Part A vessels only). ISM Safety Management Certificate. Copy of Company ISM DoC. International Ship Security Certificate. Continuous Synopsis Record file. Maritime Labour Convention (MLC) Certificate (including DMLC I and DMLC II).
Additional certificates to be issued to vessels of 1000GT and over	Civil Liability Certificate for Bunker Oil Pollution Damage (Bunkers Convention).
Additional certificates to be issued to REG Code Part B Vessels	Passenger (Yacht) Ship Safety Certificate and Form P Statement of Operational Limitations.
Periodic surveys	
Valid for 5 years in general	Load Line Certificates. Cargo Ship Safety Construction Certificates. Certificates of Compliance.
Annual, intermediate and renewal surveys in respect	Load Line Certificates. Cargo Ship Safety Construction Certificates. Certificate of Compliance. Carried out to the satisfaction of the Administration or class society as appropriate.
RO – Recognised Organisation	A classification society or other body authorised by the Administration by written agreement to undertake statutory surveys and issue statutory certificates on the Administration's behalf.

These definitions are often quoted on the ship's certificate to indicate where the vessel can operate. It should be noted that the sea areas ABCD are different to the inland waters classification of ABCD.

Larger shipping

Voyage definitions for large vessels (Ref: MSN 1676)	
Short international	When the ship is never more than 200NM from a port or place of safety, and on which there is no more than 600NM between the final departure port and the first destination port.
Long international	All other voyages between ports in two countries to which the International Convention for the Safety of Life at Sea (SOLAS) applies.
Domestic voyage	A voyage in sea areas from a port of a member state to the same or another port within that member state.
Inshore/Domestic – the sea areas around the UK for domestic passenger vessels (MSN 1811)	
Sea Area A	Ships engaged solely on domestic voyages other than ships of Class B, Class C and Class D.
Sea Area B	Domestic voyages that are at no time more than 20NM from the line of the coast where shipwrecked persons can land, corresponding to the medium tide height.
Sea Area C	Sea areas where the probability of exceeding 2.5m significant wave heights are less than 10% over a one-year period for all year-round operation, or over a specific restricted period of the year for operation exclusively in such period (e.g. summer period operation) not more than 5NM from the line of the coast, corresponding to the medium tide height.
Sea Area D	Sea areas where the probability of exceeding 1.5m significant wave height is smaller than 10% over a one-year period for all year-round operation, or over a specific restricted period of the year for operation exclusively in such a period (e.g. summer period operation), and the geographical coordinates of which are at any point no more than 3NM from the line of the coast, corresponding to the medium tide height.

Ship classification

Ships are classified by their main work type and area of operation to aid the construction and safety standards that are applied. The classes range from cruise liners to pleasure sailing yachts.

Classification of ships (Ref: MSN 1676)	
Class I	Passenger ships engaged on voyages, any of which are long international voyages.
Class II	Passenger ships engaged only on voyages, any of which are short international voyages.
Class II(A)	Passenger ships engaged on voyages of any kind other than international voyages, which are not ships of Classes III to VI(A).
Class III	Passenger ships engaged only on voyages in the course of which they are at no time more than 70NM from their point of departure and not more than 18NM from the coast of the UK and which are at sea only in favourable weather and during restricted periods.
Class IV	Passenger ships engaged only on voyages in Category A, B, C or D waters.
Class V	Passenger ships engaged only on voyages in Category A, B or C waters.

Class VI	Passenger Ships engaged only on voyages with not more than 250 passengers on board. In favourable weather and during restricted periods, in the course of which the ships are at no time more than 15NM from their point of departure, nor more than 3NM from land.
Class VI (A)	Passenger ships carrying not more than 50 passengers for a distance of not more than 6NM. Voyages to or from isolated communities on the islands or coast of the UK and which do not proceed for a distance of more than 3NM from land – this is subject to any conditions that the Secretary of State may impose.
Class VII	Ships (other than those in Classes VII(A), VII(T), XI and XII) engaged on voyages, any of which are long international voyages.
Class VII(A)	Ships employed as fish processing or canning factory ships and ships engaged in the carriage of persons employed in the fish processing or canning industries.
Class VII(T)	Tankers engaged on voyages, any of which are long international voyages.
Class VIII	Ships (other than ships of Classes VIII(T), IX, XI and XII) engaged only on short international voyages.
Class VIII(T)	Tankers engaged on voyages, any of which are short international voyages.
Class VIII(A)	Ships (other than ships of VIII(A)(T), IX, IX(A), IX(A)(T), XI and XII) engaged only on voyages that are not international voyages – this class includes small commercial vessels.
Class VIII(A)(T)	Tankers engaged only on voyages that are not international voyages.
Class IX	Tugs and tenders that go to sea but not on long international voyages.
Class IX(A)	Freight vessels and all other non-passenger vessels that do not go to sea.
Class IX(A)(T)	Tanker vessels that do not go to sea.
Class XI	Sailing ships, other than fishing vessels and ships of Class XII, which proceed to sea.
Class XII	Pleasure vessels of 13.7m length or over.

Ship certification

Ship certification is a complex subject and a ship's Master and officers should be aware of what certificates they should have on board, how long they last and what they need to do to stay in compliance. Ships certification is inspected by the Flag state and by Port state control. It would also get inspected in the event of any incident.

While we have grouped the certificates together by ship type, it is highly probable that a vessel carries other certificates to suit its operating conditions. For instance, some passenger ships will carry vehicles, whereas other may not, some small commercial vessels will carry dangerous goods, whereas others will not. Get to know your vessel and the certification on board.

Passenger ship certificates

Certificates issued to all vessels
Passenger Ship Safety Certificate, c/w Record of Equipment (Form P).
International or Domestic Safety Management Certificate, c/w copy of Company DoC.
MCA approval for manning.
MCA approval for passenger counting and recording.
Declaration on Anti-Fouling Systems (if over 24m).
International Anti-Fouling Certificate (instead of a Declaration) (400GT or over) Document of Compliance for the Carriage of Dangerous Goods (if carrying Dangerous Goods).
Certificate of Insurance or Other Financial Security in Respect of Civil Liability for Bunker Oil Pollution Damage (if over 1000GT).
Minimum Safe Manning Document (if over 500GT).

If plying on domestic voyages in the UK
United Kingdom or International Load Line Certificate (if sea-going and more than 80 net tons).
Domestic Ship Security Certificate (if sea-going and more than 250 passengers).
International Ship Security Certificate (if EU Class A domestic passengers ship).

If plying on domestic voyages in another EU state
Certificate of Registry.
International Tonnage Certificate.
Domestic Ship Security Certificate (if sea-going and more than 250 passengers).
International Ship Security Certificate (if EU Class A domestic passenger ship).
International Load Line Certificate (if sea-going and over 24m).

International voyages
Certificate of Registry.
International Tonnage Certificate.
International Load Line Certificate.
International Ship Security Certificate.
International Sewage Pollution Prevention Certificate.

+ If over 400GT
International or UK Oil Pollution Prevention Certificate.
International or UK Air Pollution Prevention Certificate.

+ If over 500GT
Minimum Safe Manning Document.

▲ Cargo vessels, such as this container ship and passenger vessels carrying cargo, would also be subject to the Cargo Stowage and Securing (CSS) code.

Cargo ship certificates (excluding tankers but including bulk carriers)

Less than 24m length	See codes for small commercial vessels SCV or SWB Code.
If on non-international voyages	
+ if over 24m	Declaration on Anti-Fouling Systems. If on Alternative Compliance Scheme, a Certificate of Inspection. UK or International Load Line Certificate (if seagoing). International Pollution Prevention Certificate for the Carriage of Noxious Liquid Substances in Bulk (if carrying bulk noxious liquids). International Certificate of Fitness for the Carriage of INF Cargo (if carrying packaged irradiated nuclear fuel or wastes). Certificate of Survey of Vessel Standing By Offshore Installations (if acting as a standby vessel at an offshore installation).
+ over 400GT	An International or UK Oil Pollution Prevention Certificate. International or UK Air Pollution Prevention Certificate. International Anti-Fouling Certificate (instead of the Declaration on Anti-Fouling Systems above).
+ over 500GT	Cargo Ship Safety Construction Certificate. Minimum Safe Manning Document. International Safety Management Certificate.
+ over 1000GT	Certificate of Insurance or Other Financial Security in Respect of Civil Liability for Bunker Oil Pollution Damage.
If on international voyages	
+ if over 24m	Certificate of Registry. International Tonnage Certificate. Declaration on Anti-Fouling Systems. If on Alternative Compliance Scheme, a Certificate of Inspection. International Load Line Certificate. International Pollution Prevention Certificate for the Carriage of Noxious Liquid Substances in Bulk (if carrying bulk noxious liquid substances). Document of Compliance for the Carriage of Dangerous Goods (if carrying Dangerous Goods).
+ over 300GT	Cargo Ship Safety Radio Certificate.
+ over 400GT	International Oil Pollution Prevention Certificate. International Air Pollution Prevention Certificate. International Sewage Pollution Prevention Certificate. International Anti-Fouling Certificate (instead of the Declaration on Anti-Fouling Systems above).
+ over 500GT	Cargo Ship Safety Construction Certificate. Cargo Ship Safety Equipment Certificates. Cargo Ship Safety Certificate may be issued in place of the Safety Construction, Safety, Radio and Safety Equipment Certificates. Minimum Safe Manning Document. International Safety Management Certificate. Copy of Company ISM DOC. International Ship Security Certificate.
+ over 1000GT	Certificate of Insurance or Other Financial Security in Respect of Civil Liability for Bunker Oil Pollution Damage.
Oil tankers, as for cargo ship but additionally:	
+ over 150GT (instead of 400GT)	International or UK Oil Pollution Prevention Certificate (Tanker).

SECTION 2

+ if carrying cargo of more than 2000 tons of persistent oil	Certificate of Insurance or other Financial Security in Respect of Civil Liability for Oil Pollution Damage.
+ if Class VIII(A)(T), over 500GT seagoing	Domestic Ship Security Certificate.
Chemical tankers or gas carriers, as for cargo ship but additionally:	
Chemical tankers	International Certificate of Fitness for the Carriage of Dangerous Chemicals in Bulk or a Certificate of Fitness for Carriage of Dangerous Chemicals in Bulk. (If carrying oil cargoes – oil tanker certification also required).
Gas carriers	International Certificate of Fitness for the Carriage of Liquefied Gases in Bulk, or Certificate of Fitness for the Carriage of Liquefied Gases in Bulk.

High-speed craft

► Typical high-speed craft covered by the High-Speed Craft Code.

High-Speed Craft (HSC)

Note: The HSC Code is not applied to vessels operating under SCV or SWB code certificates.

On any voyages	High-speed Craft Safety Certificate or a Dynamically Supported Craft Safety Certificate or a UK High-speed Craft Safety Certificate. Permit to Operate High-speed Craft (if carrying passengers or cargo). Declaration on Anti-Fouling Systems (if over 24m). International or Domestic Safety Management Certificate (if carrying passengers).
+ on UK domestic seagoing voyages	International Ship Security Certificate (if EU Class A domestic passenger ship). International or UK Load Line Exemption Certificate. MCA approval for passenger counting and recording.
+ on domestic voyages in another EU state	Certificate of Registry. International Tonnage Certificate. If seagoing, an International Load Line Exemption Certificate. MCA approval for passenger counting and recording.
+ if over 400GT	International or UK Oil Pollution Prevention Certificate. International or UK Air Pollution Prevention Certificate. International Anti-Fouling Certificate (instead of the Declaration on Anti-Fouling Systems above).

+ if over 500GT	Minimum Safe Manning Document.
+ if over 1000GT	Certificate of Insurance or Other Financial Security in Respect of Civil Liability for Bunker Oil Pollution Damage.
+ if on international voyages	If carrying Dangerous Goods and built after 1 February 1992, a Document of Compliance for the Carriage of Dangerous Goods. Certificate of Registry. International Tonnage Certificate. International Load Line Exemption Certificate. If certified for >15 persons, an International Sewage Pollution Prevention Certificate.
+ if carrying passengers	International Safety Management Certificate. Copy of Company ISM DOC. International Ship Security Certificate. If carrying Dangerous Goods and built after 1 September 1984, a Document of Compliance for the Carriage of Dangerous Goods.
+ if over 400GT	International Oil Pollution Prevention Certificate. International Air Pollution Prevention Certificate. International Sewage Pollution Prevention Certificate. International Anti-Fouling Certificate (instead of the Declaration on Anti-Fouling Systems above).
+ if over 500GT	Minimum Safe Manning Document. International Safety Management Certificate. International Ship Security Certificate. If carrying Dangerous Goods and built after 1 September 1984, a Document of Compliance for the Carriage of Dangerous Goods.
+ if over 1000GT	Certificate of Insurance or Other Financial Security in Respect of Civil Liability for Bunker Oil Pollution Damage.

Section 3
General responsibilities of the Master

When being examined, the emphasis is on what you would do in your role, whether you are the Master or the Officer of the Watch. It is also worth bearing in mind that the OOW is the Master's representative when the Master is not on the bridge. Therefore, knowing what your legal responsibility is and what is expected of you is of high importance. The sections below give a good idea of what to expect. Some are taken from good practice, while others are laid down in law.

Considerations prior to arrival on board

Details sent to a Master prior to appointment:

- **SEA** — Seafarers Employment Agreement. Identifying standard contractual terms as per Maritime Labour Convention and any particular requirements of the Master from the Company.
- **Deficiencies** — Any problems or repairs that are happening with the ship.
- **Ship info** — Type, size, machinery, draught etc.
- **SMS** — Company Safety Management System. Paying particular attention to the Master's responsibilities.
- **Crew** — Manning of ship. Who is new joining and how long have the critical staff been in place. Any new crew need inducting?
- **Voyage information** — Estimated time of departures and arrivals.
- **Handover** — Who will be carrying out handover and induction – when do they leave.
- **Cargo/job** — What the cargo is or what the job entails.

First impressions

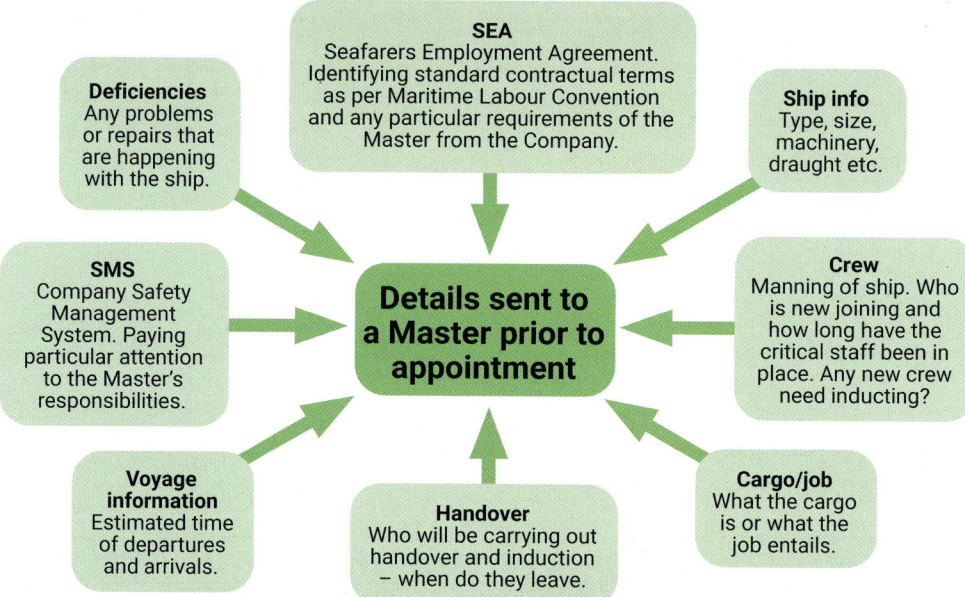

▶ First impressions count and build a picture for the Master or Officer of the Watch approaching a vessel for the first time.

Walking towards your vessel, how are you forming a first impression – visual checks

Condition	Stability	Berthing	Crew	Access
Rust	Clarity of markings	Sufficient lines	Correct PPE	Safe access to vessel
Frayed lines	Load line not overloaded	Protected from chafe	Good safety culture	Slip and trip hazards
Dents	Trim (Draught marks)	Not ranging	Look engaged in work	Nets rigged
Paintwork	List	Fendering	Attitude	Security in place
Anchor stowage/clean	Any outboard covers in place	Lines correctly adjusted	Smoking on the job?	Safe movement on deck

SECTION 3

Handover

These are general common-sense requirements that a Master would consider when taking over a vessel. Exactly how applicable some of these points are will depend on the size and complexity of the vessel. The end result should be the Master having a good grip on the current operational status of the equipment, vessel and crew.

Taking over a vessel – handover			
Taking over a ship	Meet outgoing Master. Receive familiarisation training according to STCW & ISM. Receive bridge handover. Discuss handling characteristics and tug requirements. Discuss any defects, and any action planned or ongoing to rectify them. Discuss manning requirements. Any Permits to Work in place. Inspect the muster list and ensure that it is updated. Read relevant clauses of bill of lading or charter party. Establish safety surplus of fuel required to be carried on board ships. Provide the standing orders for their crew.		
Consult	• Chief Engineer on condition of machinery and quantity of bunker fuel and lubricating oil. • Chief Officer on cargo, stability, ballast, freshwater, stores, maintenance of the ship etc. • Navigating Officer on the passage plan. • Safety & Security Officers on any relevant issues.		
Checks	• Present ship condition, both on the interior and exterior. • Condition of load lines, draught lines to ensure they are visible. • Condition of safe access to the vessel. • Condition of the life-saving equipment and fire-fighting appliances. • Check nautical charts and publications are updated. • Check SMS for any pending or recently rectified non-conformities. • Practically inspect the ship to satisfy that it is seaworthy.		
Official Logbook	• Make an entry in the Official logbook along with the off-going Master. • Enter your details such as name, CoC and reference number. • Check the past records of the ship and recent activities that have been carried out from the official logbook. • Note the amount of ship's money and enter the amount. • Check that drills and checks have been carried out. • Review narrative section to establish any disciplinaries.		
Check documentation	Class certificate	Continuous Synop. Rec.	SOPEP approval
	Load line	EPIRB registration	IOPP
	Int. tonnage certificate	EPIRB annual	Safe manning
	Radio licence	Compass adjustment certificate	Stability manual
	DOC	Liferaft certificate	Fire equipment certificate
	SMC	Safety construction certificate	Safety equipment certificate
	Oil record book	Official logbook	Safety radio certificate

These are the legal requirements of the Master (there are others). Responsibility is often applied to the Owner/Managing Agent to ensure the vessel is equipped and has the procedures in place, and then to the Master to implement the procedures and ensure they are complied with.

The Master's responsibilities

To ensure the Owner's best interests are protected at all times.
To ensure the safety of the ship, crew, passengers and cargo at all times.

STCW Definitions of Command. IMO states:	
Master	The person having command of the ship.
Chief Mate	Means the officer next in rank to the Master and upon whom the command of the ship will fall in the event of the incapacity of the Master.
Officer	Member of the crew, other than the Master, designated as such by national law or regulation or, in the absence of such designation, by collective agreement.
Deck Officer	Means an officer qualified in accordance with the provisions of Chapter II of STCW Convention.
Rating	Means a member of the ship's crew other than an Officer or Master.[1] (Excerpt).
Master's responsibilities – STCW	
A-II/2	IMO states: Bearing in mind that the Master has ultimate responsibility for the safety of the ship, its passengers, crew and cargo, and for the protection of the marine environment against pollution by the ship.[2] (Excerpt).
A-VIII/2 pt2 (Also SOLAS V/34)	IMO states: Prior to each voyage the Master of every ship shall ensure that the intended route from the port of departure to the first port of call is planned using adequate and appropriate charts and other nautical publications.[3] (Excerpt).
STCW B-I/14 – 3	IMO states: Prior the Master should take all steps necessary to implement any company instructions issued in accordance with STCW AI/14. Such steps should include: Identifying all seafarers who are newly employed on board ship before they are assigned to any duties. Providing the opportunity for all newly arrived seafarers to: 2.1 Visit the spaces in which their primary duties will be performed; 2.2 get acquainted with the location, controls and display features of equipment that they will be operating or using; 2.3 activate the equipment when possible and perform functions using the controls on the equipment; and 2.4 observe and ask questions of someone who is familiar with the equipment, procedures and other arrangements, and who can communicate information in a language that the seafarer understands; and 3. provide for a suitable period of supervision when there is any doubt that a newly employed seafarer is familiar with the shipboard equipment, operating procedures and other arrangements needed for the proper performance of his or her duties.[4] (Excerpt).
Ch VIII Anchor Watch	If the Master considers it necessary, a continuous navigational watch shall be maintained at anchor.
Master's responsibilities – SOLAS V	
Regulation 31 Danger messages	IMO states: The Master of every ship that meets with dangerous ice, a dangerous derelict, or any other direct danger to navigation, or a tropical storm, or encounters sub-freezing air temperatures associated with gale-force winds, causing severe ice accretion on superstructures, or winds of Force 10 or above on the Beaufort Scale for which no storm warning has been received, is bound to communicate the information by all means at his disposal to ships in the vicinity, and also to the competent authorities.

SECTION 3

GENERAL RESPONSIBILITIES OF THE MASTER

Regulation 33 Distress situations: Obligations and procedures	IMO states: The Master of a ship at sea that is in a position to be able to provide assistance on receiving information from any source that persons are in distress at sea, is bound to proceed with all speed to their assistance, if possible informing them or the search and rescue service that the ship is doing so. This obligation to provide assistance applies regardless of the nationality or status of such persons or the circumstances in which they are found.
Regulation 34-1 Master's discretion	IMO states: The owner, the charterer, the company operating the ship as defined in regulation IX/1, or any other person shall not prevent or restrict the Master of the ship from taking or executing any decision that, in the Master's professional judgement, is necessary for safety of life at sea and protection of the marine environment.[5] (Excerpt).
Master's responsibilities – ISM Code	
5 Master's responsibility and authority **5.1**	IMO states: The Company should clearly define and document the Master's responsibility with regard to: 1. Implementing the safety and environmental-protection policy of the Company; 2. motivating the crew in the observation of that policy; 3. issuing appropriate orders and instructions in a clear and simple manner; 4. verifying that specified requirements are observed; and 5. periodically reviewing the SMS and reporting its deficiencies to the shore-based management.
5.2	The Company should ensure that the SMS operating on board the ship contains a clear statement emphasising the Master's authority. The Company should establish in the SMS that the Master has the overriding authority and the responsibility to make decisions with respect to safety and pollution prevention and to request the Company's assistance as may be necessary.[6] (Excerpt).
INTERNATIONAL REGULATIONS FOR PREVENTING COLLISIONS AT SEA, 1972	
Rule 2(a) Responsibility	IMO states: Nothing in these Rules shall exonerate any vessel, or the owner, Master or crew thereof, from the consequences of any neglect to comply with these Rules or of the neglect of any precaution that may be required by the ordinary practice of seamen, or by the special circumstances of the case.[7] (Excerpt).
Merchant Shipping and Fishing Vessels (Health and Safety at Work) Regulations, 1997	
MGN 636 3.3	The ship's Master should ensure that the shipowner's health and safety policy and procedures are implemented on board ship and clearly communicated to all those working on board. The Master sets the tone for the safety culture on board, and so it is particularly important that they are seen to prioritise health and safety and to encourage others to do the same. The day-to-day implementation of many of the specific duties set out in this notice will be delegated to the Master. The Master may in turn delegate duties but retains overall responsibility on board.
MGN 636 9.5	As workers themselves, the Master and the crew also have a responsibility to report any safety concerns, and they should be encouraged to do so where such concerns arise from the activities of contractors or sub-contractors, as well as any deficiencies of on-board equipment or procedures relating to their own duties.
Means of Access (Ref: MGN 533 & MGN 591)	
1.2	Providing a safe means of access to the ship is considered to be an integral part of that duty. The duty is placed on the shipowner, the employer and any other person 'in control of the matter', which – in respect that the equipment provided is properly used – will include the Master.

Hours of Work and Rest (Ref: MSN 1842)	
3.1	The Regulations require that the shipowner, the employer (in the case of an employed seafarer) and the Master must ensure that seafarers are provided with at least the minimum hours of rest.
3.3 Additional guidance	Day-to-day monitoring of compliance with minimum hours of rest is likely to be part of the duties of the Master. However, on ships with many different departments, the Master may delegate the monitoring of hours of rest to department managers, including the managers of franchises, who are responsible for the personnel working for the franchise, and any employer of a seafarer working on board the vessel. However, the legal responsibility remains with the shipowner, employers and the Master to ensure that the Regulations are complied with.
ISPS Code	
4.10	IMO states: At all times the Master of a ship has the ultimate responsibility for the safety and security of the ship. Even at security level 3 a Master may seek clarification or amendment of instructions issued by those responding to a security incident, or threat thereof, if there are reasons to believe that compliance with any instruction may imperil the safety of the ship.[8] (Excerpt).
6 Obligations of the Company	IMO states: 6.1 The Company shall ensure that the ship security plan contains a clear statement emphasising the Master's authority. The Company shall establish in the ship security plan that the Master has the overriding authority and responsibility to make decisions with respect to the safety and security of the ship and to request the assistance of the Company or of any Contracting Government as may be necessary. 6.2 The Company shall ensure that the company security officer, the Master and the ship Security Officer are given the necessary support to fulfil their duties and responsibilities in accordance with chapter XI-2 and this Part of the Code.[9] (Excerpt).
MAIB/Incident reporting	
MGN 564	The Master/Skipper or senior surviving officer of a UK ship must notify the MAIB of any marine casualty or marine incident. The Master/Skipper or senior surviving officer of *any* ship must notify the MAIB of any marine casualty or marine incident if: the ship is within UK waters and carrying passengers to/from the UK or the marine casualty is within the jurisdiction of a UK harbourmaster.
Cargo Securing Code	
General elements to be considered by the Master	IMO states: Having evaluated the risk of cargo-shifting, the Master should ensure, prior to loading of any cargo, cargo transport unit or vehicle that: 1. the deck area for their stowage is, as far as practicable, clean, dry and free from oil and grease; 2. the cargo, cargo transport unit or vehicle appears to be in suitable condition for transport, and can be effectively secured; 3. all necessary cargo securing equipment is on board and in good working condition; and 4. cargo in or on cargo transport units and vehicles is, to the extent practicable, properly stowed and secured on to the unit or vehicle.[10] (Excerpt).

Section 4
Safe working

All persons operating a vessel, whether it is the Owner, Master or crew have responsibilities under Health and Safety (H&S). To give some sort of priority, all works will be subject to the avoidance of risks – therefore all seafaring begins with H&S and all have a responsibility and should be aware of their responsibilities. MGN 636 sums it up nicely: The ship's Master should ensure that the shipowner's H&S policy and procedures are implemented on board the ship and are clearly communicated to all those working on board. The Master sets the tone for the safety culture on board, and so it is particularly important that they are seen to prioritise H&S and to encourage others to do the same. The day-to-day implementation of many of the specific duties set out in this notice will be delegated to the Master. The Master may in turn delegate duties but retains overall responsibility on board.

Responsibilities

Masters, owners and seafarers have responsibilities under: Merchant Shipping and Fishing Vessels (Health and Safety at Work) Regulations 1997 (SI 1997/2962 & MGN 636)	
Application	It covers work activities on UK ships anywhere in the world and to non-UK ships when in UK waters.
Responsibility	Regulations require the shipowner or employer to ensure the health and safety of 'workers and other persons'.
Shipowners	Should ensure that Masters have adequate support to carry out their responsibility for health and safety management effectively while on board.
Ship's Master	Ensures the Shipowner's health and safety (H&S) policy and procedures are implemented on board ship and are clearly communicated to all those working on board. Sets the tone for the safety culture on board Seen to prioritise health and safety and encourage others to do the same. Day-to-day implementation of specific H&S duties may be delegated by the Master, but the Master retains overall responsibility.
Seafarers and other workers	Must co-operate with the Master and Shipowner to implement prescribed health and safety policies and other measures. Participate in developing and promoting risk assessments and safe and healthy working practices and working conditions. Take reasonable care for their own health and safety and that of others on board who may be affected by their acts or omissions. Co-operate with anyone carrying out H&S duties. Comply with control measures identified during risk assessment. Report serious hazards or deficiencies immediately to an officer or authorised person. Make proper use of plant and machinery and treat any hazard to health or safety (such as a dangerous substance) with due caution.
Shipowner's duty	To protect the health and safety of workers and others affected by their activities so far as is reasonably practicable.
By...	The principles for ensuring health and safety are: (a) the avoidance of risks, which among other things includes the combating of risks at source and the replacement of dangerous practices, substances or equipment by non-dangerous or less dangerous practices, substances or equipment; (b) evaluation of unavoidable risks and taking action to reduce them; (c) adoption of work patterns and procedures that take account of the capacity of the individual; (d) adaptation of procedures to take account changes in working practices, equipment, the working environment and any other factors; (e) a coherent approach to management of the vessel or undertaking, taking account of health and safety at every level of the organisation; (f) giving collective protective measures priority over individual protective measures; (g) the provision of appropriate and relevant information and instruction for workers. Following these principles, risk assessment forms the basis of all safety measures. Those measures should include: (h) provision and maintenance of safe plant, machinery and equipment; (i) ensuring articles/substances can be used, handled, stowed or transported safely; (j) providing information, instruction, training and supervision as necessary to ensure the safety of workers and other persons on board ship; (k) providing a safe working environment on board ship.

H&S policy (more than five employees) (SI 2962 1997)	Employers are required to produce a written H&S policy and the arrangements and organisation in place for carrying out that policy. The policy must be brought to the attention of the employer's workers. Health and safety policy is linked to Master in ISM section 5, as it is the Master's responsibility to implement the H&S policy on board ship.
Safety Officer	The Safety Officer is normally the competent person on board ship. On all seagoing ships on which there are five or more seafarers, other than fishing vessels, a Safety Officer must be appointed. The Safety Officer should be provided with sufficient resources to carry out their role effectively, including training. It is not advisable for either the Master or the officer with responsibility for medical care on board to be the ship's Safety Officer.
Safety Committee (MGN 636)	Required on every ship with five or more seafarers. Chaired by the Master. Committee will include Safety Officer and elected safety representatives. Master must record safety committee appointment in the official logbook. Committee should have records (minutes). When fewer than five seafarers on board, the Master should ensure that information sharing, training and consultations on H&S issues are carried out.
'Reasonably practicable'	Balancing the level of risk against the measures needed to control the real risk in terms of money, time or trouble. A particular course of action may not be required if it would be grossly disproportionate to the level of risk.

Code of Safe Working Practices

On the basis of a risk assessment, it is probable that best safe working practice will be sought to enable the procedure to go ahead. That is where the Code of Safe Working Practices (COSWP) comes in as it shows the best practice and legal requirements for most types of work on board a vessel. It should be remembered that the COSWP's Chapter 1 is 'Managing Health and Safety'. It can therefore be surmised that it is the highest priority from the MCA in managing a vessel. The COSWP is a free download and all seafarers should have access to it. Chapters 1, 2 and 4 are a must-read for any seafarer.

The Code of Safe Working Practices (COSWP)	
Published by Maritime and Coastguard Agency	
Aim	Best practice guidance on implementing statutory regulations for improving health and safety on board ship and best practice when no regulation is in force.
Audience	It is intended primarily for merchant seafarers on UK-registered ships. It is also for everyone on a ship regardless of rank or rating, and those ashore responsible for safety, to ensure effective co-operation and implementation.
Requirement	COSWP must be carried on all UK ships other than fishing vessels and pleasure vessels. Seafarers with safety responsibilities should have immediate access; the Code must also be available to ALL other workers and seafarers. It can be electronic or hard copy. Should be in the mess room and other areas as required.

COSWP chapters (as of 2002)	
1. Managing occupational health and safety 2. Safety induction 3. Living on board 4. Emergency drills and procedures 5. Fire precautions 6. Security on board 7. Health surveillance 8. Personal protective equipment 9. Safety signs and their use 10. Manual handling 11. Safe movement on board ship 12. Noise, vibration, other physical agents 13. Safety officials 14. Permit to work systems 15. Entering dangerous (enclosed) spaces 16. Hatch covers and access lids 17. Work at height 18. Provision, care of and use of work equipment	19. Lifting plant and operations 20. Work on machinery and power systems 21. Hazardous substances and mixtures 22. Boarding arrangements 23. Food preparation and handling in the catering department 24. Hot work 25. Painting 26. Anchoring, mooring, towing operations 27. Roll-on/roll-off ferries 28. Dry cargo 29. Tankers and other ships carrying bulk liquid cargoes 30. Port towage industry 31. Ships serving offshore oil and gas installations 32. Ships serving offshore renewables installations 33. Ergonomics

Safety Management Systems

While SOLAS, MARPOL, STCW, MLC and many codes, conventions and regulations state how the vessel is built, equipped and manned, a Safety Management System (SMS) is required to ensure that the vessel is then used and maintained correctly so that it is operated safely and stays that way.

There are two main types of certificated SMS and recommendations for many others. The good news is that they all follow the same principles.

Safety Management Systems	
There are two main types of safety management system that require external certification and inspection: International Safety Management System (ISM) and Domestic Safety Management Code (DSM).	
ISM	International Safety Management System – international waters
Required on	Ships engaged on international voyages that are: passenger vessels; vessels 500GT or more; high-speed craft; mobile offshore drilling units 500GT or more.
DSM	Domestic Safety Management Code.
Required on	Passenger vessels operating in UK inland and domestic waters.

ISM chapter	Contains
	The objectives and functional requirements of both ISM and DSM are the same. However, certification differs. Listed below are the main headings for ISM; DSM is very similar.
1. General	Definitions, objectives, application and functional requirements. Requires compliance with regulation and safe working practices based on findings of a risk assessment.
2. Safety and environmental protection policy	Policy that the whole SMS hinges upon. Overarching view of how the safety of the company and vessels will be managed by the company. Signed by the CEO/Owner.
3. Company responsibilities and authority	Outlines the company's responsibilities to ensure that adequate resources are available to ensure safety and that they should have a SMS in place.
4. Designated person(s)	Monitors the safety and pollution-prevention aspects of the operation of each ship and ensures that adequate resources and shore-based support are applied. Access to highest level of management.
5. Master's responsibility and authority	Master has to implement the company's safety and environmental policy and ensure that the crew follow procedures. Statement from the company emphasising Master's authority.
6. Resources and personnel	Company ensures that the Master and crew are qualified, trained and have sufficient knowledge to execute SMS duties. Procedures to identify and provide appropriate training, and to ensure crew can communicate effectively.
7. Shipboard operations	On the basis of a risk assessment, procedures for undertaking key shipboard operations should be drawn up to ensure a safe working environment and safe systems of work.
8. Emergency preparedness	Emergency operating procedures should be in place, trained and exercised both on the ship and emergency management ashore.
9. Reports and analysis of non-conformities, accidents and hazardous occurrences	Reporting of non-conformities, accidents. Company should investigate and improve safety in the future. Procedures in place for implementing corrective action. Lessons learned should be shared with the staff to prevent reoccurrence.
10. Maintenance of the ship and equipment	Procedures for ship maintenance. Timings for inspections, defects recorded and action taken. Safety critical equipment identified, with enhanced maintenance procedures.
11. Documentation	Ensuring valid documents are on board, certificates, latest copies of procedures and old documents removed.
12. Company verification, review and evaluation	Internal checks and audits by the company at intervals not exceeding 12 months to ensure that the safety management system is effective. Checks that non-conformities have been 'closed out' and resolved. Periodic review of SMS with aim of continual improvement.

If a vessel requires a certificated SMS, then it will have to prove this with current certification. An Owner, Master and Chief Officer will need to have a good grip on when the certification is valid to and what is required to keep it in date.

Safety Management System certification and internal audit

Audit	Initial	Annual	Mid-term	3 years	5 years
ISM	International Safety Management System requires audit and certificate by the MCA. ISM Document of Compliance (DOC) issued to company for ship types. ISM Safety Management Certificate (SMC) issued to each individual ship. Ship also carries a copy of the company's DOC.				
Shore DOC Vessel SMC	Initial audit by MCA may lead to an Interim DOC or SMC	Audit by MCA + Company			Renewal MCA
		Company audit	Vessel audit between 2nd or 3rd anniversary of SMC certification		
Interim DOC and SMC certificates can be issued to new ISM companies and new ISM ships to enable them to gradually comply so long as they meet ISM objectives and have a plan for implementation. This is for new ship types, new ships on delivery, when a ship changes flag etc.					
Interim DOC is valid for up to 12 months. Interim SMC is valid for up to 6 months.					
Audit	Initial	Annual	Mid-term	3 years	5 years
DSM	Domestic Safety Management System requires audit and certificate by the MCA. A DSM Safety Management Certificate (DSMC) will be issued after both the company and the vessel have been audited.				
Shore Vessel	Initial audit of vessel by MCA	DSM self-assessment and DSM checklist sent to MCA annually	Vessel audit between 2nd or 3rd anniversary of DSM certification	Internal company review within 3 years. Records kept	Office or Company Ship Audit by MCA every 5 years

Risk assessment

Risk assessment	
Hazard	Source of potential harm or injury.
Risk	1) Consequences; and 2) severity of the hazard.
Reasonably practicable	Shipowners and employers are required to do what is 'reasonably practicable' to ensure the health and safety of seafarers, workers and other persons.
5 steps to risk assessment	Identify the foreseeable hazards. Decide who might be harmed. Evaluate the risks and decide precautions. Record your findings and implement them. Review the risk assessment and update if required.

SECTION 4

Control measure hierarchy Most effective ▲ to least effective ▼	Elimination. Substitution. Engineering control. Procedural/admin control. Personal protective equipment.
'Suitable and sufficient'	A risk assessment should be suitable and sufficient if: A proper check was made. You asked who might be affected. You dealt with the significant risks, taking into account the number of people. The precautions are reasonable and the remaining risk is low. You involved your workers or their representatives.
'Significant findings'	Significant findings of the assessment shall be brought to the attention of the workers (hazards, risks and control measures).
Assessment review	Periodically (annually as a minimum). If a process changes (new equipment or environmental changes). In the event of a near miss or accident. If it is no longer required.
Competent person	Has special responsibility for health and safety and consultation with workers. They will be a person who has sufficient training and experience or knowledge and other qualities, to enable them to properly undertake the duty imposed. Normally competent person ashore/Safety Officer afloat.
Toolbox talk	Conducted prior to any work being carried out that involves more than one person and where there is significant risk to persons or assets: Talk through the procedures of the job in hand with those involved. Discuss the findings of any task-based risk assessment. Discuss the findings of dynamic risks on the day, weather – visibility etc. Encourage all parties to contribute and ask questions. Confirm that all know their role in the job in hand. Ensure clear communications and stop/go work requirements. Recorded that the talk took place with any findings.

▲ Control measure hierarchy identifies the most effective ways of reducing risk.

SAFE WORKING

Permit to work

Permit to work	
Why	A 'permit to work' (PtW) system reduces the risk of accidents on board ship. Under this system, seafarers must get written permission from a senior officer before they can perform hazardous tasks.
Tasks	Working aloft and over the side. Working with boilers. Hot work (resulting in the ignition of flammable material, for example welding, grinding and metal cutting). Working in unmanned machinery spaces. Entry into enclosed/dangerous spaces. Electrical testing. Working on elevators. Diving operations. Any other task as identified and defined in Company SMS.
Competent person	A person designated and authorised for the task covered by a permit to work under the safety management system. They should sign the PtW. The competent person carrying out the specified work should not be the same person as the authorised officer.
Authorised officer	A person designated and authorised for the purposes of issuing and closing permits to work under the SMS. They should sign the PtW. They retain responsibility for the work until they have either closed the permit or formally transferred it to another authorised officer who should be made fully conversant with the situation. Anyone who takes over from the authorised officer, either as a matter of routine or in an emergency, should sign the permit to indicate transfer of full responsibility.
PtW should state	Job location. Details of work to be done. Nature and results of any preliminary test done. Safeguards that should be in place, lock outs, toolbox talks, no conflicts with other works and risk assessments carried out. Safety equipment to be used and PPE. Cancellation of the PtW when work not completed or finished.
Time	PtW should state the period of validity (Max 24 hours).
Posting	PtW should be posted on the noticeboard and discussed with any crew or contractors that may be affected.
On completion	The competent person should notify the authorised officer and get the permit closed.

SECTION 4

Dangerous spaces

The terminology has moved slightly over the years on dangerous spaces – however, the result is the same. The regulation covers any enclosed or confined space that is, or may become, a dangerous space. It is important to remember that any all-sided space can become dangerous if fumes are added to it or oxygen is deprived from it.

Dangerous (Enclosed) Spaces (Ref: SI 2022/96 – Entry Into Enclosed Spaces Regulations, 2022 & MGN 659)	
Definition	*UK definition:* Any enclosed or confined space in which it is foreseeable that the atmosphere may at some stage contain toxic or flammable gases or vapours, or be deficient in oxygen, to the extent that it may endanger the life or health of any person entering that space. *IMO definition:* • Has limited openings for entry and exit. • Has inadequate ventilation. • Is not designed for continuous worker occupation.[11] (Excerpt).
Examples	Dangerous space may not necessarily be enclosed on all sides, e.g. ships' holds may have open tops, but the nature of the cargo makes the atmosphere in the lower hold dangerous. cargo pump rooms; cargo compressor rooms; cofferdams; boilers; chain lockers; void spaces; duct keels; fuel tanks; ballast tanks; cargo spaces; double bottoms; inter-barrier spaces; engine crankcases; engine scavenge air receivers; CO_2 rooms; battery lockers; sewage tanks.
Problem	A single inhalation with a 5% oxygen content may result in instantaneous loss of consciousness and subsequent death. Similarly, small concentrations of a toxic substance may result in loss of consciousness and subsequent death.
Oxygen content	The normal level of oxygen in the atmosphere is 20.8%. Variation may indicate a problem and should be investigated.
Identification	Dangerous (enclosed) spaces on board ship should be identified using risk assessment and reviewed. An inventory is kept of enclosed spaces seafarers may enter that might become dangerous.
Entrances	Should be kept locked, hatches or entrances to have warning sign.
Training (all crew)	Statutory two-monthly training exercises required, including: Identification of the hazards likely to be faced during entry into enclosed spaces; knowledge of the procedures for assessment of the space; knowledge of the procedures for safe entry; and recognition of the signs of adverse health effects caused by exposure to hazards during entry. Practising the rescue plan.

Risk assessment will show	On the basis of a risk assessment, the authorised officer should decide the procedures to be followed for entry into a potentially dangerous space. These will depend on whether the assessment shows that: 1) there is minimal risk to the life or health of a person entering the space then or at any future time; 2) there is no immediate risk to health and life, but a risk could arise during the course of work in the space; or 3) the risk to life or health is immediate.
If (2) there is no immediate risk	To make the space safe for entry without breathing apparatus and to ensure it remains safe while persons are within the space. A competent person should make an assessment of the space and an authorised officer to take charge of the operation. The potential hazards should be identified. The space should be prepared, vented and secured for entry. The atmosphere of the space should be tested remotely. A permit to work system should be used. Procedures for preparation and entry should be agreed. Emergency procedures should be in place. Workers should wear a personal atmosphere-monitoring device, sludge or deposits liable to give off fumes cleaned out.
Other precautions before entry	Illuminated. No source of ignition. Rescue plan in place – to include: • appropriate breathing apparatus, with spare air cylinders; • lifelines and rescue harnesses; • torches or a lamp (intrinsically safe); • means of hoisting an incapacitated person from the space. At least one competent person, with equipment, posted to remain as an attendant at the entrance to the space while occupied. Agreed and tested system of communication.
Additional where 'risk to life or health is immediate' or where atmosphere is suspect or unknown	Only entered if it is essential for testing purposes or for the safety of life or of the ship. Breathing apparatus should always be worn. The number of persons entering the space should be the minimum compatible with the work to be performed. Two air supplies – one from outside the space and a spare cylinder.
Small vessels under 24m working close to shore or those vessels operating on inland waters	Seafarers may never be expected to enter a dangerous space, because shore-based companies or personnel may be engaged to carry out any inspection or other work in dangerous spaces. However, all seafarers should have on-board training to help them recognise the risks from dangerous spaces and to familiarise them with any applicable procedures.

SECTION 4

Lifting and work equipment

Lifting Equipment and Lifting Operations Regulations (LOLER) and Provision and Use of Work Equipment Regulations (PUWER) tend to go hand in hand. However, it is worth remembering that all work equipment will tend to come under PUWER in one way or another if it is not covered by a similar protective regulation.

Lifting Equipment and Lifting Operations Regulations (LOLER) (Ref: MGN 332)	
Overview	LOLER regulations place duties on shipowners, people and seafarers who own, operate or have control over lifting equipment.
Lifting equipment	Work equipment used for lifting or lowering loads and includes the attachments used for anchoring, fixing or supporting it; cranes, gantries, davits, deck bolts, scissor lifts, forklifts and hoists etc.
Loose gear or accessories for lifting	Any gear by means of which a load can be attached to lifting equipment, but which does not form an integral part of either the lifting equipment or the load: slings, chains, hooks, shackles etc.
Certification	Certificate of testing and thorough examination by a competent person should be in force for every item of lifting equipment, accessory for lifting and loose gear. Person is often an outside contractor as they have the testing equipment and are not biased. Items should be tested, thoroughly examined and certificated for use: • after manufacture or installation; • after any repair or modification that is likely to alter the safe working load (SWL) or affect the strength or stability of the equipment.
Thorough examination in service timings	Lifting equipment, at least every 12 months. Lifting equipment for lifting persons at least every 6 months. Accessory for lifting, at least every 6 months. Records of thorough examination and certifications, reports kept for 2 years.
Examination scheme	The shipowner and employer should devise a documented system/procedure to ensure that all parts of lifting equipment exposed to conditions causing deterioration to such equipment are properly examined, at the required intervals.
Other lifting terms	
WLL	Working Load Limit is the maximum working load designed by the manufacturer.
SWL	Safe Working Load is a figure lower than the WLL. It may be necessary for the competent person to reduce the WLL to a practical SWL because of the application. SWL may be the same or less than WLL but may never be more.

SAFE WORKING

55

Provision and Use of Work Equipment Regulations (PUWER) (Ref: MGN 331)

Overview	Places the responsibility on the shipowner and employer to ensure that all work equipment is appropriate for its intended purpose and is safe to use.
Work equipment	Means any machinery, appliance, apparatus, tool or installation for use at work.
Employer to ensure the work equipment:	Is suitable for the work to be carried out; or properly adapted for that purpose. Workers may use it without impairment to their health or safety.
Employer shall ensure that:	Work equipment is maintained in an efficient state. Maintained in efficient working order and in good repair. Where machinery has a maintenance log, the log is kept up to date.
Inspection	On first installation (if critical such as welding, bolting etc.). Regular intervals (by best practice or manufacturer's requirement). After exceptional circumstances, modifications, damage, weather stress etc. Could be daily, weekly, monthly. Results to be recorded and retained.

Hours of work and rest

Close to all seafarers' hearts is ensuring that they get enough rest and that it is of sufficient quality. While systems and engineering are making vessels generally safer, this is having an impact on the amount of manning on board. Fatigue is therefore a major problem and something that both seafarers and companies should try to avoid as it leads to issues occurring due to the human element.

Hours of work and rest (Ref: MSN 1877)

Applies to	All seafarers, including Masters, employed, engaged or working in any capacity on board a seagoing ship, and whose normal place of work is on a ship.
Do not apply to	Seafarers on fishing vessels, pleasure vessels, warships or naval auxiliaries, vessels not engaged in commercial activities; or seafarers subject to the Working Time: Inland Waterways Regs 2003 (Seafarers mainly working in Categories A–D inland waters).
Responsibility	Shipowner, employer and the Master to ensure that Hours of Work and Rest Regulations are met.
General	Seafarers should ensure they are properly rested when they begin duty on a ship and obtain adequate rest when not on duty.
Hours of rest	The minimum hours of rest shall be not less than: (a) 10 hours in any 24-hour period; and (b) 77 hours in any seven-day period.

Splits	Daily hours of rest cannot be divided into more than two periods, one period must be at least 6 hours. The two periods must provide at least 10 hours' rest.
On-call time	On-call time is not counted as 'hours of work' unless the seafarer is required to work during that time. A seafarer whose normal period of rest on board ship is disturbed by a call-out, should have compensatory rest.
Posting of watchkeeping duties and hours of rest	Shipowners must ensure that a table of scheduled watchkeeping duties and hours of rest is produced, setting out the hours of work and rest periods. It must be in English and in the working language of the ship. The Master or a person authorised by the Master must ensure that the table is posted in a prominent and easily accessible place in the ship.
	The table must contain, for every seafarer, the following information: • The daily schedule of duties at sea and duties in port. • The daily minimum hours of rest as required by the regulations.
Records	Master or authorised person must maintain records of hours of rest for seafarers on board. Records in English and signed by the Master and seafarer to whom it refers.

The 'human element'

The human element incorporates the interaction between a human and any system aboard ship. The RMS *Titanic* was 'unsinkable', but humans found a way to do it...

Some factors affecting the human element:	
Leadership	Communication
Organisational and safety culture	Safety management systems
Operational systems	Crew competence, training and experience
Situational awareness	Stress and fatigue
Culture of continuous improvement	Workforce engagement
Manning levels and hours of work	Design, construction and ergonomics
Living and working conditions	Conditions of service, motivation and morale

Near miss, accident and incident reporting

It is important to have clearly understood procedures for reporting near misses, accidents and incidents. When an incident occurs, there is often too much going on to remember a process if it is not written down and important points are easily missed without clear procedures and guidance.

Near miss, accident and incident reporting

General principle
The key in incidents is to investigate why they happened, stop their reoccurrence and promulgate the information for others. (It is safer to learn from others' mistakes than your own).

Internal
Safety Management Systems should include procedures ensuring that non-conformities, accidents and hazardous situations are reported to the company, investigated and analysed with the objective of improving safety and pollution prevention.

MCA, class and certifying authorities
Vessel problems, pollution, groundings, fire or other major event that causes damage often require reporting to the authority – depending on requirement.

Insurance, associations, builders and manufacturers and the Police.
The list of people to whom you report will depend on the type of incident and who and what was involved.

Ports
There are often byelaws that require vessels to also report incidents to the port or harbour authority.

MAIB
If applicable report the incident to the Marine Accident Investigation Branch.

▲ While going aground is always seen as a reportable incident, there are many less serious events that are now reportable to the MAIB.

SECTION 4

Marine Accident Investigation Branch (MAIB) (Ref: MGN 564)

MAIB investigates marine casualties involving UK vessels worldwide and vessels of any flag in UK territorial waters. Its purpose is to help prevent further avoidable accidents from recurring. MAIB does not seek to apportion blame or establish liability.

Who must report	Master/Skipper (or senior surviving officer) of a UK ship. Master/Skipper (or senior surviving officer) of *any* ship if: a) the ship is in UK waters and carrying passengers to and from the UK; b) the incident occurs within the jurisdiction of a UK harbourmaster. The ship's owner, unless satisfied that the Master has already reported to harbour authorities, for incidents in/near their harbour area. The person, authority/body responsible for an inland waterway. An official of the MCA, for all occurrences in UK waters.
Does not apply to	Recreational craft unless operated under Intended Pleasure Vessel Code. Recreational craft hired on a bareboat basis. Commercial craft <8m operating in a harbour/inland waterway, not carrying passengers. Unless it involves an explosion, fire or capsize of a power-driven vessel, or results in death, serious injury or severe pollution.
Marine casualty	The death of, or serious injury to, a person. The loss of a person from a ship. The loss, presumed loss or abandonment of a ship. Material damage to a ship. Ship unfit to proceed (requires flag/class approval before proceeding). At sea: A breakdown of the ship, requiring towage. Stranding or disabling of a ship, or involvement in a collision. Material damage to marine infrastructure external of a ship that seriously endangers ship safety, another ship or any individual. Pollution, caused by damage to a ship or ships.
Marine incident	Close-quarters situations where urgent action is required to avoid collision. Any event that had the potential to result in a serious injury. A fire that did not result in material damage. Unintended temporary grounding on soft mud, where there was no risk of stranding or material damage. A person overboard who was recovered without serious injury. Snagging of fishing gear resulting in a dangerous heel.
When and how to report	As soon as practicable, by the quickest means available. The MAIB's 24-hour accident reporting line: **+44 (0)23 8023 2527**. MAIB's online 'Accident Report Form' (ARF).
Evidence	MAIB may require access to additional information and evidence. charts, logbooks, recorded data (hard copy or electronic), all other documents, records and equipment that may be pertinent to the marine casualty or marine incident must be preserved. Voyage Data Recorder data must be saved immediately, and precautions taken to prevent the data being overwritten.

SAFE WORKING

Section 5
Records and logbooks

Record-keeping is often a legal requirement and, if not on your vessel because of size or area of operation, it is still good practice. Usually records are required after an incident and if they have not been kept it is then too late. Records can help prove good practice in the event of a failure and are a welcome sight to an arriving Master, Safety Officer or Auditor. When first joining a ship as a Master or OOW, the records and logbooks will give a very good idea of how the vessel was being run.

Official logbook

Records and logbooks: Official logbook (OLB)
(Ref: SI 1981/569 The Merchant Shipping (Official Log Books) Regulations, 1981 & MSN 1391)

Applies to	Records/Logs	When and who notes
A vessel over 25GT but not pleasure yacht or a ship belonging to General Lighthouse Authority	Official logbook	Entries signed by the Master
	Births and deaths	Master when a return is made
	Musters, drills and LSA and FFA checks	Master and crew after each event
	Ships main and emergency steering	Master and Officer after event
	Crew accommodation	Master and crew after each event
	Food and water	By person inspecting
	Load line, depth of loading	Master and officer before preceding to sea

Narrative examples	
<ul><li>Changes of Master.</li><li>Appointments of Safety Officers, Representatives and Committees.</li><li>Meetings of safety committees. Promotions and demotions.</li><li>Annexing of documents to OLB.</li><li>Accidents.</li><li>Casualties.</li><li>Disciplinary matters.</li><li>Discharge of seafarers (when they sign off the list of crew).</li><li>Details of crew left behind.</li><li>Desertions.</li><li>Complaints.</li><li>Wages disputes.</li><li>Criminal convictions during a voyage.</li><li>Illness.</li><li>Deaths.</li><li>Closing of OLB.</li></ul>	Master and another Officer when entry made

Other records and logbooks

Other records and logbooks		
Official Log Book Part II (passenger ships)		
Passenger ships	Doors, openings and other devices	Master at log opening
	Watertight door drills	Master and Officer at least weekly
	Inspections of watertight doors, devices and valves	Master and Officer at least weekly
	Load line and depth of loading	Master
	Departures and arrivals, draught, freeboard and stability (Form MSF 2004)	Master and Officer
	Opening and closing of doors, plates etc. and closing accesses below the bulkhead deck	Master and Officer
All ships except pleasure vessels and fishing vessels	Hours of Work and Rest	Monthly by the Master
Over 80GT Not General Lighthouse Authority Not pleasure yacht with no more than 4 paid crewmembers	ALC – A List of Crew MLC – List of Crew	As required when a seafarer is signed on or discharged from the vessel. ALC for Crew Agreements on ships not subject to MLC, otherwise MLC List of Crew
Oil tanker 150GT or more All ships 400GT or more	Oil Record book part 1 Machinery space operations	Each entry by officer in charge. Page end signed by Master
Oil tanker over 150GT or more (Also require Part 1)	Oil Record book part 2 Cargo/ballast operations (oil tankers)	Each entry by officer in charge. Page end signed by Master
Ships certified to carry noxious liquid substances in bulk	Cargo record book – ships carrying noxious liquid substances in bulk	Page end signed by Master. Each entry by officer
All ships 400GT or more 15 or more persons	Garbage record book	Page end signed by Master. Each entry by officer

SECTION 5

Every ship 400GT and above carrying water ballast of quantity 8m³ or greater and engaged in voyages to ports in areas of different jurisdiction, shall be provided with a Ballast Water Record Book	Ballast Water Record Book	Responsible Officer to sign each page
Cargo ships 300GT or more Passenger vessels Not pleasure vessels	*GMDSS radio log	Days entries signed by the Master
All ships	Passage plans	Approved by the Master
Over 150GT on international voyages	Record of navigational activities	Positions recorded periodically checked by Master
Any commercial vessel	Cadet training records Training record books	Signing off competencies and tasks
Any commercial vessel	Testimonials/discharge book	When crew leave the ship

*These are general requirements, for specifics please consult the regulation or logbook

Continuous synopsis record

Continuous Synopsis Record (CSR)			
CSR	Logbook that stays with a ship for its whole life		
It records (example)	Owner	Changes of owner	Class and changes
	Flag	ISM Certificates issued by	Registration
Required on	Passenger ships on international voyages. Cargo ships of 500GT and above on international voyages. Class A passenger ships operating domestic services within UK waters.		
Responsibility	Master is responsible for the proper upkeep of the CSR on board UK ships. It is important that the details are always correct as Port State Control will check the CSR as a matter of routine at inspections.		

63

Section 6
Seaworthiness and seamanship

Seaworthiness has a few definitions; however, in general terms a seaworthy vessel is a vessel in compliance with all rules and regulations; is manned, equipped and 'in class' and in such a condition to safely complete the intended voyage.

SECTION 6

Safe access and movement

Safe access and safe movement are presently very hot topics due to the number of injuries and incidents. It seems strange that vessels are getting safer, but we have an increasing chance of entrapment, injury or falling in the water just in the process of getting on board.

Safe access (Ref: MGN 533 & 591)	
Responsibility	Is with the person providing the access: Master, shipowner or berth operator, or whoever is 'in control of the matter'. However, the Master still has responsibility for ensuring a safe means of access, even if the equipment is provided from the shore side.
General provision	Carry out a risk assessment. Access is properly rigged and secured. Adjusted as necessary from time to time. Well illuminated. Lifebuoy with self-activating light and buoyant safety line and quoit. Ensure access and egress is free of slip and trip hazards. Net provided when access equipment is in use.
Step directly	Vessel(s) moored securely – no gaps and not ranging fore and aft. Not to cross at vessel tapers/ends. Ensure mooring lines/obstructions do not cross access point. Avoid access near deck shelters and equipment. Provide adequate handholds where practicable.
Fixed ladders on a quay wall	Check ladder condition. Ensure ladder does not have slippery surface.
Portable ladder	Only used when there is no safer access to the vessel. Angle of 75 degrees from horizontal. Ladder should extend 1m above the upper landing place unless other suitable handholds. Clearance of 150mm behind the rungs. Properly secured against slipping.
Gangway	Required if vessel is 30m or more. No greater than 30 degrees angle from quay to vessel. Check before use: for any material defects and surface condition. Check SWL on equipment. Ensure stanchions rigged correctly. Ensure guardrails taught and good condition. Fenced on both sides. Secured to vessel. Mooring lines not allowed to go slack. Test certificates in place if appropriate.
Accommodation ladder (then general condition as gangway)	Required if vessel is 120m or more. SWL and/or maximum numbers marked on plates at either end. Angle of slope no more than 55 degrees. Fenced along its length.
LOLER	Gangways, accommodation ladders and winches used should be treated as lifting equipment and tested and recorded as such.

SEAWORTHINESS AND SEAMANSHIP

Safe movement (Ref: MGN 532 & COSWP Ch. 11)

Requirement	The employer and Master shall ensure that safe means of access is provided and maintained to any place on the ship to which a person may be expected to go.
This includes	Lighting. Ventilation. Guarding against slips, trips and falls. Adequate safety signs. Guardrails or fencing. Condition of ladders and companionways. Movements of vehicles.
General principles	Passageways, walkways, stairs maintained and kept free of slip and trip hazards. Adequately lit and ventilated areas. Safety signs where appropriate for slip hazards, reduced height etc. Openings, open hatchways, dangerous edges fitted with guards/fencing (unless inappropriate). Drains, deck channels and scuppers inspected. Specific walkways clearly marked and closed when dangerous. Walkways non-slip surface where practicable. Lifelines rigged on deck areas in rough areas. Hazards – pipes, low door arches – painted in contrasting colour. At sea: Loose gear lashed or stowed. Ropes coiled and secured. Guardrails should be 1m high with mid rail 0.5m. Vehicles secured or safe walkways established where they operate.

Pilot ladder
(Ref: MGN 533 & IMO Resolution A.1045(27) – Pilot boarding arrangements)

General requirement	Constructed to SOLAS standards (Reg V/23). Identified with tags to enable identification for survey, inspection and record-keeping. Properly maintained, stowed and inspected.
General rigging	Supervised by a responsible officer. Officer has comms with bridge. Crew rigging are trained and equipment inspected. Safety line and harness worn by riggers. A lifebuoy with self-igniting light, buoyant line and quoit nearby. Heaving line. Adequately lit.
Safe rigging	Rigged so steps are horizontal. Correct height. Ladder should rest firmly against ship side. When c/w accommodation ladder, pilot ladder should extend at least 2m above the bottom platform. Any retrieval line leading forward and attached at or above the lowest spreader.
Where	On the lee side of the vessel (sheltered side). Rigged ideally near amidships, but away from bow/stern overhangs. Clear of any discharges on the ship. The person climbing climbs no more than 9m (over 9m only with a combination of accommodation ladder). Any illumination shining forward so as not to blind pilot boat coxswain.

SECTION 6

Components and dimensions	Two 28mm main ropes. Two 18mm side ropes. Steps slip resistant. Steps made from hardwood, resilient plastic or rubber. If made from wood – no knots and not painted. Foothold minimum 400 x 115 x 25mm. Step intervals 310mm +/- 5mm. Lower four steps made from rubber. 1.8m spreader at intervals that shall not exceed nine steps. Spreader at fifth step from the bottom.

Watertight doors

Water- and weathertight doors (Ref: SOLAS II-1/13)	
SOLAS Def. (Ref: II-1/2.17)	Watertight doors are capable of preventing the passage of water in any direction under the head of water likely to occur in intact and damaged conditions. Often below the waterline, shaft tunnels, engine compartments, ballast tanks. Weathertight is defined as that in any sea conditions water will not penetrate the ship. Therefore, above the waterline, bridge or external accommodation doors, hatch covers, ventilator covers etc.
Operation	Powered-type watertight doors can be operated locally (at the door) or remotely on the bridge. When closed remotely from the bridge, all doors must close within 40 seconds; audible and visual alarms at the door. Indicators on the bridge show the status of watertight door closure. Powered-type doors require manual pump-operated back-up system, both locally and from a remote station above the bulkhead deck. Controls for local operation are on both sides of the door.
Category/type of watertight door (Ref: IMO Circular MSC.1/Circ. 1380)	
D	A door must always be kept closed during navigation, except at the urgent discretion of the Master.
C	A door that should be closed during navigation, but may be opened to permit passage through it of passengers and crew, but then immediately closed.
B	A door that should be closed during navigation, but left open for the length of time personnel are working in the adjacent compartment.
A	A door that may be kept open during navigation, if considered absolutely necessary for the safe and effective operation of the ship's machinery or allow passengers unrestricted access throughout the passenger area. This judgement will be made by the administration/flag state. It should always be in a state of ready closure in an emergency.
Discretion	The Administration may authorise that particular doors can be opened at the discretion of the Master, for the operation of the ship or the embarking and disembarking of passengers when the ship is at safe anchorage and provided that the safety of the ship is not impaired.
Markings	A, B, C, D and the meaning should be marked either side of the watertight door and on the navigational bridge.
Stability information	Watertight doors that can remain open should be marked as such on the ship's stability information and plan.

SEAWORTHINESS AND SEAMANSHIP

67

Factors restricting the opening of watertight doors	IMO states: 1. In waters with high traffic density; 2. near coastal waters; 3. in heavy weather; 4. in dangerous ice conditions; 5. in waters where soundings are unreliable; 6. during periods of restricted visibility; 7. within port limits or compulsory pilotage waters; 8. when loose objects are nearby, which could potentially prevent the watertight door from being closed; or 9. under any condition when the ship's Master considers the situation to necessitate all watertight doors to be closed.[12] (Excerpt).
Records	Hinged doors, portable plates, side scuttles, gangway, cargo and bunkering ports and other openings, which are required by SOLAS regulations to be kept closed during navigation, shall be closed before the ship leaves port. The time of closing and the time of opening (if type permissible under regulations) shall be recorded in such logbook as may be prescribed by the Administration. A record of drills, inspections and defects recorded in the logbook.
Drills, inspections and additional requirements	Passenger ships: Weekly if the voyage exceeds one week duration, a complete drill held before leaving port, then once a week thereafter. Weekly – mechanisms, valves and indicators inspected. Daily – all watertight doors in watertight bulkheads, in use at sea, operated daily. Recorded in OLB Part II. Ro-ro: Ro-ro spaces continuously monitored so that movement of vehicles or unauthorised access can be detected.
Maintenance	Free of dirt and obstruction, lubrication of mechanical parts (wheels, bearings and hinges), check seals, hydraulic hoses, structural damage of frame or lip, check signage ABCD is in place, check operation of manual pump closures, check for signs of corrosion, warning light operation and alarms.
Timings	Power-operated doors must be capable of closing from the bridge and ship control centre in not more than 60 seconds when the ship is upright. Once the door starts to close it shall do so no less than 20 seconds and no more than 40 seconds. Local accumulator sufficient for three complete movements of the door. Hand-operated pump closure during power outage, the door should shut in 90 seconds. Remotely operated doors will sound an audible alarm for at least 5 seconds before the door moves. The door will move in no more than 10 seconds.

Stability

▶ Key terms in defining stability: Gravity, Buoyancy, GZ and Metacentre

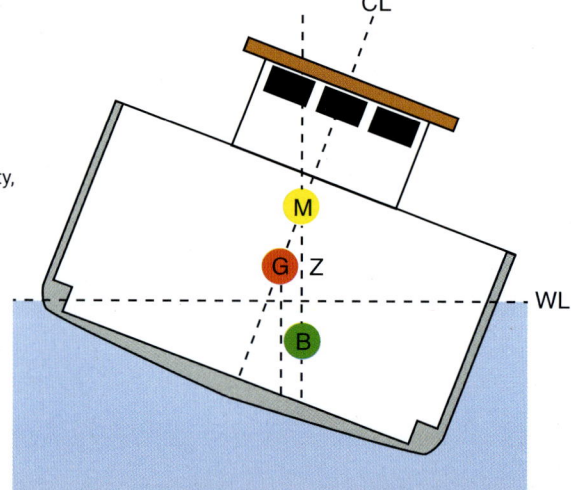

SECTION 6

Stability terms and definitions

Abbreviation	Term	Definition
G	Gravity	The point at which the mass of the ship (and everything on board) may be assumed to be concentrated, and through which the force of gravity acts vertically downward.
∇	Volume	The volume of the portion of the ship's hull below the waterline (m^3).
B	Buoyancy	The geometric centre of the underwater volume. The point through which the force of buoyancy is assumed to act vertically upward.
ρ	Density	The mass per unit volume of a substance. Normally measured in kg per m^3 (kg/m^3). Density of seawater is 1025 kg/m^3. Density of freshwater is 1000 kg/m^3.
TPC	Tonnes per centimetre	Tonnes per centimetre immersion is the mass that must be loaded or discharged to change a ship's mean draught in salt water by 1cm. For example, a barge with a TPC of 2.4 means the barge will sink 1cm for every 2.4 tonnes of cargo loaded. (TPI, tonnes per inch immersed, was also used before metrification. TPI is still seen today, but it may also mean tonnes per cm immersed.)
FWA	Fresh water allowance	The number of millimetres by which the mean draught changes when a ship passes from salt (1.025) to fresh water (1.000).
DWA	Dock water allowance	The dock water allowance is the proportion of the FWA that the load line can be submerged when the ship is floating in dock water of a density between 1.000 and 1.025 (fresh and seawater mix).
M	Metacentre	The metacentre is a theoretical defined point at the intersection of successive verticals through the Centre of Buoyancy for small angles of heel. It is generally used as a reference point to express a value between Gravity and Metacentre (GM).
	Transverse stability	Dealing with list, heel and the ability of the ship to stay upright.
	Longitudinal stability	Dealing with trim, draughts and optimum loading conditions.
LBP or LPP	Length between perpendiculars	Datum length of ship used in trim and stability calculations. The perpendiculars of a vessel are defined as the intersection of the summer load waterline with verticals through the forward edge of the stempost, and the after end of the rudder stock or, if no rudder stock, then the axis of the rudder post. The after perpendicular tends to be the 'zero' point for all longitudinal measurements within the ship.
GZ	Sum	The perpendicular distance between the parallel lines of force created by B and G is known as the GZ or righting arm. The greater the GZ the greater the righting lever.
GM	Sum	Vertical distance between the centre of gravity and the metacentre. Also known as the metacentric height. The greater the distance between G and M, the greater the righting lever and hence the more stable the vessel. GM gives a measure of the vessel's stability.
KG	Sum	The height between the keel and the centre of gravity.
	Stiff	Vessel with a fast roll period. Vessel that rights itself quickly. Often a large GM or small KG.

SEAWORTHINESS AND SEAMANSHIP

CRAMMER FOR DECK OFFICER ORAL EXAMS

	Tender		Vessel with a slow roll period. Rights itself more slowly. Smaller GM or larger KG.
	Positive equilibrium or stability		Centre of gravity is lower than metacentre. This means the vessel will return to upright every time as there is a positive righting lever.
	Neutral equilibrium or stability		Centre of gravity is at the same level as the metacentre. An angle of heel will stay the same and there is no righting lever. Dangerous.
	Negative equilibrium or stability		Centre of gravity is higher than metacentre. The vessel is unstable and has negative righting lever so the vessel will continue to list until either a stable equilibrium is reached, or more likely, the vessel will capsize.
	Heel		Angle to port or starboard due to external forces such as wind or waves.
	List		Angle to port or starboard due to internal forces such as placement of cargo or stores.
	Loll		Angle of loll is when a vessel is initially unstable when upright and can take on a heel to port or starboard.
	Trim		Fore and aft angle of the vessel – trimmed by the bow means the vessels bow is lower than the stern. Trimmed by the stern means the vessel's stern is lower than the bow.
	Damaged stability		Compartments and tanks that could be flooded due to damage and predicted draught, trim and list in those conditions.
FSE	Free surface effect		The unchecked movement of fluids; water, fuels, liquids on deck or in tanks that change the centre of gravity as the fluid flows from one side to the other.
	Lifting loads		As soon as a load is raised, the weight of the load transfers to the head of the crane.

Load lines

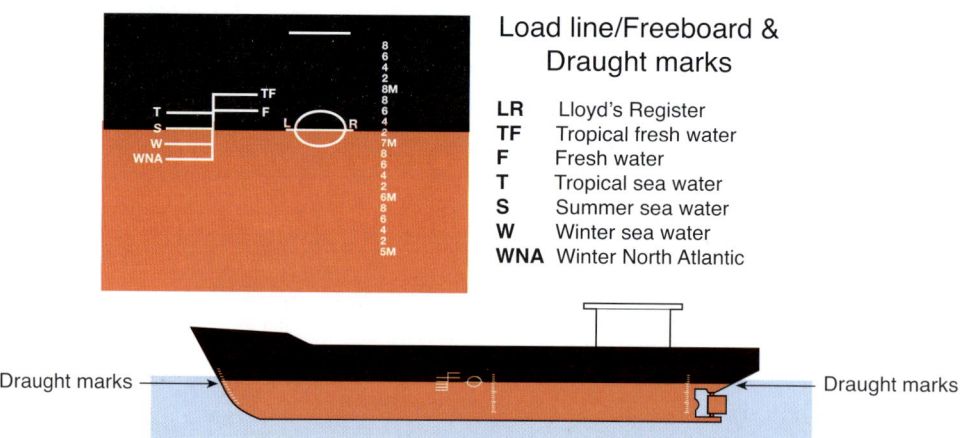

Load line/Freeboard & Draught marks

LR Lloyd's Register
TF Tropical fresh water
F Fresh water
T Tropical sea water
S Summer sea water
W Winter sea water
WNA Winter North Atlantic

▲ International load line and draught marks on the side of the ship.

SECTION 6

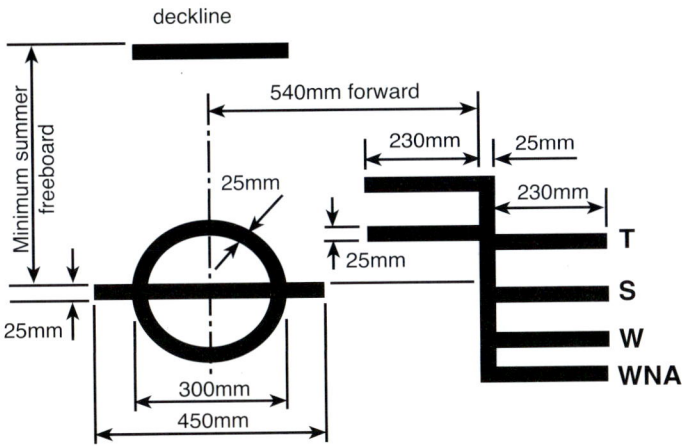

▲ Load and deck line measurements are displayed in a contrasting colour.

Hull markings – load line	
Colours and general requirement	Marked on each side of the ship. Should be plainly visible.
Markings	Load line (sometimes known as 'freeboard mark' – small vessels). Load line ring. Deck line.
Deck line	A line on the side of the ship at the same level as the uppermost continuous watertight deck (line 300mm x 25mm). Often a raised mark, such as a welded steel strip.
Load line, or Plimsoll Mark	A line placed at a distance below the deck line equal to the minimum freeboard as assigned to the vessel by the Certifying Authority. 450mm x 25mm. Line is usually marked with a ring (300mm).
Markings that adjust working load line due to season, salinity and area	LR Lloyd's Register or two letter initials of class society/flag TF Tropical fresh F Fresh water T Tropical sea water S Summer sea water W Winter sea water WNA Winter North Atlantic
Load line zone chart	IMO produce a 'zone chart' defining the load line areas (T, S, W, WNA etc.) and when they apply seasonally. In general terms, IMO define the following: Summer – not more than 10% winds of F8 or more. Tropical – not more than 1% winds of F8 or more. Winter and Winter North Atlantic are given times when they apply, depending on the area and hemisphere. In basic terms, more freeboard is required for rougher seas.

SEAWORTHINESS AND SEAMANSHIP

Inland waters load lines or freeboard marks	On inland waters vessels, and on those vessels under 24m, the load line is occasionally without the load ring – this single line is often referred to as a freeboard mark. Occasionally there may not be a corresponding 'deck line'. On the River Thames the inland category of water that the vessel is able to operate within (C or D) is also noted alongside the load line/freeboard mark. Category D waters have greater maximum wave heights than Category C, therefore the allowable amount of passengers or loads carried may differ between C and D vessel operation. In European inland waters the categorisation of inland waters are Zones 1, 2, 3 and 4, therefore numbers may be marked next to the corresponding load line.
Load line certificate	Three types of survey – Initial, Renewal and Annual. Certificate validity – not exceeding 5 years and subject to annual surveys. Annual surveys recorded/endorsed on the original Load Line Certificate. International Load Line Certificate for vessels over 150GT (or 24m) or; UK Load Line Certificate for vessels under convention size but not pleasure vessels, fishing vessels, those that do not go to sea. Details from the Load Line Certificate are transferred to the vessel's official logbook (load line, depth of loading, etc.). The Load Line Certificate should be kept framed and posted in a conspicuous place on board ship. If the vessel complies with a small vessel code (SCV or SWB), the code certificate becomes a legal alternative to a load line certificate.
Notice of Load lines (Posted)	Along with the Load Line Certificate, Notice 'MSF 2004' (Draught of water and freeboard) should be posted on board before sailing.
Draught marks	Marked on each side of a ship's stem and near the sternpost. In figures in two-decimetre increments. In figures at every metre denoted with a 'M' (metres).
Freeboard (also known as reserve buoyancy)	Distance measured vertically downwards at amidships from the upper edge of the deck line to the actual waterline to give actual freeboard. Ship's general freeboard quoted from the deck line to the load line.
Freeboard notes	More freeboard will often result in: More reserve buoyancy. Less chance of down flooding because of the greater height. Greater height from the water of intakes and ventilators. Greater angle of deck edge immersion. Greater range of stability. Greater GZ. Greater GM.
Draught survey hydrometer	Measures the relative density of the water. Often used to establish water salinity for Dock Water Allowance. Hydrometer should be calibrated and certificated.
Draught	The depth to the bottom of the keel from the waterline.
Air draught	The distance from the waterline to the top of the vessel including antennae, usually required for calculating vertical clearances. Air draught changes as draught changes.
Gross tonnage (GT)	A measure of volume inside a vessel. Includes all areas from bow to stern and keel to funnel. The volume is multiplied using a formula to give the gross tonnage (GT).
Net tonnage (NT)	A measure of the available volume of cargo and passenger spaces; the earning capacity of the ship.

SECTION 6

Lightship tonnage	The weight of the ship as built, including boiler water, lubricating oil and cooling water systems full.
Deadweight (Dwt)	The amount of weight a ship can load; it is the difference between the lightship and loaded displacements. Includes cargo, ballast, fuel, potable water, stores, crew and effects.
Displacement tonnage	The weight of the volume of water displaced by the ship stated in tonnes.
Freshwater density	1000kg/m^3.
Seawater density	1025kg/m^3.

Tonnage definitions

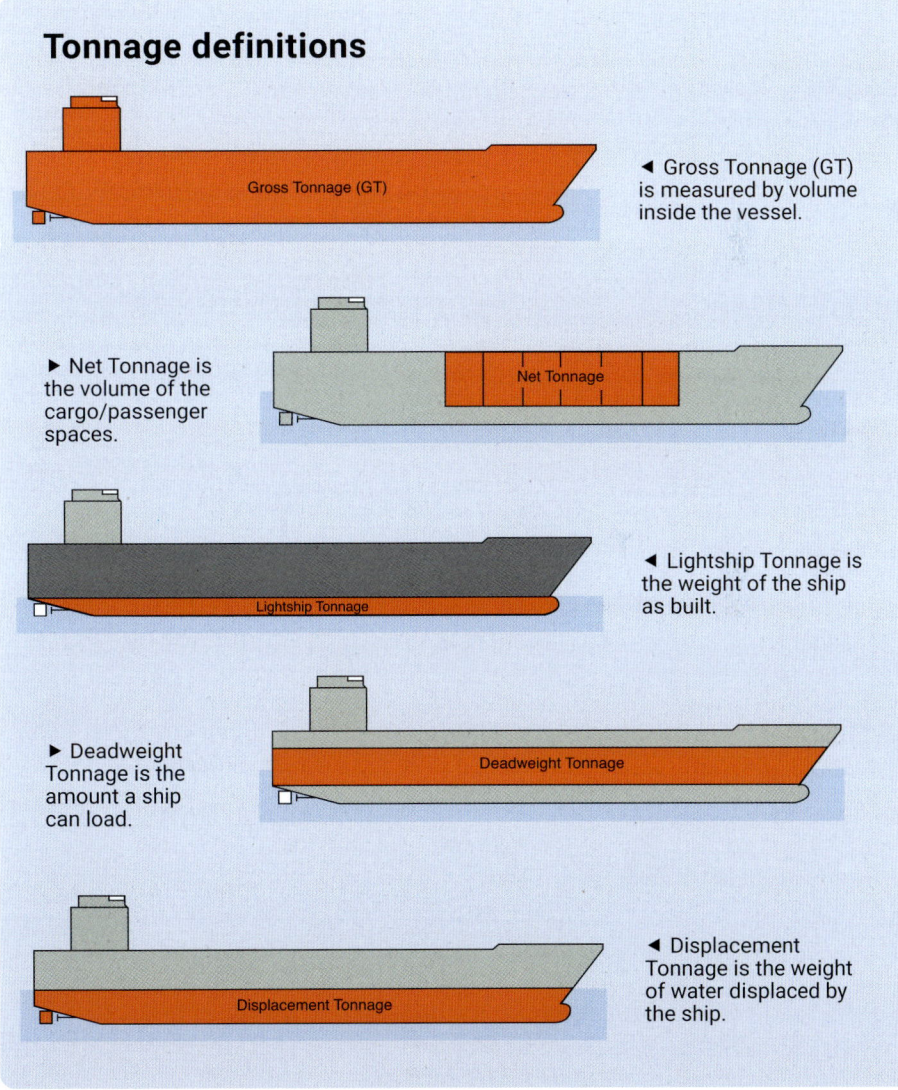

◄ Gross Tonnage (GT) is measured by volume inside the vessel.

► Net Tonnage is the volume of the cargo/passenger spaces.

◄ Lightship Tonnage is the weight of the ship as built.

► Deadweight Tonnage is the amount a ship can load.

◄ Displacement Tonnage is the weight of water displaced by the ship.

SEAWORTHINESS AND SEAMANSHIP

Stability information book

The stability information book is often overlooked, especially on some smaller vessels, but careful use of this book is paramount to ensuring the vessel's safety.

Stability Information Book (SIB)	
General	Mandatory book on any vessel to which the load line regulations apply (or applicable Small Commercial/Workboat Vessels). SIB contains information on the ship's stability for the guidance of the Master. The stability book is drawn up by an authorised Naval Architect and then approved on a case-by-case basis by the Administration.

Contents
 	
Note: A similar but simplified list for small workboats is in the Workboat code.
	1. General particulars.
	2. Plans showing cargo spaces, storerooms and tanks.
	3. Special notes regarding the stability and loading of the ship.
	4. Metric conversions.
	5. Hydrostatic particulars.
	6. Capacities and centres of gravity of cargo spaces, storerooms, crew and effects.
	7. Capacities, centres of gravity and free surface moments of oil and water tanks (sheet 1 – cargo oil and oil fuel).
	8. Capacities, centres of gravity and free surface moments of oil and water tanks (sheet 2 – engine room and fresh + ballast).
	9. Notes on use of Free Surface Moments.
	10. Container ships – capacities and centres of gravity.
	11. Cross curves of stability (KN Curves).
	12. Example showing use of cross curves (KN).
	13. Deadweight scale.
	14. List of conditions required.
	15. Typical condition sheet.
	16. Statical stability curve for condition.
	    Simplified stability information.
	17. General note.
	18. Deadweight moment curve + table.
	19. Typical loading sheet.
	    Damaged stability
	20. Flooding and damaged stability; requirements for Type 'A' and Type 'B' ships I.
	21. Flooding and damaged stability; requirements in the flooded condition.
	22. Flooding and damaged stability; information to be presented from flooding calculations.
	23. Flooding and damaged stability; typical sketches required.

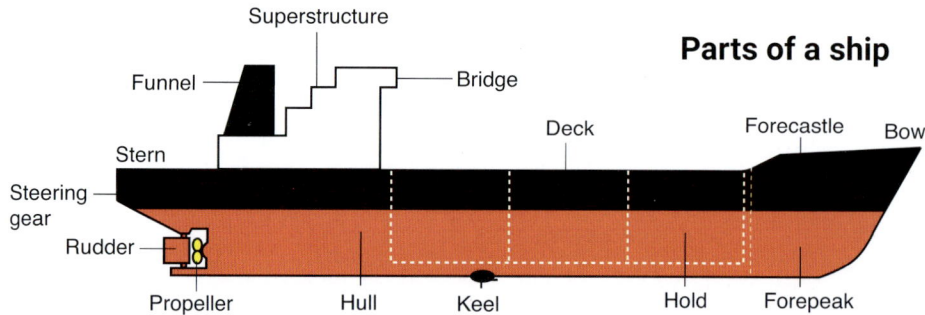

Parts of a ship

SECTION 6

Critical measurements, especially for navigation

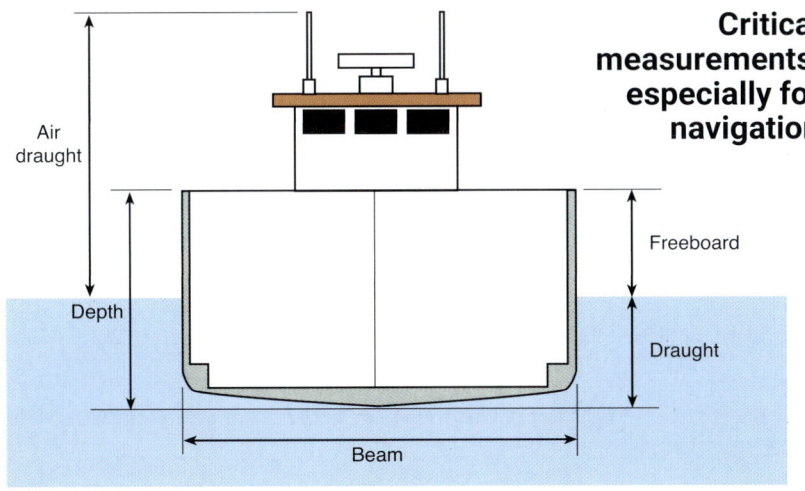

Basic nautical terminology

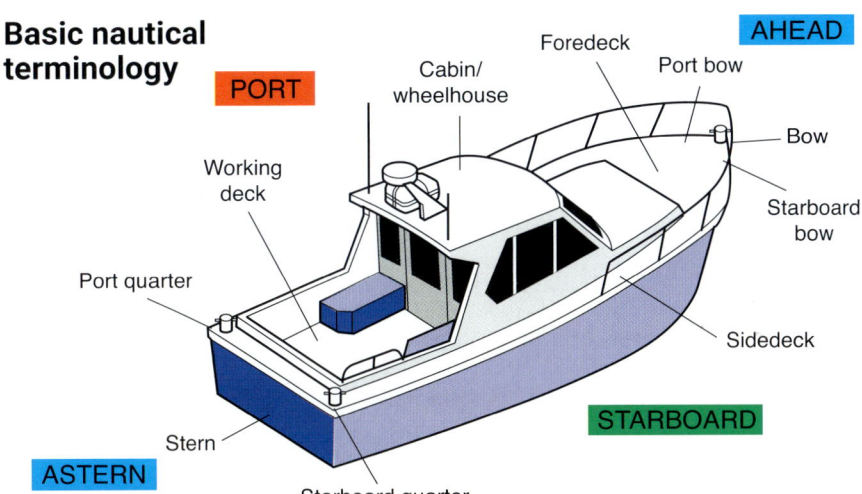

Basic measurements of ship length

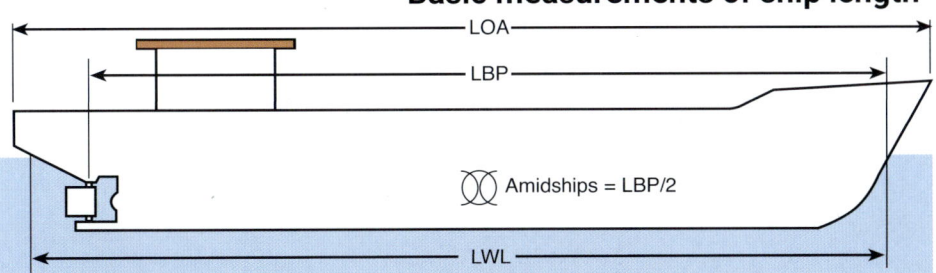

LOA – Length over all
LBP – Length between perpendiculars
LWL – Length water line

Dock water allowance

Dock water allowance (DWA) and effect

A vessel at sea, proceeding upriver where the salinity and relative density of the water is less, will sink lower in the water, increasing its draught. This is because seawater relative density is 1025 and freshwater has a relative density of 1000.

Definition	DWA of a ship is the number of millimetres by which the mean draught changes when a ship passes from saltwater to dock water, or vice versa, when the ship is loaded to the summer displacement.

DWA (Dock Water Allowance)

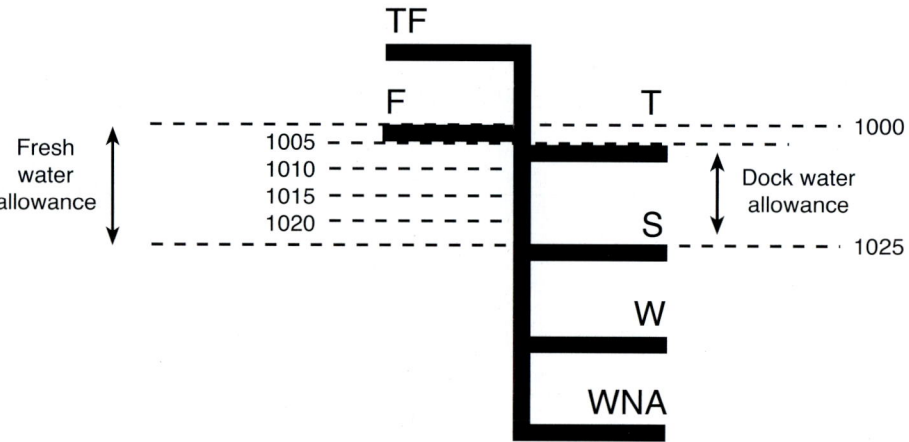

▲ Calculation of Dock Water Allowance when a change in salinity is present, such as when in a dock.

Section 7
Pollution prevention

Depending on the type and size of vessel you are operating, it is likely that not all the conditions listed in MARPOL will apply. Annex I, IV, V and VI usually apply in some way to all vessels to a greater or lesser extent.

Useful mnemonics: MARPOL

Oil	Oh
Noxious substances	No,
Harmful substances	High Spirits
Sewage	Start
Garbage	Going
Air	Around

International Convention for the Prevention of Pollution from Ships

MARPOL Annex I	Regulations for the prevention of pollution by oil.
MARPOL Annex II	Control of pollution by noxious liquid substances in bulk.
MARPOL Annex III	Prevention of pollution by harmful substances carried by sea in packaged form.
MARPOL Annex IV	Regulations for the prevention of pollution by sewage from ships.
MARPOL Annex V	Regulations for the prevention of pollution by garbage from ships.
MARPOL Annex VI	Regulations for the prevention of air pollution from ships.

IMO (MARPOL) Special Areas

Special area	I Oil	II Nox	IV Sewage	V Garbage	VI Air emission control
Mediterranean Sea	x			x	
Baltic Sea	x		x	x	SOx and NOx
Black Sea	x			x	
Red Sea	x			x	
'Gulfs' area	x			x	
Gulf of Aden	x				
Antarctic area	x	x			
North West European Waters	x				
Oman area of the Arabian Sea	x				
Southern South African waters	x				
North Sea				x	SOx and NOx

SECTION 7

POLLUTION PREVENTION

Antarctic area (south of latitude 60 degrees south)				x	
Wider Caribbean region, including the Gulf of Mexico and the Caribbean Sea				x	
North American ECA					(SOx and PM) (NOx)
United States Caribbean Sea ECA					(SOx and PM) (NOx)

Particularly Sensitive Sea Areas (PSSAs)

PSSA	Protective measure	PSSA	Protective measure
Great Barrier Reef	IMO-recommended Australian system of pilotage; mandatory ship reporting system	Torres Strait as an extension to GBR PSSA Australia and Papua New Guinea	IMO-recommended Australian system of pilotage; two-way route
Archipelago of Sabana-Camagüey Cuba	Area to be avoided	Canary Islands Spain	Areas to be avoided; traffic separation systems; recommended routes; mandatory ship reporting system
Sea Area around Malpelo Island, Colombia	Area to be avoided	Galapagos Archipelago, Ecuador	Area to be avoided; mandatory ship reporting system; recommended tracks
Marine Area around the Florida Keys, USA	Areas to be avoided; mandatory no anchoring	Baltic Sea Area Denmark, Estonia, Finland, Germany, Latvia, Lithuania, Poland and Sweden	Traffic separation schemes, deep-water route, areas to be avoided, mandatory ship reporting system, MARPOL Special Area; MARPOL SOx Emission Control Area
Wadden Sea Netherlands, Denmark, Germany	Mandatory deep water route	Papahānaumokuākea Marine National Monument (North-western Hawaiian Islands)	Areas to be avoided; recommended/ mandatory ship reporting system
Paracas National Reserve, Peru	Area to be avoided	Strait of Bonifacio	Recommendation on navigation
Western European Waters	Mandatory ship reporting system	Saba Bank (Caribbean Island of Saba)	Area to be avoided; mandatory no anchoring

79

Oil

Oil record books

Oil record book Part I Requirement	Oil tanker of 150GT or more and every ship of 400GT or more.
Oil record book Part II Requirement	For oil tankers, oil record book part II shall also be provided to record relevant cargo/ballast operations).
LIST OF ITEMS TO BE RECORDED	a. Ballasting or cleaning of oil fuel tanks. b. Discharge of dirty ballast or cleaning water from oil fuel tanks. c. Collection, transfer and disposal of oil residues (sludge). d. Non-automatic starting of discharge overboard, transfer or disposal otherwise of bilge water that has accumulated in machinery spaces. e. Automatic starting of discharge overboard, transfer or disposal otherwise of bilge water that has accumulated in machinery spaces. f. Condition of the oil filtering equipment. g. Accidental or other exceptional discharges of oil. h. Bunkering of fuel or bulk lubricating oil.

Sample, part I

Date	Code	Item	Record of operations/signature of officer in charge

Signature of Master ....

Oil record book Part II

Requirement	For oil tankers, oil record book part II shall also be provided to record relevant cargo/ballast operations. They shall also carry oil record book Part I.
LIST OF ITEMS TO BE RECORDED	a. Loading of oil cargo. b. Internal transfer of oil cargo during voyage. c. Unloading of oil cargo. d. Crude oil washing (COW tankers). e. Ballasting cargo tanks. f. Ballasting of dedicated clean ballast tanks (CBT Tankers). g. Cleaning of cargo tanks. h. Discharge of dirty ballast. i. Discharge of water from slop tanks into the sea. j. Disposal of residues and oily mixtures not otherwise dealt with. k. Discharge of clean ballast contained in cargo tanks. l. Discharge of ballast from dedicated clean ballast tanks (CBT tankers). m. Condition of oil discharge monitoring and control system. n. Accidental or other exceptional discharges of oil. o. Additional operational procedures and general remarks. p. Loading of ballast water. q. Reallocation of ballast water within the ship. r. Ballast water discharge to reception facility.

SECTION **7**

POLLUTION PREVENTION

Sample, part II			
Date	Code	Item	Record of operations/signature of officer in charge

Signature of Master ………………………………………………………………..

Garbage

Garbage requirements and logs (Ref: MGN 632)	
Garbage placards	Required on every ship 12m or more. (Vessels shall display a placard displaying the legal requirements of dumping waste in accordance with MARPOL).
Garbage management plan	Every ship 100GT and above and certified to carry 15 persons or more.
Garbage management plan, written procedures for:	1) Minimising, collecting, storing and processing of garbage. 2) Disposing of garbage. 3) The use of the garbage equipment on board. 4) Designating the person or persons in charge of carrying out the plan.
Garbage record book (GRB)	
Requirement	Every ship 400GT and certified to carry 15 persons or more on passages to areas under the jurisdiction of another party (international).
Description of the garbage	Garbage is grouped into categories for the purposes of the garbage record book (or ship's official logbook) as follows: **Part 1** A Plastics B Food wastes C Domestic wastes D Cooking oil E Incinerator ashes F Operational wastes G Animal carcasses H Fishing gear I E-waste **Part 2** J Cargo residues (non-HME) K Cargo residues (HME)
Entries	When garbage is discharged to a reception facility ashore or to other ships. When garbage is incinerated. When garbage is discharged into the sea in accordance with regulations 4, 5 or 6 of MARPOL Annex V. Accidental or other exceptional discharges or loss of garbage into the sea, including in accordance with regulation 7 of MARPOL Annex V.

Example							
Date/time	Position of the ship/Remarks (e.g. accidental loss)	Category	Estimated amount discharged incinerated	To sea	To reception facility	Incineration	Certification Signature

Master's signature .... Date ....

MARPOL certificates, plans and records

International Oil Pollution Prevention Certificate (IOPP)	
Who needs it	Issued to oil tankers of 150GT or more, or any vessel 400GT or more after survey by the Flag administration or organisation duly authorised by it.
Valid	5 years (maximum).
Survey – initial	Requires initial survey before ship is put into service to include full survey of its structure, equipment, systems, fittings, arrangements, and that materials comply with Marpol Annex I.
Renewal	Survey at 5 years.
Intermediate	Survey within 3 months before or after second anniversary or 3 months before or after 3rd anniversary of the certificate, to be carried out to coincide with the annual survey.
Annual	Survey within 3 months before or after each anniversary date of the certificate.
Repair/alteration	Additional survey to ensure repairs are effective and to regulation.

Shipboard oil pollution emergency plan

Shipboard oil pollution emergency plans (SOPEP) realistically apply to nearly everyone going for a certificate and they are often the emergency procedure and drill most forgotten.

Shipboard oil pollution emergency plan (SOPEP)	
Who needs it	Every oil tanker of 150GT and above and every ship other than an oil tanker of 400 GT and above shall carry on board a shipboard oil pollution emergency plan.
Approved by	The SOPEP plan should be approved by the Administration.

SECTION 7

POLLUTION PREVENTION

What should it cover	1. Procedure to be followed by the Master or other persons having charge of the ship to report an oil pollution incident. 2. List of authorities/persons to be contacted in the event of an oil pollution incident. 3. A detailed description of the action to be taken immediately by persons on board to reduce or control the discharge of oil following the incident. 4. The procedures and point of contact on the ship for co-ordinating shipboard action with national and local authorities in combating the pollution.
SOPEP action plan should include	Crew members SOPEP duty and emergency muster and actions. Procedure to contain the discharge of oil into the sea. Location, contents and inventory of SOPEP locker. Vessel drawings of fuel/oil lines, positioning of vents and scuppers. General arrangement plans with location of tanks. Authorities to contact and external reporting requirements (port state control, harbour authority, oil spill response team). On board reporting procedure and requirement. Guidance for record-keeping (for liability and insurance). Procedure to maintain required SOPEP records. Procedures for testing SOPEP plan. Details of when and how to review the plan.

Noxious liquid substances

Shipboard marine pollution emergency plan for noxious liquid substances

Who needs it	Every ship of 150GT and above and certified to carry noxious liquid substances shall carry on board a noxious liquid emergency plan approved by the Administration.
What should it cover	1. Procedure to be followed by the Master or other persons having charge of the ship to report a noxious liquid substances pollution incident. 2. List of authorities/persons to be contacted in the event of a noxious liquid substances pollution incident. 3. Detailed description of the action to be taken immediately by persons on board to reduce or control the discharge of oil following the incident. 4. Procedures and point of contact on the ship for co-ordinating shipboard action with national and local authorities in combating the pollution.

MARPOL Annex II: Categorisation of noxious liquid substances

Category	Hazard level if discharged into sea from cleaning or de-ballasting	Amount that can be discharged
Category X:	Major hazard	Prohibited
Category Y:	Hazard	Limitation of quality and quantity
Category Z	Minor hazard	Less stringent on the quality and quantity of the discharge
OS (Other Substances)	No harm	No limits under Annex II

International Pollution Prevention Certificate for the Carriage of Noxious Liquid Substances in Bulk

Who needs it	Any ship intended to carry noxious liquid substances in bulk and engaged in voyages to ports or terminals internationally.
Valid	5 years (maximum).
Survey – initial	Requires initial survey before ship is put into service, including survey of its structure, equipment, systems, fittings, arrangements and materials to comply with Annex II.
Renewal	Survey at 5 years.
Intermediate	Survey within 3 months before or after second anniversary or 3 months before or after 3rd anniversary of the certificate, to be carried out to coincide with the annual survey.
Annual	Survey within 3 months before or after each anniversary date of the certificate.
Repair/ alteration	Additional survey to ensure repairs are effective and to regulation.

Shipboard marine pollution emergency plan for noxious liquid substances (SMPEP – NL)

Who needs it?	Every ship of 150GT or more certified to carry noxious liquid substances shall carry an approved shipboard marine pollution emergency plan for noxious liquid substances. (This follows a similar format to the SOPEP plan).

Cargo record book for ships carrying noxious liquid substances in bulk

LIST OF ITEMS TO BE RECORDED	a. Loading of cargo. b. Internal transfer of cargo. c. Unloading of cargo. d. Mandatory prewash in accordance with the ship's Procedures and Arrangements Manual. e. Cleaning of cargo tanks except mandatory prewash (other prewash operations, final wash, ventilation, etc.). f. Discharge into the sea of tank washings. g. Ballasting of cargo tanks. h. Discharge of ballast water from cargo tanks. i. Accidental or other exceptional discharge. j. Control by authorised surveyors. k. Additional procedures and remarks.

Useful mnemonics

IMDG classes	1. Explosives 2. Gases 3. Flammable Liquids 4. Flammable Solids 5. Oxidising 6. Toxic / Infectious 7. Radioactive 8. Corrosive 9. Miscellaneous	Every Gust Flies Flags On The Riggers Centre Mast

SECTION 7

POLLUTION PREVENTION

Sample

Plan view of cargo and slop tanks	Identification of the tank	Capacity – cubic metres
Pump room		

Cargo and ballast operations

Date	Code Letter	Item Number	Record of operations/signature of officer in charge/name of and signature of authorised surveyor

Signature of Master..

Note	• Ship's Masters should obtain from the operator of the reception facilities, which include barges and tank trucks, a receipt or certificate specifying the quantity of tank washings transferred, together with the time and date of the transfer. • The receipt or certificate should be kept together with the cargo record book.

MARPOL Annex III
Prevention of pollution by harmful substances carried by sea in packaged form

IMDG Code	Much of the requirements of Annex III are contained in the IMDG Code International Maritime Dangerous Goods Code.	
Dangerous goods are substances or articles that may:	Kill or injure people. Damage the environment. Damage ships or transport. Damage cargo.	
Cargo	Transport as **cargo** by sea – in **any** vessel – is ONLY permitted under the terms of the Document of Compliance (DoC). Ships **stores** would normally be covered by Material Safety Data Sheets (MSDS) rather than the IMDG code.	

Classification of Dangerous Goods (DGs)

Class 1		Explosives (six sub-divisions 1.1, 1.2, 1.3, 1.4, 1.5, 1.6)
Class 2		Gases
	Class 2.1	Flammable gases
	Class 2.2	Non-flammable, non-toxic gases
	Class 2.3	Toxic gases
Class 3		Flammable liquids
Class 4		Flammable solids
	Class 4.1	Flammable solids
	Class 4.2	Substances liable to spontaneous combustion
	Class 4.3	Substances which, in contact with water, emit flammable gases
Class 5		Oxidising substances and organic peroxides
	Class 5.1	Oxidising substances
	Class 5.2	Organic peroxides
Class 6		Toxic and infectious substances
	Class 6.1	Toxic substances
	Class 6.2	Infectious substances
Class 7		Radioactive material
Class 8		Corrosive substances
Class 9		Miscellaneous dangerous substances and articles

SECTION 7

POLLUTION PREVENTION

IMDG Codes (Vol 1, 2 and Supplement) – International Maritime Dangerous Goods Code

Volume 1	Part 1 – General provisions, definitions and training
	Part 2 – Classification
	Part 3 – Dangerous Goods List (special provisions and exceptions)
	Part 4 – Packing and tank provisions
	Part 5 – Consignment procedures
	Part 6 – Construction and testing of packaging
	Part 7 – Transport operations
Volume 2	Appendix A – List of generic and N.O.S proper shipping names
	Appendix B – Glossary of terms
	Index – Alphabetical list of PSNs
Supplement	EmS Guide – (Emergency situations) Emergency response procedures
	MFAG – Medical First Aid Guide
	Reporting procedures
	Recommendations on the safe use of pesticides
	Safe carriage of INF, plutonium and radioactive wastes
	Appendix – Resolutions and circulars relating to IMDG
Terms	
UN Number	IMO states: Four-digit United Nations Number is assigned to dangerous, hazardous and harmful substances, materials and articles most commonly transported.[13] (Excerpt).
PSN	Proper Shipping Name is the name of the DG as listed by the IMDG and conforming to the UN Number.
Packing group	I, II or III: assigned by degree of hazard: higher risk, lower number (Classes 3, 6, 8 and 9).
Subsidiary risk	A product that has other risks, such as it is both flammable and corrosive.
Segregation	IMO states: Separating two or more substances or articles that are considered mutually incompatible when their packing or stowage together may result in undue hazards in case of leakage, spillage or any other accident.[14] (Excerpt).

A key point with IMDG compliance is the difference between what dangerous goods are carried as ship's stores, as these would just fall into Control of Substances Hazardous to Health and the application of Safety Data Sheets. As opposed to what is carried as cargo, which falls into IMDG and the requirements for a Document of Compliance.

IMDG Document of Compliance

	Cargo ships	Passenger ships
Who needs it	All other ships 500GT or more constructed on or after 1/09/84. All other ships of under 500 tons constructed on or after 1/02/92.	Passenger ships constructed on or after 1/09/84.
	Which are intended, or which have cargo spaces that are intended for the carriage of dangerous goods on international voyages.	
IMDG DoC validity	No more than 5 years and not to be extended beyond the expiry date of the Cargo Ship Safety Construction Certificate.	One year and should not be extended beyond the expiry date of the valid Passenger Ship Safety Certificate.
What surveys are required?	An initial survey. An annual survey, in conjunction with Safety Equipment Certificate or SCV survey. A renewal survey.	An initial survey. A renewal survey, in conjunction with the passenger ship survey.
Information on a DoC	Name of ship. Distinctive number or letters. Port of registry. Ship type. IMO Number (if applicable). • Schedule 1: A table of the dangerous goods approved for carriage and their stowage locations. • Schedule 2: A of list of the special requirements for this ship to carry dangerous goods.	
Small vessels	On small commercial vessels and workboats when issued with a DG DoC, they can only carry certain cargo types and only on the weather deck.	

Anti-fouling

Anti-foul
The International Convention on the Control of Harmful Anti-fouling Systems on Ships

Anti-foul declaration	Over 24m – under 400GT engaged in international voyages (excluding fixed or floating platforms, FSUs and FPSOs carry a Declaration of Anti-fouling Systems signed by the owner or authorised agent. The Declaration should be accompanied by a paint receipt or contractor invoice.
Anti-foul survey and certificate	Over 400GT engaged in international voyages. Initial survey before the ship is put into service or before the International Anti-fouling System Certificate is issued for the first time; and a survey when the anti-fouling systems are changed or replaced.

SECTION 7

Air pollution

MARPOL Annex VI Prevention of Air Pollution from Ships

Sulphur	The emissions of sulphur are strictly controlled and special Sulphur Emission Control Areas ('SECAs') are set up where strict limits must be observed. See MARPOL Special Areas section (air emission control). In addition to MARPOL Annex VI listed SECAs, the EU require 'that after 1st January 2010 all ships berthed or at anchor for longer than two hours in EU Ports must use low sulphur fuel of less than 0.1%' (Ref: Council Directive 2016/802/EC). Similar limits exist in Turkish ports, Icelandic territorial waters, certain Chinese and South Korean waters (check local requirements) (Ref: Britannia P & I). Panama Canal requires use of marine distillate fuels (MGO or MDO), NOT residual fuels (IFO, HFO). More and more areas are becoming designated as SECAs in an effort to slow climate change. Check before arrival.
Bunker delivery note (Ref: MARPOL Annex VI/18.1, (b), iii, 3 & 4. & Appendix V)	Must contain details of the sulphur content of the fuel delivered. Should be kept with either the oil record book or sulphur record book. Retention period 3 years. Should be produced to PSC officers when required.
Maximum fuel sulphur content	Within SECAs and EU ports: 0.1% m/m. / Outside SECAs and EU ports: 0.5% m/m.

Example of a marine fuel sulphur record book

Ship's name		IMO number		Distinctive numbers/letters	
SECA	Date and time of entry into SECA	Date and time changeover completed	Position changeover completed	Volume of low sulphur fuel remaining per tank	Signature

Master's signature.. Date........................

International Air Pollution Prevention Certificate (IAPPC)

Application	Every ship of 400GT and above.
Emissions covered by the certificate	Ozone depleting substances. Nitrogen oxides. Sulphur oxides (SOx) and particulates. / Volatile organic compounds (VOCs). Shipboard incineration.
Surveys required	An initial survey. A renewal survey at intervals not exceeding five years. / An intermediate survey. An annual survey.

POLLUTION PREVENTION

89

Information contained on the certificate	Particulars of ship. Name of ship. Distinctive number or letters. Port of registry. Gross tonnage. IMO Number. A statement that the survey shows that the equipment, systems, fittings, arrangements and materials fully comply with the applicable requirements of Annex VI of MARPOL. Date of survey that certificate is based.
Information contained in the IAPP Supplement	Particulars of ship. Control of emissions from ships. Ozone depleting substances. Nitrogen oxides (NOx). Sulphur oxides (SOx) and particulate matter. Volatile organic compounds (VOCs). Shipboard incineration.

Engine International Air Pollution Prevention Certificate (EIAPPC)

Engines requiring compliance with NOX regulations (engine age and tier)	All marine diesel engines (power output more than 130kW) installed on a ship. Caveats international voyages, not emergency machinery.
NOX engine tiers	Tier I 2000–11. Tier II 2011 after. Tier III in an emission control area.

Section 8
Emergencies

If there are questions that will always rear their head in an exam, it will be those on emergency procedures. With all emergency drills, the maintenance and checking of the equipment as well as the drill should be recorded, usually in the official logbook.

MGN 71 has for years been the reference for emergencies and drill. However, at the time of writing this book, new editions of COSWP are starting to have clearer definitions of what is required. Therefore, the author suggests you read COSWP and MGN 71 for full clarity.

▼ Performing the regular fire drill exercise.

Drills

Drills (MGN 71)		
Drill	**Frequency not exceeding**	**Notes**
A fire or other emergency drill should be held simultaneously with the first stage of the abandon ship drill.		
Abandon ship drill **Fire drill**	At least every month	**Within 24 hours of leaving port** if more than 25% of the crew have not taken part in drills on board the ship in the previous month. Drills for emergencies other than fire, e.g. collision, damage control, grounding, cargo or bunker spillage, rescue of personnel from dangerous spaces, or medical treatment, may be conducted in lieu of or in addition to a fire drill, provided each crew member participates in at least one fire drill each month.
Abandon ship drill and a fire drill		**In addition to above**, ships of Classes I, II, II(A) and III must hold these weekly, such that every crew member attends at least one drill per month.
Fire drills should be varied		1. Cargo fires in holds or other spaces. 2. Fires involving oil, gas or chemical cargoes as appropriate. 3. Fires in engine, pump or boiler rooms. 4. Fires in crew or passenger accommodation. 5. Galley fires due to oil or cooking fat.

Fire drill contents	Weekly	**Fire pumps in/outside** of the machinery spaces are prepared for operation, started, and the fire main(s) fully pressurised.
		
		 Lay out hoses – Where practicable run water through them.
		
		 A number of portable fire extinguishers should be available and members of the fire party should be instructed in their use for particular types of fire. The crew trained in the closing of openings, doors, ventilating shafts, fire doors, to reduce the supply of air to a fire and isolate it from other parts of the ship. Position and operation of remote controls for ventilation fans, oil fuel pumps and oil tank valves.
		
		 Fire party trained in use and checks on BA sets, protective clothing and emergency appliances (axes and safety lamps). Recommended that persons using BA sets practise in pairs.
		
		 At each fire drill at least one extinguisher discharged by a different crew member so both crew members in fire parties and other crew members gain experience in using extinguishers.
		 Crew members not in fire parties familiar with:
		   Types of fire extinguisher in their accommodation/work areas.
		   Location/means of activating alarms in their areas.
		
		 Escape routes from any part of the ship they are likely to be in when on or off duty.

SECTION 8

EMERGENCIES

Post fire drill	**Weekly**	**Fire protection systems** and appliances should at all times be in good order and available for immediate use during the voyage and in port. **Compressed air bottles** of breathing apparatus and fire extinguishers should be refilled after any drill. Where refilling facilities are not available on board additional equipment may be carried to facilitate training. **Discharged equipment** should be clearly marked and stored separately for refilling when in port. Equipment dedicated for training purposes should be marked 'for training purposes only'.
Survival craft muster and drill	**Three months**	**Crew muster** wearing lifejackets at their lifeboat station. **First/second in command have a list of crew.** **Life/rescue boat engine** should be run for 3 minutes (if possible) and gears tested. **Davits swung out** and winches tested. **Emergency lighting** for muster tested. **Lifeboats must be lowered** and launched every three months (or launched annually if trading patterns dictate).
Freefall lifeboats	**Six months**	Lowered to water.
Davit launched liferaft	**Four months**	Should include inflation and lowering.
Rescue boat drills	**Every month but not exceeding three months**	**Launched with crews**. Drill should include recovery of object/person in the water. Class 1 ship – rescue/emergency crews mustered on first day of voyage and then drilled every seven days.
Enclosed space entry/rescue	**Two months**	Each enclosed space entry and rescue drill shall include: • Checking and use of personal protective equipment required for entry. • Checking and use of communication equipment and procedures. • Checking and use of instruments for measuring the atmosphere in enclosed spaces. • Checking and use of rescue equipment and procedures. • Instructions in first aid and resuscitation techniques.
SOPEP or spillage leakage	**Three months**	**Shipboard Oil Pollution Emergency Plan.** **Shipboard Pollution Emergency Plan Noxious Liquids.** These plans and procedures should be exercised.

Security	Three months	Vary the content each time so the drills practise the procedures for: • Stowaway search. • Piracy attack, including retreat to Citadel. • Bomb threat and searching for devices. • Changes to ISPS Security Levels. • Any other circumstances or threats as identified by the CSO/SSO.
Steering gear	Three months	**Emergency steering** to be tested at sea. Test to be recorded in official logbook.
Damage control	Three months	**Passenger ships only** (Ref: SOLAS II-1/19-1 & IMO Resolution) Resolution MSC.421(98) Each damage control drill shall include: 1. For crew members with damage control responsibilities, reporting to stations and preparing for the duties described in the muster list required by regulation III/8. 2. Use of the damage control information and the on board damage stability computer, if fitted, to conduct stability assessments for the simulated damage conditions. 3. Establishment of the communications link between the ship and shore-based support, if provided. 4. Operation of watertight doors and other watertight closures. 5. Demonstrating proficiency in the use of the flooding detection system, if fitted, in accordance with muster list duties. 6. Demonstrating proficiency in the use of cross-flooding and equalisation systems, if fitted, in accordance with muster list duties. 7. Operation of bilge pumps and checking of bilge alarms and automatic bilge pump starting systems. 8. Instruction in damage survey and use of the ship's damage control systems.
Marine Evacuation Systems (MES)	Monthly	**Monthly training** for designated launch crew.
	2-yearly	**Designated launch crew** to descend chute
	3-yearly deployment; 6-yearly individually;	**At least one MES unit to be deployed** every three years such that there is a maximum interval of not more than six years for each individual unit, i.e. two units on board – one deployed alternate three years; four units on board – two deployed alternate three years; etc.

SECTION 8

Muster list

It is of vital importance that everyone knows their duty in the event of an emergency on board and the muster list is key to this. There are several points that a muster list must contain:

Muster list (MGN 71)	

Master's responsibility	Compiling the muster list.
	Updating it.
	Ensuring copies are exhibited in conspicuous places:
	    Bridge.
	    Engine room.
	    Crew accommodation.

Must contain	Details of the emergency alarm(s).
	Other emergency signals.
	Action by the crew and passengers on hearing alarm.
	How the 'order to abandon' is given.
	Comms equipment, channels and reporting chain (as appropriate).
	Duties of each member of crew, e.g.
	    Prep and deploying survival craft.
	    Closing of water/fire tight doors.
	    Use of communications.
	    Equipping of survival craft.
	    MOB and rescue boat.
	Location of crew's survival craft/launching station/evacuation position.
	Duties within LSA (if any).
	Must show the rank of the person responsible for maintaining the LSA and FFA in 'ready for use'.
	Designation of substitutes.
	Personnel responsible for the release of fixed fire-fighting installations.
	Additional for passenger vessels:
	    Damage control personnel.
	    Personnel responsible for care of disabled passengers and/or casualties.
	    Flag state approval.

Sound signals	Signals for incidents not requiring a muster of the passengers or whole crew are at the Master's discretion. • **Abandon ship signal is at the Master's discretion** – a signal or by voice. • **General emergency alarm** – 7 short and 1 long blast • **Person overboard** – 3 long blasts
Instruction and training	STCW 95 VI/1 states all persons shall receive familiarisation training. Crew with key safety tasks should be trained in that role. Training should be ship specific. Training complemented with training manual.
Small Vessels Workboat Code requirement	Prior to the first occasion of working on the vessel, each employee must receive appropriate familiarisation training and proper instruction in on board procedures. This should include, but not necessarily be, limited to: Mooring and unmooring. Launching and recovery of survival craft. Evacuation from all areas of the vessel. Donning of lifejackets. Use and handling of fire-fighting equipment.

Training Manual	Training manual accessible to all crew (mess, recreation rooms or each cabin). Training manuals in appropriate language for crew.
Training manual contents **(Ref: SOLAS III/35)**	1. Donning of lifejackets, immersion suits and anti-exposure suits. 2. Muster at the assigned stations. 3. Boarding, launching and clearing the survival craft and rescue boats and, where applicable, use of marine evacuation systems. 4. Method of launching from within the survival craft. 5. Release from launching appliances. 6. Methods and use of devices for protection in launching areas. 7. Illumination in launching areas. 8. Use of all survival equipment. 9. Use of all detection equipment. 10. With assistance of illustrations, the use of radio life-saving appliances. 11. Use of drogues. 12. Use of engine and accessories. 13. Recovery of survival craft/rescue boats, including stowage and securing. 14. Hazards of exposure and the need for warm clothing. 15. Best use of the survival craft facilities in order to survive. 16. Methods of retrieval, inc. the use of helicopter rescue gear (slings, baskets, stretchers), breeches-buoy and shore life-saving apparatus and ship's line-throwing apparatus. 17. All functions contained in the muster list and emergency instructions. 18. Instructions for emergency repair of the life-saving appliances.
MES	Every ship fitted with a Marine Evacuation System shall be provided with on-board training aids in the use of the system.
Small vessels	A shorter Training Manual is required on Small Commercial Vessels.

Life-saving appliances

Inspection of life-saving appliances (LSA) (Ref: SOLAS III/20)

Weekly inspections	Monthly	3-monthly
- Survival craft, rescue boats and launching appliances. - Rescue boat and lifeboat engines run up. - The general emergency alarm system tested.	- All life-saving appliances including lifeboat and rescue boat equipment. - Examination and testing of any radio installations and searchlight equipment.	- Lifeboats with water spray system.

Records in official logbook	Date of musters, drills and training sessions are held. The type of drill training. When life/rescue boats/davit-launched rafts lowered or launched. When any required drills that were not held, and reason.

Fire

The fire or combustion triangle shows the necessary ingredients for most fires:

Heat, fuel and an oxidising agent (usually oxygen). Obviously, these three elements do not normally combust, unless there is a chain reaction between them to ignite the fire. This is called the fire tetrahedron, the chain reaction being the fourth element.

A fire is prevented, extinguished or reduced by removing one of the ingredients.

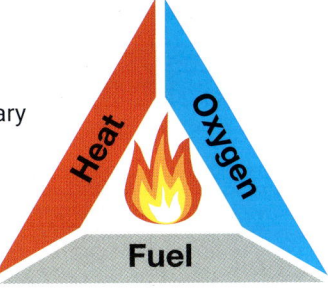

▲ Fire triangle, although sometimes now known as a fire tetrahedron, to introduce the chemical reaction to get ignition.

Fire class and extinguishers	
A	Solid material – wood paper (carbonaceous)
B	Flammable liquids
C	Flammable gases
D	Flammable metals
No (E)	There is no E, although there is an electrical sign on some extinguishers, indicating safe for use on 'live' equipment. (Electricity is the source of heat, not the fuel.)
F	Cooking oils

Type	Ability	Basic service	Extended discharge test	Overhaul Hydraulic test
Water	**Use**: Primarily for dealing with fires fuelled by wood, paper or fabrics, not liquids or electrical fires. Often cost effective to buy and service. **Dangers**: Do not use on electrical fires for risk of electric shock. Cumbersome and requires a lot of water to fight a fire.	Annually	Five years	Ten years
Foam	**AFFF (Aqueous Foam Forming Film) foam fire extinguishers** **Use**: Smother the fire to starve it of oxygen. Effective on liquid-fuelled fires. **Dangers**: High water content so sometimes problematic with electricity. Check the label.	Annually	Five years	Ten years
CO_2	**CO_2 fire extinguishers** **Use**: Electrical and gas fires, works by starving the fire of oxygen. **Dangers**: By starving a fire of oxygen, in a confined or engine space they also reduce the amount of oxygen available to breathe. If the source of the fire is not removed, once the CO_2 has dispelled, the fire could reignite.	Annually	Five years	Ten years

Dry Powder	**Dry powder fire extinguishers** **Use**: For liquid, wood and electrical fires. The powder debilitates a fire by stopping the chemical reaction from occurring. **Dangers**: Vision reduces massively. Dry powder chokes a fire, but has limited cooling effect, so if the fire is not fully extinguished it could return. Hard to breathe if inhaled, so caution if used in a confined space. Clean-up is difficult – the powder can damage furnishings, electrics and engine areas.	Annually	Ten years. Returned to manufacturer for recharge	Ten years
Wet C Chemical	**Wet chemical fire extinguishers** **Use**: Kitchens where oil is used to cook. Designed to stop specialist Class F fires, which other types of extinguisher cannot handle. **Dangers**: While designed for cooking oil fires, they can be used for all other types of fires, too. The chemicals are dangerous, so brief well so accidental activation is reduced.	Annually	Five years	Ten years
Class D Powder	**Special (L2)-type extinguishers.** Metal fires including lithium. Usually can be used on Class A and electrical fires.	Annually	Ten years	Ten years

Fire drills and testing (MGN 71)
Periodic checks performed to ensure ready availability of fire protection systems & appliances.

Monthly testing and inspection should be carried out to ensure that:	1. Fireman's outfits, fire extinguishers, fire hydrants, hose and nozzles are in place and in serviceable condition. 2. Escape routes, including stairways and corridors, are free of obstructions and properly maintained. 3. Public address system and ship's alarms are serviceable. 4. Fixed fire-fighting installation valves are set in the correct operational position. 5. Dry pipe sprinkler systems are pressurised, where appropriate, and gauges indicate correctly. 6. Sprinkler system pressure tank water levels are correct as indicated by glass gauges. 7. Sprinkler system pumps operate automatically on pressure loss in the systems. 8. Fire pumps are operational. 9. Fixed gas fire extinguishing installations are free from leakage.
Quarterly testing and inspection should be carried out to ensure that:	1. Fire extinguishers are at correct pressure and not due for servicing. 2. Automatic alarms for sprinkler systems activate using section test valves. 3. International shore connection is serviceable. 4. Fire-fighting equipment lockers contain their full inventory and the equipment they contain is in serviceable condition. 5. Fire doors, fire dampers and closing devices can be operated locally.

SECTION 8

Annual testing and inspection should be carried out to ensure that:	1. Fire doors and ventilation dampers, where appropriate, operate remotely. 2. Aqueous foam/water spray fixed fire installations operate correctly. 3. Accessible components of fixed fire-fighting systems, typically nozzles, are free from damage or obstruction on visual inspection. 4. Fire pumps, including sprinkler system pumps, develop correct pressures and flow rates. 5. Hydrants operate. 6. Antifreeze solutions are correctly maintained and cross connection between fire main and sprinkler system operates correctly. 7. Fixed fire detection systems operate correctly, according to manufacturers' test instructions.
Fire Training Manual SOLAS II-2	• A training manual shall be provided in each crew mess room and recreation room or in each crew cabin. • The training manual shall be written in the working language of the ship.
Fire Training Manual contents	The training manual shall explain the following in detail: 1. General fire safety practice and precautions related to the dangers of smoking, electrical hazards, flammable liquids and similar common shipboard hazards. 2. General instructions on fire-fighting activities and fire-fighting procedures, including procedures for notification of a fire and use of manually operated call points. 3. Meanings of the ship's alarms. 4. Operation and use of fire-fighting systems and appliances. 5. Operation and use of fire doors. 6. Operation and use of fire and smoke dampers. 7. Escape systems and appliances.

Digital distress alerting

Most long-term survival at sea happened before the advent of the Global Maritime Distress and Safety System (GMDSS). The arrival of EPIRBs, SARTs and Digital distress alerting has given mariners much reassurance. Now if we do encounter a problem and have to call the emergency services, help will have a good chance of knowing who is in danger and where they are.

Emergency Position Indicating Radio Beacon (EPIRB)	
Frequency	406MHz to COSPAS SARSAT satellites. 121.5MHz homing signal for SAR and aircraft to close location. COSPAS SARSAT Low Earth Orbiting (LEOSAR). EPIRBs can have GNSS and/or AIS for better accuracy and local response. Some new EPIRBs (2022) are also Medium Earth Orbiting 'MEOSAR ready'. They offer quicker beacon detection, faster speed of location, return signal to acknowledge receipt of distress.
Battery	Four to five years, can depend on make. Battery life (operational 48 hours).

Registration	Needs registration with radio authorities and National EPIRB Registry or COSPAS SARSAT if no National Registry.
Testing inspection	Monthly inspection on board. Annual testing either by a service agent or by crewmembers with the appropriate experience and test equipment. Service five years by an approved service station/manufacturer.
Records	Monthly, annual records and certificates of five-year inspections kept on board. Monthly test should be logged in the GMDSS logbook or official logbook.
Types	Cat I – Auto water-activated when released from bracket, often by Hydrostatic Release Unit. Cat II – Manually activated.
Other	Highly visible colour, lanyard, buoyant, flashing light (0.75cd) and have a test facility.

Search And Rescue Transponder (SART)

Frequency	9GHz (3cm X-Band). Note: Some new-generation SARTs use AIS instead of radar.
Battery	Four to five years, can depend on make. Standby 96 hours. Respond to radar transmissions for eight hours.
Range	5NM to a vessel (vessel antenna height 15m (IMO)). 30NM to an aircraft (10kW radar 3000ft (IMO)). Usually fitted with a telescopic pole to increase height/range.
Registration	Needs registration with radio authorities.
Testing inspection	Monthly inspection on board. Annual testing or as per manufacturer's requirement. Service 5 years by an approved service station/manufacturer. Test logged in GMDSS logbook or official logbook.
Testing note	When a full test is carried out, the SART is often activated and the ship's radar is used to see if it picks up the SART signal. Should be done in port and Port Operations should be consulted. If at sea, the area should be clear on a 3–6NM range.
SART signal	12 dots, then 12 arcs, then concentric circles.
Records	Monthly, annual records and certificates of 5-year inspections kept on board.
Other	Highly visible colour, lanyard, buoyant and have a test facility. Indicator that it is being 'pinged' by radar.

▲ Search And Rescue Transponders (SARTs) traditionally operated with 9Ghz radar, but AIS SARTs are becoming more common.

SECTION 8

AIS SART differences	• Range 5NM over water – no greater range given in standard. • Operates for 96 hours – no lesser level. • Have a unique identifier (9 digit MMSI) starting 970 (AIS SART). • Symbol for AIS SART on an ECS/ECDIS/chartplotter display.	
Caution	In a liferaft, radar reflector and SART should not be used at the same time as the reflector may obscure the SART.	▲ Symbol for AIS SART on an ECS/ECDIS/chartplotter display.

GMDSS Sea Areas

A1	Sea Area A1 – an area within the radiotelephone coverage of at least one VHF coast station in which continuous digital selective calling (Ch.70/156.525MHz) alerting and radiotelephony services are available. Such an area could extend typically 30–40NM (56–74km) from the Coast Station.
A2	Sea Area A2 – an area within a coverage of at least one coast station continuous listening on MF (2187.5kHz) other than Area A1.
A3	Sea Area A3 – an area, excluding sea areas A1 and A2, within the coverage of an Inmarsat geostationary satellite. This area lies between about latitude 76° N and S, but excludes A1 and/or A2 designated areas. Inmarsat guarantees their system will work between 70° S and 70° N, though it will often work to 76° S or N.
A4	Sea Area A4 – an area outside Sea Areas A1, A2 and A3 is called Sea Area A4. This is essentially the polar regions, north and south of about 76 degrees latitude, excluding any A1, A2 and A3 areas.

MAYDAY

MAYDAY

Used in the event of grave and imminent danger AND when immediate assistance is required. Send a Digital Distress Alert using DSC (press and **hold** the button until the alert is sent), then back it up with a voice call.

Call	MAYDAY, MAYDAY, MAYDAY. This is (name of own vessel – say three times). Callsign or other identification. MMSI of own vessel.		
Message	• MAYDAY. • This is (Name, call sign and MMSI). • Position (preferably as latitude and longitude). • Nature of distress (sinking – fire, MOB). • Assistance required (immediate assistance). • Number on board. • Other information (taking to a liferaft). • Over (requesting a reply).	**M** **I** **P** **D** **A** **N** **I** **O**	Mayday Identification Position Distress Assistance Number of persons Information Over

Cancelling a false alert

If a DSC Distress Alert is broadcast in error, it must be stopped by: pressing Cancel or Stop push button or by switching the radio off, then on again after a few seconds. An all-stations voice broadcast is made to cancel the alert, indicating it was transmitted in error.

Call	ALL STATIONS, ALL STATIONS, ALL STATIONS. This is name x 3, Callsign and MMSI. Position …… Cancel my distress alert… (time of distress alert UTC). OVER.

Pyrotechnics

Flares are presently a hot topic. The burning issue is the acceptance of newer Electronic Visual Distress Signals (EVDS), which at present are not accepted commercially as there is no type approval and performance standard written for them. The downside of traditional pyrotechnics is that they are explosive, environmentally damaging and difficult and costly to dispose of effectively.

Pyrotechnics: flares and smoke signals

Flares and smoke signals are used for distress signalling, attracting attention and illumination. Coloured orange and red for search and rescue and distress signalling, and white for illumination and attention.

Orange smoke	Handheld smoke – emits dense orange smoke for 60 seconds. Used in daytime to pinpoint position to potential rescuers and gives an indication to helicopter pilots of wind direction at sea.
Floating smoke	Emits dense orange smoke for three minutes and, once activated, is thrown into the water where it floats.
Lifebuoy smoke	Emits dense orange smoke for 15 minutes. Used on large vessels for MOB marking, they are connected to lifebuoys and usually incorporate a light.
Red hand flares	60-second burn time with a luminous intensity of 15,000 candelas. Range depends on the height the flare is held, but usually about 3–4NM.
Red rockets	40-second burn time at an altitude of 300m and a luminous intensity of 30,000 candelas. Often visible for 30NM.
White hand flare	Used as a warning signal to vessels around you. Sometimes carried by small vessels, especially small vessels to warn of an impending collision.
White rocket	Collision warning signal or used at night to illuminate areas for Search and Rescue operations, primarily for use by Coastguard and life-saving services.
Using flares	Flares are very effective at night, but it can be difficult to read the instructions. Ensure the crew are familiar with the operation during the safety brief/induction. Flares often have a sensory way to help identification and use at night, such as a knurled handle or imprinted end cap. Hold flares downwind, clear of the vessel and your clothing, since molten ash often falls from the flare as it burns, therefore the entrance to an inflatable liferaft needs protecting.
Approval	Should be MED (Marine Equipment Directive) approved (Wheel marked). They should be in date (date of manufacture/expiry stamped onto the flare body). They should be in good condition with labels readable.

SECTION **8**

Liferafts

There are many types of liferafts that are accepted in commercial standards and reference to the class or type of craft you are operating will give further information. For instance, an inland waters passenger vessel may use a liferaft without a roof/canopy, whereas this would be required at sea.

Inflatable liferafts, lifejackets and hydrostatic release units (HRUs) – check code or class for exact details		
Inflatable liferaft types	SOLAS – normal required for shipping and commercial vessels. ISO 9650 Pt1, Group 1, Type A – small code vessels, except Cat 0. DoT Open Reversible Liferafts (ORILs) – for inland waters passenger vessels.	
Liferaft packs	SOLAS A – normal equipment required in a liferaft. SOLAS B – lesser kit content for vessels on short international voyages.	
Liferaft servicing	SOLAS – every 12 months, at an approved service station. ISO 9650 – to the manufacturer's instructions. ORILs – at least twice every five years (usually every second year).	
Inflatable lifejacket types	Level 150 – general use lifejacket. Level 275 – greater buoyancy for when more equipment worn.	
Standards	SOLAS – SOLAS inflatable lifejackets are twin chamber/twin bottle. ISO 12402 standards – in some cases are allowed especially on small vessels – single chamber.	
Hydrostatic release units	An HRU is a device allowing an object to float free (liferafts and EPIRBs etc.) There are two types: reusable and disposable. Reusable types need to be serviced each year. Disposable types have an expiry date when they should be replaced.	
Senhouse slip	Pelican hook/slip shackle allowing manual release of an inflatable liferaft.	
Thoughts on stowage of liferafts and HRUs (Ref: SOLAS III/11 et seq)		
Liferafts must	Display launching instructions.	Float free and automatically inflate.
	Be secured by an approved HRU*.	Clear obstructions when launched.
	Be lit by emergency lighting at the launch area and stowage position*.	Have adequate length painters for the drop height.
NOTE	* Some small craft liferafts can be stowed in a locker accessible to the sea and do not require an HRU. Lighting may be by torches on small craft.	
Do	Read the liferaft fitting instructions to establish which line is which and if any transit securing straps are fitted.	
	Consult instructions for HRU fitting.	Keep clear of propellers/thrusters.
	Stow to give protection from weather, and accidental damage.	Distribute evenly port and starboard, to provide redundancy.
	Ensure drain holes at the bottom.	Remove transport lashings.
	Inspect the container frequently for damage.	
	Ensure liferaft can be manually released by operating the senhouse slip.	

EMERGENCIES

Do not	Lash the raft to the cradle.	Concentrate on all life-saving appliances in one place.
	Stow under overhangs or awnings.	Hose down heavily.
Give thought to	If the raft will be able to float free and clear.	Ability to transfer liferafts to either side of the vessel.
	Effects on ship's compass.	Effects of icing in cold weather.
	Ensure that the risk of the painter snagging on obstructions (it's long), which might prevent it from deploying fully, is reduced.	On sailing vessels, whether the raft will float free if the vessel capsizes due to keel issues.

Liferaft use

4 key elements of survival in order of priority	**Protection** – from the elements. **Location** – how can you call for help. **Water** – to sustain life. **Food** – to sustain life (we need water more than food).	
Initial actions	**Cut** – once all on board CUT the painter and paddle away. **Stream** – the drogue/sea anchor to reduce drift and steady the raft. **Close** – the liferaft door to protect occupants, ensure regular ventilation. **Maintain** – inflate floor, check people, supplies, inflation, bail water.	
Secondary actions	Seasickness tablets.	Check survivors and use first aid.	Warm up.
	Read the liferaft manual.	Search for survivors, congregate rafts.	Keep morale – increase the 'will to survive'.
Subsequent actions	Appoint a leader.	Establish a watch system.
	Get a routine going to affect repairs, issue rations and lookout.	Care for sick.
	See what people have brought to raft.	Collect sharp objects.

▲ Crew making their way to the liferaft, wearing immersion suits, during a training exercise.

SECTION 8

Distress signals

The spoken word **'MAYDAY'** sent by radiotelephony	Radiotelegraph alarm signal DSC	Radiotelephone alarm signal DSC	Morse SOS by radio or any other signalling method
Gun or noise at 1 minute intervals	Continuous sound with fog signal	Red parachute or hand flares	Rockets or shells throwing red stars at short intervals
Flames or smoke	Orange smoke	Code flags 'N' and 'C'	A square shape above or below a ball shape
SART Radar transponder	**EPIRB** Emergency position indicating radio beacon	Outstretched arms waved slowly up and down	Dye marker

▲ Distress signals as stated in the International Regulations for the Prevention of Collisions at Sea (IRPCS).

Distress signals (Ref: ColRegs Annex IV). IMO states:

1	The following signals, used or exhibited either together or separately, indicate distress and need of assistance:
	A gun or other explosive signal fired at intervals of about a minute.
	A continuous sounding with any fog-signalling apparatus.
	Rockets or shells, throwing red stars fired one at a time at short intervals.
	A signal made by any signalling method consisting of the group ... --- ... (SOS) in the Morse Code.
	A signal sent by radiotelephony consisting of the spoken word MAYDAY.
	The International Code Signal of distress indicated by N.C.
	A signal consisting of a square flag above or below a ball or anything resembling a ball.
	Flames on the vessel (as from a burning tar barrel, oil barrel, etc.).
	A rocket parachute flare or a hand-flare showing a red light.
	A smoke signal giving off orange-coloured smoke.

105

1 (continued)	Slowly and repeatedly raising and lowering arms outstretched to each side.
	A distress alert by means of Digital Selective Calling (DSC) transmitted on: VHF Channel 70, or MF/HF on the frequencies 2187.5kHz, 8414.5kHz, 4207.5kHz, 6312kHz, 12577kHz or 16804.5kHz.
	A ship-to-shore distress alert transmitted by the ship's Inmarsat or other mobile satellite service provider ship earth station.
	Signals transmitted by EPIRBs.
	Approved signals transmitted by radiocommunications systems, including survival craft radar transponders.
2	The use or exhibition of any of the foregoing signals, except for the purpose of indicating distress and need of assistance and the use of other signals that may be confused with any of the above signals, is prohibited.
3	Attention is drawn to the relevant sections of the International Code of Signals, the International Aeronautical and Maritime Search and Rescue Manual, Volume III and the following signals:
	A piece of orange-coloured canvas with either a black square and circle or other appropriate symbol (for identification from the air).
	A dye marker.[15] (Excerpt).

Emergency actions

Emergency actions – fire

Emergency	Action	Other
Fire initial actions	• Sound alarm by shouting 'Fire'. • Call the Master. • Call engine room – prepare emergency systems. • Muster passengers and crew. • Passengers don lifejackets. • Check all persons present. • Call MAYDAY or PAN PAN at appropriate time.	Find Inform Restrict Extinguish or Evacuate
Team actions	• Establish position of fire. • Establish nature/class of fire. • Close doors and hatches to reduce air/smoke. • Prepare fire hose/fire-fighting equipment. • If appropriate send in fire party. • Fight fire. • Consider boundary cooling. • Consider flooding problems if using water.	**Small vessels:** Consider ditching oils/aerosols/gas that may make it worse. Situation may worsen quickly due to size of vessel one party fight/slow fire, the other prepare to abandon – just in case.
If situation worsens	• Consider alternative muster points for smoke/fire. • Fetch grab bag – EPIRB. • Prepare to abandon ship.	

The exact action taken will always depend on the type of vessel you operate, the amount of crew and the equipment carried. Some vessels will stand and fight the problem, while on others the best course may be to get everyone off as quickly as possible.

SECTION 8

Emergency actions – engine fire

Emergency	Action	Other
Engine Fire initial actions	• Close watertight doors and fire doors. • Sound alarm and/or shout 'Fire'. • Call the Master. • Muster crew/passengers and don lifejackets. • Call engineer if space unmanned. • Check all present. • Consider calling MAYDAY or PAN PAN. • Stop engine – stop generator. • Shut off – main engine/generator battery. • Switch off engine air blowers. • Shut off fuel. • Block engine air vents, ensure key doors shut. • Ensure engine room clear. • Start engine fire system if it has not already fired. • Retrieve extinguishers from the boat or ready the fire party. • Prepare fire hose. • Consider boundary cooling on deck. • Remember bilge pumps to reduce FSE. • Prepare to abandon ship.	**Small vessels:** Consider ditching oils/aerosols/gas that may make it worse. Situation may worsen quickly due to size of vessel one party fight/slow fire, the other prepare to abandon – just in case. Engine fires are often directly below muster points. Smoke and flames can overcome the crew quickly.

Emergency actions – flooding or collision

Emergency	Action	Other
Flooding or collision, initial actions	• Close watertight doors and fire doors. • If collision – consider staying attached to the other vessel; you may both be keeping each other afloat. • Sound general alarm. • Alert the Master. • Start pumps. • Muster passengers and crew to deck in lifejackets. • Head count. • Consider beaching if possible/necessary.	**Small vessels:** Consider clutch pump on engine. Divert fire hose to run from bilge. Divert ballast pumps to run from bilge.
	• Investigate damage. • Assign crew to pumps and damage control. • Locate leaks – sound tanks. • Check skin fittings and engine room. • Shore up hole in hull side if possible. • Divert valves in engine room while possible. • Be aware fire/explosion could start.	
	• Remove portable radios, EPIRBs, SARTs from below. • Use communication devices before water level rises above batteries. • Broadcast distress alert or urgency message. • Prepare to abandon ship.	

EMERGENCIES

107

Emergency actions – abandon ship

Abandon ship initial actions

Close watertight doors and fire doors.
Broadcast distress alert.
All to muster on deck.
Head count.
Search for missing persons if safe.
Don extra clothing, immersion suits and lifejackets.

Team actions

Fetch grab bag.
Fetch EPIRB.
Launch liferaft(s)/lifeboats – ensure liferaft painters are attached to vessel.
Master to notify all on board to abandon ship.
Embark passengers and crew in liferaft.

Rafts or lifeboats to stay together.

Emergency actions – grounding

Emergency	Action	Other
Grounding or stranding	• Close watertight doors if not already closed. • Stop engines. • Call for Master. • Sound general alarm. • Contact the engineer to prepare pumps. • Inform nearest authority on Channel 16. • Check hull damage – sound tanks and around vessel. • Check bilges for levels. • Inspect all visible compartments. • Inspect rudder and shaft where possible. • Consider ballasting down until ready to refloat. • Fix position and check chart for nature of seabed. • Determine where deep water lies. • Check tide tables. • Exhibit lights and shapes. • Consider PAN PAN or distress, if required. • Reduce draught of vessel or await tide. • Instigate SOPEP plan to check for pollution issues.	

SECTION 8

Engine or steering failure

General in harbour	Always have the anchor at the ready. Practise manual/clutched/braked anchor release to ensure familiarity. If the anchor does not stop the vessel's progress, it may slow drift, assist in turning the bow to the wind, and buy time.
General at sea	In wind, an unpowered vessel sits roughly beam to wind, this can leave it prone to beam waves and an increased rolling motion. Some smaller vessels may carry or jury rig a sea anchor (parachute deployed over the bow). This reduces drift rate, brings the bow into the sea and wind, and buys time to consider options and affect repair.

A loss of steering may follow these stages:	1. Take way off vessel.
	2. Inform Master.
	3. Inform Engineer.
	4. Can temporary steering be gained using:
	   • On twin engines – using the drives individually?
	   • Using the autopilot?
	   • By engaging emergency steering?
	5. Prepare for anchoring if in shallow water.
	6. Inform other vessels/port/reporting scheme.
	7. If in deep water hoist appropriate signal 'NUC'.
	8. On small vessels add any portable fendering to sides if in harbour and if safe.
	9. Consider immediate actions to reduce impact – going astern etc.

Using emergency steering	**Once immediate loss of steering has been made safe then:** • Emergency steering often requires switching of gear or hydraulics to enable emergency steering to operate. • The person using the emergency steering often has no idea of the whereabouts of the vessel, therefore an effective communication chain should be established with simple instructions from the bridge to the helmsperson. • Larger vessels will have a heading device at the emergency steering position. • Make ready engines for manoeuvring. • Consider making for and mooring at a sheltered anchorage or harbour wall while the problems are investigated, rather than tricky boat handling situations if the vessel is hampered. Alternatively, call a tug.
Loss of engine	1. Contact the Engineer. 2. Engine check. 3. Try start again. 4. Check tanks. 5. Check fuel switches/valves. 6. Check battery/power switches. 7. Consider anchoring if shallow or steering to safe water with momentum. 8. NUC signals. 9. Inform other vessels/port/reporting scheme.

EMERGENCIES

CRAMMER FOR DECK OFFICER ORAL EXAMS

Man overboard

Actions in the event of a man overboard depend on whether you can see the casualty and the size and nature of the vessel. In reality, the initial actions are often the same or similar. However, the way the vessel turns to return and the method of retrieval will be vessel specific.

Man overboard manoeuvres

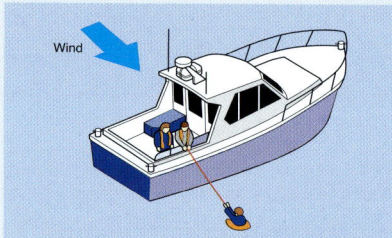

▲▶ Drift down method of person overboard recovery to provide shelter to the person in the water. There are times when this method may not be safe to use.

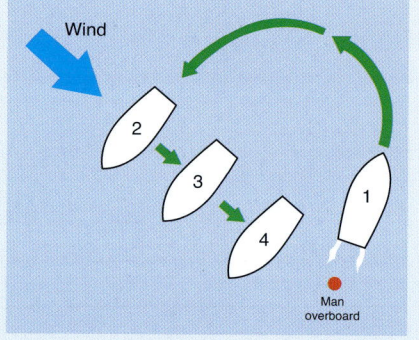

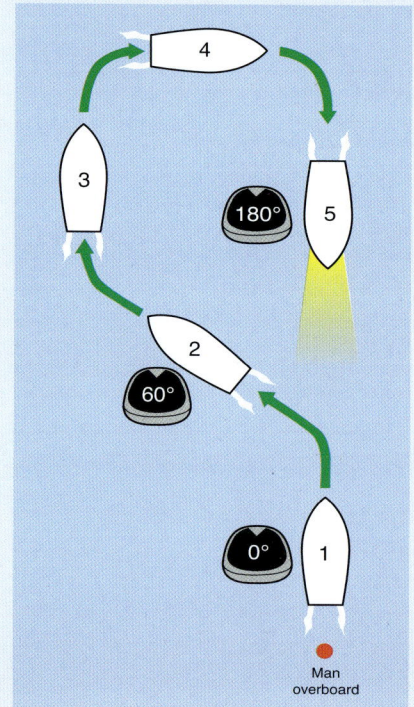

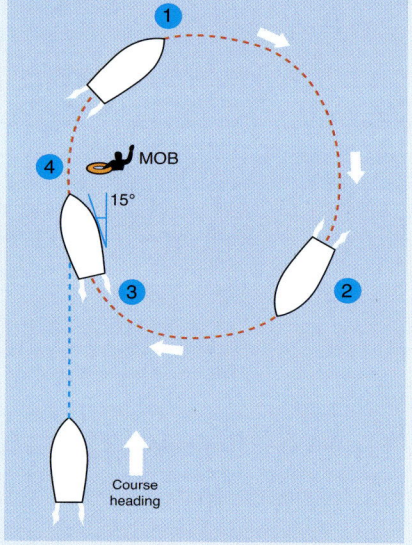

▲ **Anderson turn:** This is a fast recovery method for manoeuvrable vessels.
◀ **Williamson turn:** This is especially useful if the vessel has a large turning circle or if the person is out of sight and the wake is followed back to the area last seen.

SECTION 8

EMERGENCIES

▶ A Jason's cradle recovery device being used to recover an immobile casualty to a fast rescue craft.

Man overboard (MOB)

Initial action	Steer the vessel to the same side as the person to turn the stern away. Alert the crew, shout 'Man Overboard', sound three long blasts. Assign a spotter/s to the MOB. Throw a lifering to give a datum. Press the MOB button on the GPS or activate ECDIS MOB system.
Other actions	Call MAYDAY and DSC Alert. Prepare a recovery device for the MOB. Ensure recovery crew are wearing lifejackets.
Recovery options	Depends on the size of vessel but could include: launching/lowering of a fast rescue craft; Jason's cradle; a sling and purchase system/crane; a liferaft.
Recovery of MOB – close quarters method	Most small vessels can stop and turn around very quickly, making this method useful by day and in good visibility or at night if they are seen. After initial actions above: • Slow and establish wind direction. • Turn around and drive upwind. • Stop with the wind abeam. • Drift downwind onto the MOB. • Use only the engine furthest away from the MOB.
Recovery – Williamson turn	The Williamson turn is an initial action after a person has fallen overboard. It turns the boat back towards its wake where the MOB should be located. It is designed for large vessels travelling at speed but works for all vessels and is a useful strategy at night. 1. Rudder hard over to the side of the casualty – this moves the props away from the person in the water. 2. Continue to turn 60 degrees from the original course. 3. Put the rudder hard over to the opposite side. 4. When on reciprocal course, rudder amidships and steady upon reciprocal. 5. Slow down and look for MOB. Initiate recovery directly or with fast rescue boat. Treat casualty.
Anderson (single) turn	**Fast recovery method:** • Tight turning characteristic required. • Difficult for large single-screw vessel as turn radius may be too large. • Difficult as approach to person is not straight. • Must have eye on the casualty as you will not come exactly back on the wake track. • Single turn 270 degrees. • Rudder hard over to the side of the casualty. • Once at about 250 degrees, rudder amidships and stop/slow down.

111

Piracy

Piracy/armed robbers	
GMDSS	On DSC and Inmarsat-C GMDSS equipment, 'Piracy' is a category of distress message. However, vessels may have to covertly send out a 'piracy' message for their own safety using the SSAS. A Rescue Co-ordination Centre will then advise appropriate agencies and care will be taken regarding any communications sent back to the vessel so as not to warn the pirates. Under pirate command, pirates often stop the vessel making radio calls.
Two attack categories:	1. Pirates are spotted prior to boarding of the vessel. 2. Pirates board unnoticed. Take hostages and make threats to the crew.
Pirates board unnoticed	Vessel should comply with order by pirates not to use the radio. Pirates may be able to pick up VHF/MF radio signals. They might not intercept satellite communication. Best activated by means of concealed push buttons located in: 1. Wheelhouse; 2. Master's cabin; 3. Engine room. Pre-programmed button should select/transmit attack message to the authority.
Considerations when planning a route through known areas	
Company planning prior to entry	• Register ship with reporting centre. • Obtain latest threat and risk warnings. • Review ship security assessment and ship security plan. • Enforce ship protection measures. • Monitor piracy websites for threats. • Offer guidance to the Master on best routes. • Ensure security of critical information so exact details of transit are not made public. • Ensure vessel reporting system is registered with authorities before transit.
Master's planning	• Implement Ship Protection Measures as required through risk assessment. • Brief crew, check equipment and conduct drills. • Ensure emergency communication plan is in place (phone numbers pre-programmed etc.). • AIS is suggested to be left on: but only transmit position, course, speed, nav status and safety-related information.
Master's special standing orders 'entry to area of risk'	• Maintenance restricted in critical areas so engine/machinery always available. • Consider increasing speed to reduce transit time and make boarding harder. • Consider manoeuvring to make it difficult to board. • Low freeboard areas need extra protection. • Increase vigilance and lookouts. • Submit daily positions to reporting authorities. • Use convoys where practicable.

SECTION 8

EMERGENCIES

Special Protection Measures	**Primary defense:**
	    Shorter watches, extra lookouts, thermal imaging and radar.
	    Razor wire, especially at prone points.
	    Dummies at side decks to give the impression of large crew.
	    Manoeuvring to make boarding difficult.
	    Speed increases to out-run, delay or get to safer waters.
	    Approaching vessels challenged for their identity.
	    Water cannons – deck and anchor wash, fire pumps.
	
	Secondary defense:
	    Door and window hardening.
	    Motion sensors and Closed Circuit TV monitoring.
	    Gratings over windows.
	    Gates inside doors to limit access.
	    Limiting the use of doors and entrances – keeping others secured.
	
	Last defense:
	    Internal door hardening.
	    Safe muster points and citadel.
	    Communication.

Event of an attack or suspicious approach	• Increase speed to increase distance. • Manoeuvre away from approaching vessel. • Steer a straight course to maximise distance. • Manoeuvre when close to deter boarding. • Warn ships' crew. • Alert area controlling station. • Activate emergency communication plan. • Ships whistle to auto to show ship is aware of attack and to attract other ships. • Ensure AIS is on. • Secure external doors.
When under attack	1. Make a distress call. 2. Confirm the attack has been reported to reporting centre. 3. Consider course alterations to deter boarders and create wash. 4. All crew except those required on bridge move to citadel or safe muster point.
Action if ship is boarded	• Stop engines and take all way off if safe to do so. • Remaining crew to go to citadel. • Ensure all crew are present. • Contact company.
If pirates take control	• Be compliant. • Leave CCTV on. • Don't take photos. • Don't confront the attackers. • Don't be aggressive or make rapid movements.
Post attack	• Preserve the crime scene. • Avoid contaminating the area. • Do not touch anything or throw anything away.

Search and rescue

SOLAS states that a Master has an obligation to assist other vessels or persons in distress. Therefore there is a high probability that you will be asked to perform a search pattern to try to find the casualty from their last known position.

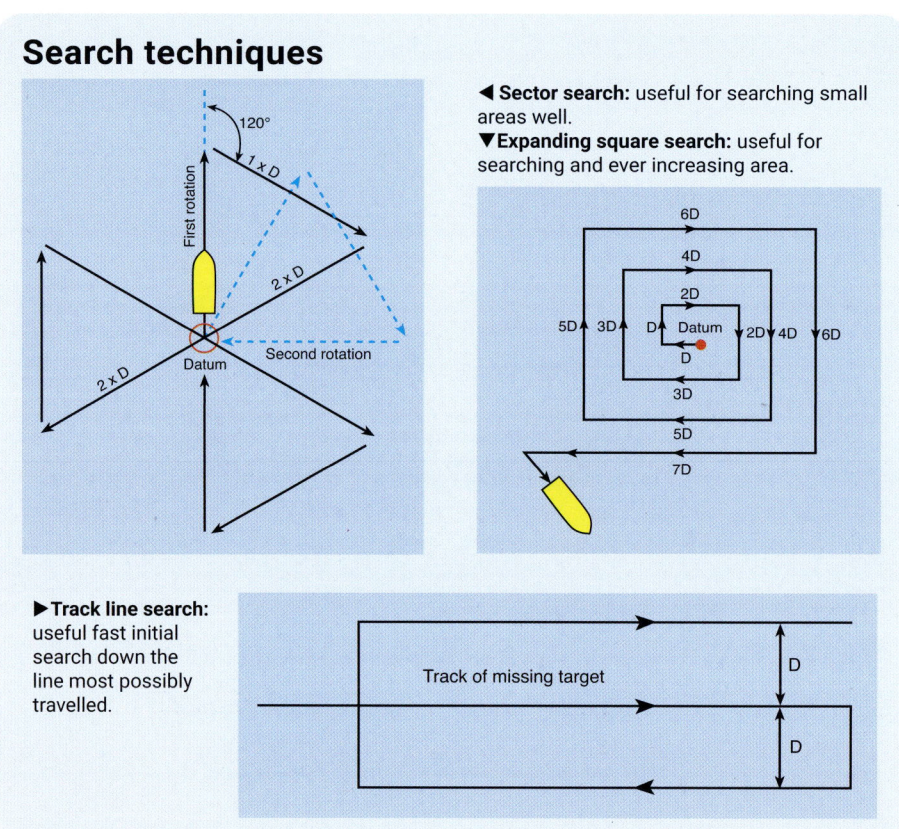

Search techniques

◀ **Sector search:** useful for searching small areas well.

▼ **Expanding square search:** useful for searching and ever increasing area.

▶ **Track line search:** useful fast initial search down the line most possibly travelled.

Search and Rescue techniques – search patterns

IAMSAR	The International Aeronautical & Maritime Search and Rescue Code (IAMSAR). Volume 3 (Mobile units) contains information about the vessel's actions, responsibilities, signals and search patterns in a search operation.
Why	SOLAS V Reg 31 Distress situations: obligations and procedures require the Master to provide assistance. SOLAS V Reg 21 requires vessels to carry IAMSAR Vol III, which tells Masters how to provide assistance.
Search techniques	Wind and currents quickly move a casualty away from their last known position and estimating their drift and estimated position may indicate their approximate location. There are many patterns used to search for a person or object in the water, starting with the Williamson turn already covered in the MOB section on page 111.

SECTION 8

EMERGENCIES

Search techniques (continued)	Four others are: sector search, expanding square, creeping line search and track line. The sector search and expanding box might be used if you are the first on scene, such as in the event of a MOB. The track line and creeping line ahead may be carried out under the guidance of the Coastguard and in conjunction with other vessels in the area.
Sector search	Effective when the search area is small or the last known position of the object is recent. After each completion of a sector, the original datum is passed, therefore the immediate area is covered comprehensively and the extremities of the area are searched less thoroughly at first. Sector searches comprise timed turns of 120 degrees. It is simpler to start the first run at North (000) so the sums are easier (000 – 120 – 240). However, if you are quick with your mathematics, an initial course downwind or downtide of the start position could bring faster results. 1. Go to the datum, and drop a visual marker such as a horseshoe lifebuoy. 2. Motor away from the lifering, steering (000) at a steady speed and count until the lifering nearly disappears. This is the Detection Range (D). 3. Then turn 120 degrees to starboard. 4. Continue on this course (120) for 1x (D), and then turn to starboard again. 5. After the datum is passed on course (240), continue on that course for another 1x (D), then turn to starboard. 6. If the casualty is not found after one complete circuit, rotate the pattern by 30 degrees to fill in the initial quadrants of the search area.
Detection range (D)	IAMSAR give tables that show recommended track spacing and sweep widths to give an indication on how long each leg should be so you will be able to see the missing target. A simple detection range can be estimated by putting a datum in the water of a similar size (lifering) and motoring away at a set speed and counting how long you can see it. When it is starting to be hard to see, this is the detection range. This can be used to indicate your track spacing.
Expanding square	Effective if the datum of the object is known to have moved a short distance or as a secondary search after a sector search. It searches an ever-increasing area. The initial leg is 75–100% of (D). The (D) range for a MOB is likely to be less than a cable depending on conditions and height of eye. 1. A datum mark, such as a lifering, will give valuable information on visibility. 2. Each leg consists of a 90-degree course alteration, increasing in length after every second turn. 3. North, East, South and West can be used for simplicity or motor downwind for the first leg, then turn to keep the wind on the beam for the second, then into the wind for the third, and so on. 4. If the vessel only has sails available, an expanding box search can be carried out under sail by a series of broad reaches and close hauled courses; however, speed and visibility will need careful monitoring.
Track line search	Run down the estimated drift track of the casualty. Then turn and run up either side of the track at a spacing of the estimated detection range. This is often used as a fast initial search of an area because of its ease of use and it searches the exact route and variables of the route first.

115

Search and Rescue Co-operation Plans (SARCo)

Requirement	Passenger vessels, even those that operate in categorised waters, are required to carry and practise a SARCo plan.
SARCo objectives	Early and efficient contact in the event of emergency between: The passenger ship. Its operator's shore-based emergency response system. The SAR services. The SAR co-operation plan should ensure that all relevant contact details are known to each of the three parties beforehand, and these details stay up to date. The plan is of use when a passenger ship has an emergency, but also when the passenger ship is acting as a SAR facility, particularly when taking on the role of On Scene Co-ordinator.
To provide	SAR services with easily accessible and up-to-date information on: The ship and its assets. The intended voyage. Communications. Emergency response systems. The ship and its operators with easily accessible information on: SAR and other emergency services in the ship's area of operation to assist in decision making and contingency planning.
SARCo plans held at	International SARCP Index, HM Coastguard, Pendennis Point, Castle Drive, FALMOUTH TR11 4WZ, UK. The plans themselves will often be constructed and held locally by liaising with the local or national Coastguard office, with the local MCA office or with a local maritime port authority.
Required plan details	Details vary depending on the distance the passenger vessel ventures: Operator details. 24-hour contact details, or those during the vessel's operation period. Chartlet(s) showing details of route(s) and service(s) provided. Liaison arrangements between operator and local emergency services The vessel's: Gross tonnage, length overall, draught and speed. Maximum persons allowed on board – number of crew normally carried. Communications equipment carried. Plan of decks and profile of the vessel. Life-saving equipment – firefighting equipment. The SAR provider adds to the plan with their details, so that knowledge of each other's resources and remit is known and shared.
Periodic exercises	SARCo regulation requires periodic exercises to be undertaken to test its effectiveness. Frequency and type of exercise depends on the circumstances in which the ship operates, availability of SAR service resources, etc. SARCo ship/shore exercises should be held once in any 12-month period.
SARCo exercise records	Exercises recorded by key participants: ship, company and SAR service. Records should include: Date, location and type of exercise, and a list of the main participants. A copy of the record should be available aboard the ship.

SECTION 8

Emergency preparedness teams

This is a quick guide to how a Master may consider organising teams in the event of an emergency and what those teams may be doing. The 'basic considerations' section identifies what may be on the priority list when in these situations.

Emergency preparedness teams – example

Who	What would they be doing
Command team Master Chief Engineer Any key personnel for decisions	Comms to shore, reviewing plans, building a picture of what is going on, contacting DPA, organising teams on board, discussions with SAR, plotting positions.
Emergency team 1 Chief Officer Bosun	Establish extent of damage and report back. Advise on action. Advise on assistance and equipment required.
Engineering team 2nd Engineer, Electro Technical Officer	Supply Emergency services. Pumps and power. Flooding and oil (SOPEP).
Emergency team 2 3rd Engineer 2nd Officer	Prep LSA and FFA. Back up for fire teams. Assist with command team.
Interior/catering Chief Steward Chief Housekeeping Chef	First Aid. Passenger control. Food. Missing persons.

Basic considerations per issue – Comms – Distress or Urgency

Fire Fire alarm Ventilation/Eng flap Doors BA Sets Boundary cooling (six sides) Flood system	**Flood – Damage Control team** GA Plans Sound tanks Stability Shore up/reduce flow Pumps
Collision – Damage Control team GA Plans Stay together Info exchange Shore up bulkhead Sound tanks Lights NUC – two A/R reds	**Grounding – Damage Control team** GA Plans Sound tanks Shore up Reduce Flow Lights Three Balls/Two reds + Anchor 3 str, 5 sec bell, 3 str, gong

MOB (Man Overboard) – Recovery team		**Salvage**
Turn vessel to side of MOB Spotters GPS position 3 long blasts Lifering/lifebuoy	Williamson turn or stop/slow/turn search patterns Lower recovery device First aid	Lloyd's Open Form No cure – no pay Scopic Clause – pay for trying Keep log – show control Continue to be on watch if towed

EMERGENCIES

117

Towage and salvage

At the end of an emergency situation occurring on your vessel, it is possible that a vessel will need a tow. It is better that the vessel, cargo and crew get to port in one piece and the lawyers argue the outcome in a court of law, rather than a loss of life, cargo or vessel.

Towage and Salvage	
Salvage	If your vessel is in real danger then a vessel or person coming to your aid to: tow, pilot, navigate, advise or stand-by, can be termed as a salvageable act.
Pay	The amount a salvor is paid is determined by the risk they take and what life or property they save. Proving that real danger existed is down to the salvor. Danger is often proved by the state of the salvaged boat, the lack of ability of the skipper/crew and the conditions and the circumstances of the event.
Towage	If a vessel is in difficulty and requires another vessel's assistance, the Master should initially arrange a towage contract with a tug. Towage is a contract for assisting the voyage of a vessel when nothing more is required than 'accelerating her progress'. There is little chance of a tug claiming salvage if it is contracted to tow, unless the towing situation seriously deteriorates through conditions.
No cure – No Pay	Try to agree a towage fee first, if not state 'No Cure – No Pay' because the overarching principle of salvage is that the property or part of it must be saved for a salvage fee or claim to be made.
Agreement	Simple forms of salvage agreement such as **Lloyd's Open or Standard Form** where the salvage fee can be fixed by negotiation or arbitration after the event. They are useful to have on board.
If in duress	If communication is difficult ensure any verbal agreement is witnessed by the crew and entered in the log. If no agreement has been made, once ashore, again try to settle a fee for towage and get a receipt.
Control	Try to show that you still have some control of the situation by doing the following, if you can: • Use your own line and help where you can in the operation. • If being towed, establish comms with the tug en route. • Gather and record forecasts en route. • Keep an accurate log. • Recording this information can be used in your defence.
Fee	To decide how much a salvor is rewarded, a court will consider: • Dangers exposed to the salvor and assisted vessel. • Expertise displayed by the salvor. • What was salvaged and its value. • Damage caused by negligence of the salvors. • The state of the assisted craft and its crew.
SCOPIC clause (Special Compensation P&I Clause)	The 'No Cure – No Pay' principle led to a problem where a salvor may choose not to go out because there was little chance of success of saving the vessel. This was apparent in pollution cases where the vessel would be a total loss, but the danger to environment was large. To encourage salvage, the SCOPIC clause was brought in to at least cover the costs incurred by the salvor for trying to help with anti-pollution events. A SCOPIC clause can be invoked on most salvage agreements.

Section 9
Manoeuvring

All vessels manoeuvre differently. In this section we have mainly concentrated on the manoeuvring of single-screw vessels as these are often the most problematic and have the least manoeuvrability. However, much of the section is generic about how all vessels operate and the checks that should be applied in all cases.

CRAMMER FOR DECK OFFICER ORAL EXAMS

Steering

Steering gear tests and drills (Ref: SOLAS V Reg 26). IMO states:

Within 12 hours before departure, the ship's steering gear shall be checked and tested by the ship's crew.	
The test procedure shall include the operation of the following:	• Main steering gear. • Auxiliary steering gear. • Remote steering gear control systems. Steering positions located on the navigation bridge. • Emergency power supply. • Rudder angle indicators showing the actual position of the rudder. • Remote steering gear control system power failure alarms. • The steering gear power unit failure alarms. • Automatic isolating arrangements and other automatic equipment.
The checks and tests shall include:	• The full movement of the rudder according to the required capabilities of the steering gear. • A visual inspection for the steering gear and its connecting linkage. • The operation of the means of communication between the navigation bridge and steering gear compartment.
Diagrams	• Operating instructions and block diagrams showing the change-over procedures for remote steering gear control systems and steering gear power units. • Permanently displayed on bridge and steering compartment.
Familiarity	Officers concerned with steering systems shall be familiar with the system and change-over requirements.
Ships engaged on voyages of short duration	The administration may allow these vessels to test steering weekly rather than before departure.
Emergency steering drills intervals	At least once every three months in order to practise emergency steering procedures.
Drills shall include	• Communication between bridge and emergency steering area. • Operation of alternative power supplies. • Direct control within the steering compartment.[16] (Excerpt).

Propellers and rudders

Propellers

▶ Propellers are defined by their pitch and diameter.

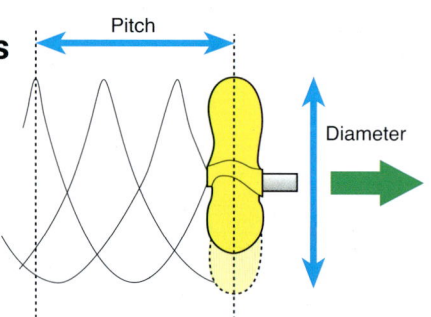
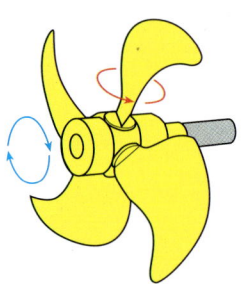

▲ Controllable pitch propellers always rotate in the same direction, but the pitch is changed to go from forward to astern.

SECTION 9

MANOEUVRING

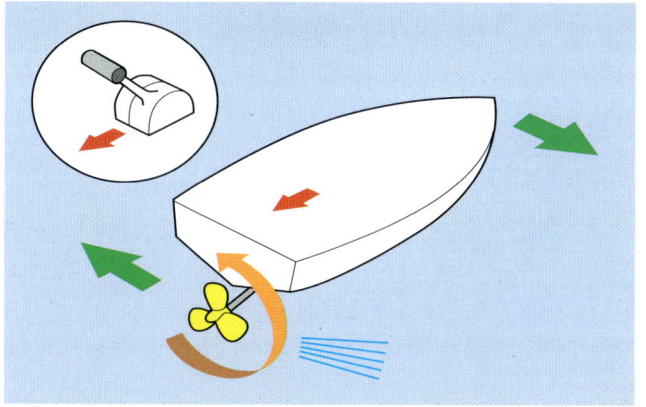

▲ Propwalk or transverse thrust is often 'felt' more when going astern.

Props and rudders

Rudders – Steering is only effective when there is water flowing over the rudder blade.

Water flow over the rudder is gained in three ways	1. The vessel moving through the water. 2. From the propeller (propwash). 3. When the vessel is stationary over ground but water is flowing over the rudder, such as tidal/river stream.
Therefore a single screw, rudder-steered vessel...	a. When stopped in the water, has no steerageway. b. If vessel stopped over ground, but head to stream (tide or river), has some steerageway depending on the strength of the stream. c. If motoring forwards has steerageway, depending on boat speed and size of rudder. d. At slow speed when turning, propwash is required to assist the turn. This is achieved by using the wheel first, then applying a short burst of power to divert the propwash into turning moment.
Rudders going astern	Propwash does not flow across the rudder when going astern, so steering relies on water flow gained by moving astern. Rudders are often quite ineffective astern until way is gained and then less effective than when going forwards.

Propellers – Measured by diameter and pitch

Pitch and diameter	Amount of twist in the propeller and measured by the theoretical amount that it would drive forward in a solid for each revolution. A propeller measuring 20in x 30in would be 20in diameter and would drive forward 30in per revolution.
Fixed pitch propeller (FPP)	A fixed pitch propeller is a one-piece propeller and the pitch set at the time of manufacture. Designed to be most efficient at a particular speed/RPM, therefore at all other times it suffers power wastage. To go astern, a gearbox is fitted to enable the shaft to rotate in the opposite direction. This type of propeller is very common.
Controllable pitch propeller (CPP)	Often fitted to larger ships. The shaft and the propeller rotate in a constant direction and astern power is achieved by altering the pitch of the blades, thus removing the necessity to have reverse gearing. Also the pitch can be changed to suit the RPM/speed, therefore giving greater efficiency.

121

Transverse thrust (propwalk)	Effect the propeller has on the direction of the vessel at slow speed. For a single-propeller vessel, when the engine is moving ahead or astern, the twisting rotation of the propeller tends to turn the vessel to port or starboard, when the rudder is amidships.
Effects of transverse thrust	• In ahead the effect does not last long because the rudder soon has propwash over its surface and steerage negates the effect. • In astern it has a much greater effect as the rudder has no effect until steerageway is gained. For example, going ahead, a right-handed prop walks the stern to starboard while also moving the vessel forwards. However, the effect is negligible. Going astern, a right-handed prop walks the stern to port and has greater effect.

Effects of water pressure

Water pressure and the effects of squat, interaction, canal and bow cushion effect can have some serious consequences, especially in restricted waterways.

Interaction, squat and bow cushion effects

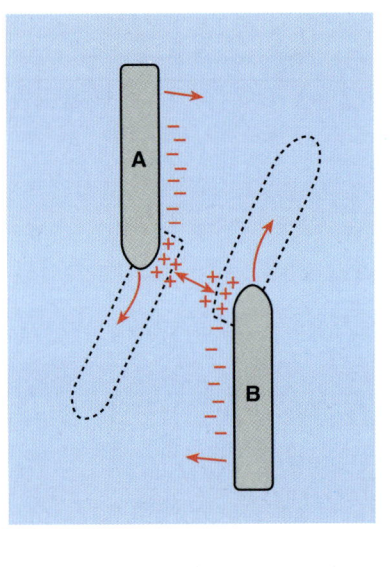

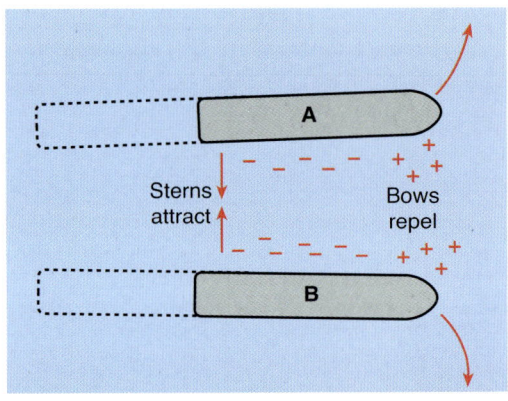

◀ ▲ Dangers of interaction: pulling boats together. The positive pressure wave that comes from the bow of vessel A repels the bow of vessel B, sheering its bow and turning vessel B stern towards vessel A.

▼ Squat: normally a shallow water issue that makes a boat sink lower in the water reducing its under-keel clearance.

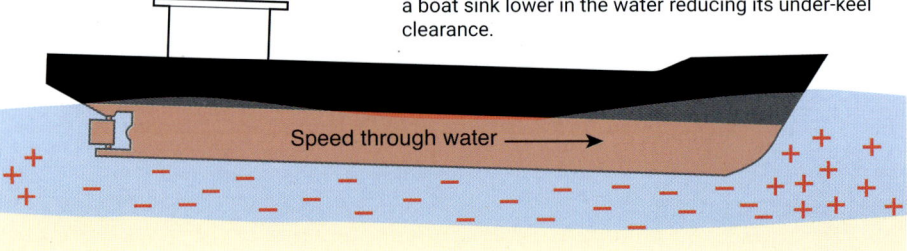

SECTION 9

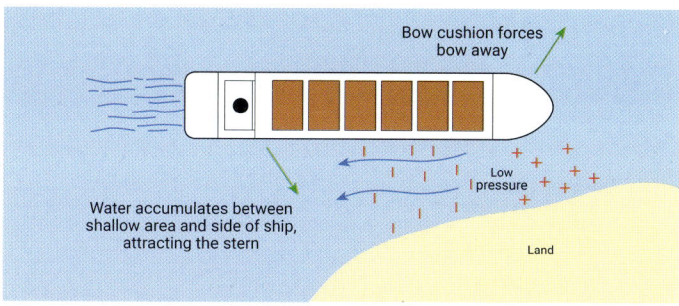

◄ Bow cushion effect can push a bow off a bank making the vessel change direction uncontrollably.

Effects of water pressure

As a vessel's hull cuts through the water, it experiences different water speeds locally around its hull. These localised water speed changes also change the pressure around the hull and create high and low pressure areas.

At the bow	The bow pushes water forward and out of the way.
Along the sides	Water accelerates as it is pulled back along the sides of the vessel.
At the stern	Then it recovers after initial turbulence as it comes away at the stern.
Underneath	In shallow water, water accelerates between the hull and seabed.
Bernoulli's principle	An increase in (water) speed leads to a decrease in (water) pressure. If water travels faster in one place around a vessel, water pressure drops at that point. Low pressure areas attract objects that are in high or normal pressure areas.
Interaction	1. Vessels closely passing or overtaking each other can get drawn closer to each other as they enter the low pressure area. 2. The positive pressure wave that comes from the bow of vessel A repels the bow of vessel B, causing a sheer, and turning vessel B stern towards vessel A. Cause: excess speed, often combined with shallow water and proximity to another vessel.
Squat	Vessels travelling at speed in shallow water experience an increase of water speed between hull and the ground, therefore a lowering of water pressure, thus reducing under-keel Clearance (UKC). Draught will reduce at the bow, stern and along the length of the vessel, the magnitude of the sinkage and change of trim (squat) dependent upon the initial trim and depth-to-draught ratio. Cause: excess speed combined with shallow water. Halve the speed and you quarter the squat.
Bank effect	Vessels near banks encountering an increase of water speed/ lowering of pressure between their hull side and bank. This seemingly sucks the vessel towards the bank. Cause: excess speed, often combined with shallow water and proximity to a river or canal bank.
Bow cushion	Bow cushion is the effect of the build-up of high water pressure as the bow closes with a bank, bridge arch, dock wall or canal. This makes the bow sheer away from the solid construction as high pressure builds up between its bow and the obstruction. Cause: excess speed, often combined with shallow water and proximity to a river or canal bank.

Combined effects	In rivers, for instance, while the bow is sheered away from the obstruction with bow cushion effect, the increase in water speed flowing down the hull creates a low-pressure area between the obstruction and the hull side. Therefore, the hull side and stern is drawn into the bank.
	In rivers, particularly through bridge arches, the flow of the current itself creates pressure zones around a constriction. Navigation through bridge arches therefore need special care, as the vessel's bow high-pressure zone will meet another high-pressure area of water passing around the bridge arch causing the vessel to sheer.
Other factors affecting under-keel clearance	• Cargo. • Relative density/salinity. • Swell/sea state. • Trim. • List/heel. • Heel due to turning. Local barometric pressure (high pressure reduces sea level, low pressure increases sea level). 10mb (hPa) changes height by approx. 0.1m. Standard barometric pressure is approximately 1013mb.

Factors reducing draught

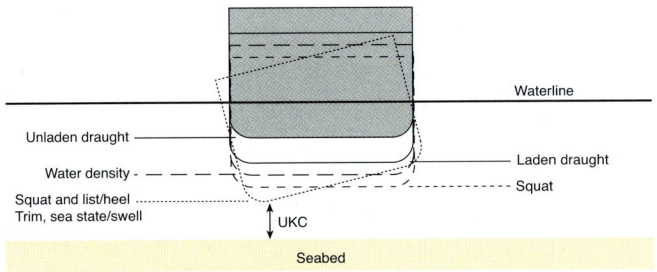

▲ There are many factors at work that can reduce under-keel clearance.

Handling characteristics

Handling characteristics	
Pivot points	A vessel has three main pivot points: Going ahead, the pivot point is roughly 1/3 from the bow. Going astern, the pivot point moves back to roughly 1/3 from the stern. When stalled, the pivot point is roughly amidships.
Result	Stern is steered rather than the bow because the rudder is aft.
Turning in ahead	Beware colliding with obstructions with the stern quarters, as this area has the greatest swing when turning ahead. For example, if a 30-metre vessel turns to port, 20 metres behind the forward pivot swings to starboard and only 10 metres turns to port.
In astern and turning	In astern the pivot point moves to a point roughly 1/3 from the stern. Now on a 30-metre vessel, 20 metres of bow swings and only 10 metres of stern. Also, the turn is harder as there is smaller leverage because of the respective positions of the rudder and pivot point.

SECTION 9

Pivot points when going ahead and astern

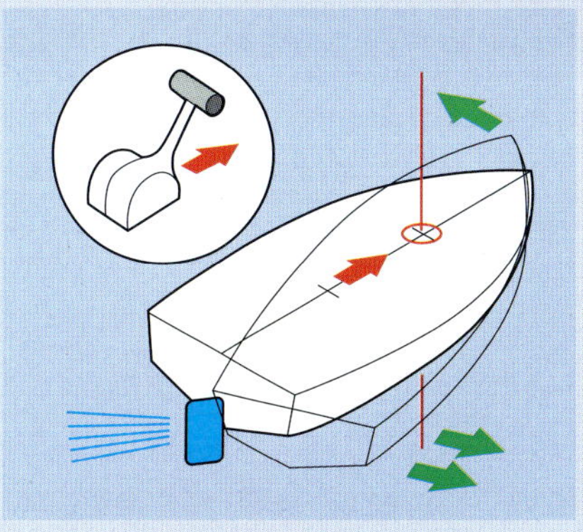

▲ Pivot point when going ahead is approximately one third from the bow.

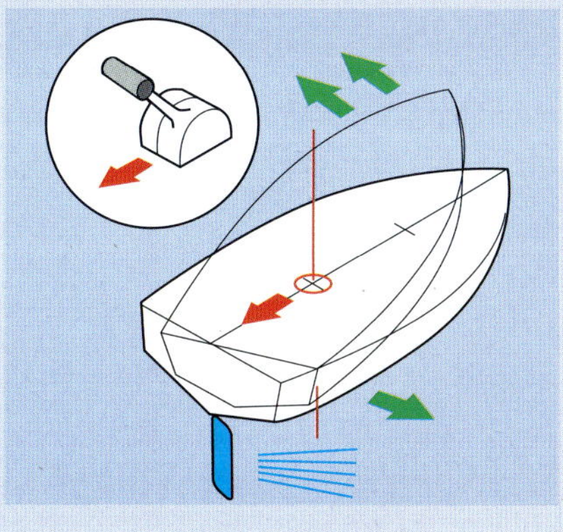

▲ Pivot point when going astern is approximately one third from the stern.

Wind, stream and hydrodynamic effects

Wind effects

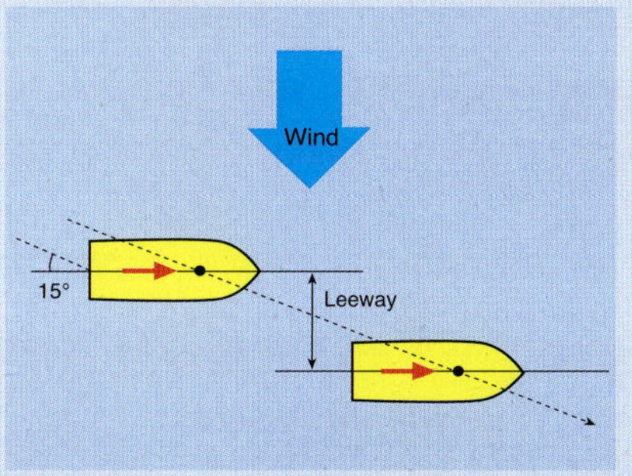

▲ As a vessel slows, leeway (sideways drift) increases. Greater windage on the vessel coupled with less draught increases leeway.

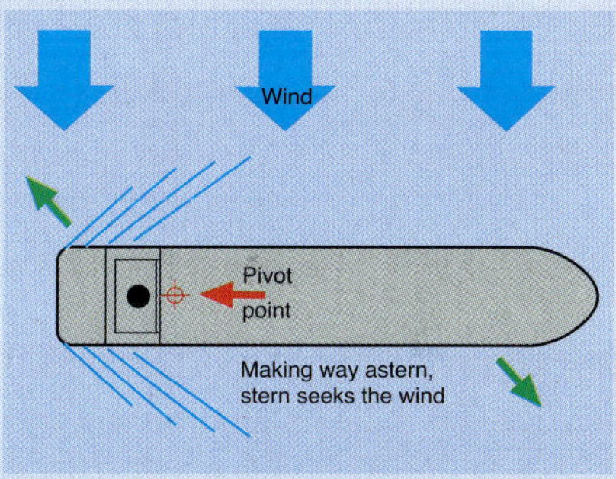

▲ A crosswind on the vessel can make the stern seek the wind as the windage forward is greater than the windage aft.

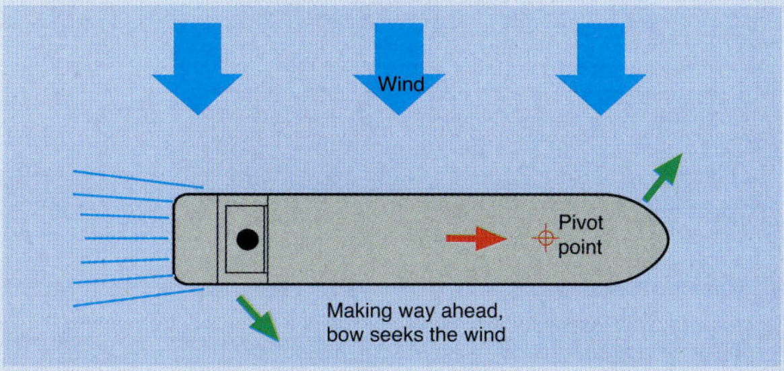

◀ A crosswind on the vessel can make it turn towards the wind as the windage aft is greater than the windage forward.

125

CRAMMER FOR DECK OFFICER ORAL EXAMS

External effects on manoeuvring	
Wind	Wind has a considerable effect on manoeuvring at slow speed, especially when a vessel is in a light condition, or with smaller planing hull boats, with lots of windage above the waterline and little grip below.
Direction	Be aware of wind direction; flags around a port, wind indicators and smoke and gusts on the water surface are all useful indicators.
Leeway and windage	A vessel is affected by a side wind force and makes leeway or sideways drift. Leeway increases as speed decreases. In navigation, leeway angle is estimated by comparing the angle between the wake and the reciprocal of the vessel's heading/fore and aft line.
Pivot points in wind – stopped	When the vessel is stopped in the water, the pivot is amidships and the vessel will sit roughly beam to wind, unless it has more windage fore or aft.
Pivot points in wind – going ahead	If the vessel moves from stopped to ahead the pivot point moves forward, therefore the relative amount of windage aft of the pivot increases and the bow turns towards the wind as the aft sections are blown downwind. As momentum increases and the rudder gains steerage, the effects of windage and pivot reduce.
Pivot points in wind – going astern	When going astern the pivot point moves aft. The relative windage forward increases, the bow swings downwind as the stern seeks the wind. The rudder is very ineffective when going astern at slow speeds because the stern is much closer to the pivot point than when going ahead and has little leverage. At slow speeds going astern, the wind effect is more noticeable making a vessel more difficult to control. Tugs or bow thrusters can help.
Streams caused by	Streams are caused by either tide, natural river flow, or by local movement of water, such as sluices around locks.
Stream effect	Streams have a similar effect as stepping onto a conveyor belt, they move you bodily in one direction. Therefore, if you are travelling through the water at the same speed: Going with the stream, vessel A travels faster over the ground and reaches the destination quicker. Going against the stream, vessel B takes longer to reach the destination; the speed over the ground will be less.
Streams best use	When coming alongside a pontoon or berth a boat pointing into the stream is slower over the ground while retaining good steerageway as there is both the boat speed and speed of the stream flowing over the rudder; this allows much more control. Therefore, given the opportunity, always berth driving into the stream for best control.

Berthing and wind

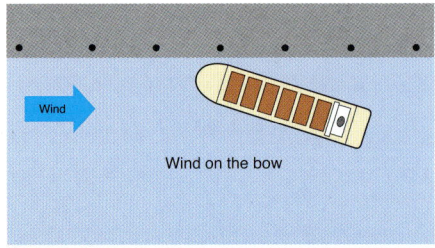

Wind on the bow

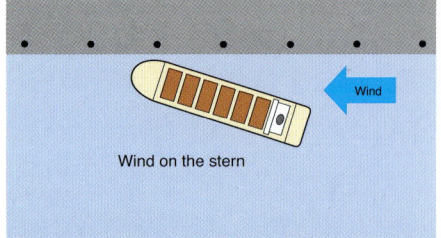

Wind on the stern

▲ Going into the elements is always good news, but beware the bow blowing on to the quay too early.

▲ Often a difficult approach as the wind starts to blow the stern away and this occurs more as the vessel slows.

SECTION 9

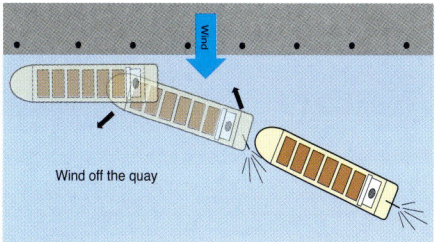

▲ Wind off the quay often requires a more positive approach.

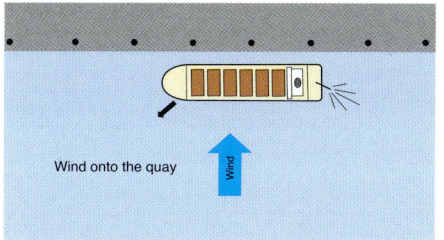

▲ Wind on to the quay means that you are committed, so ensure you're positioned correctly before getting blown alongside.

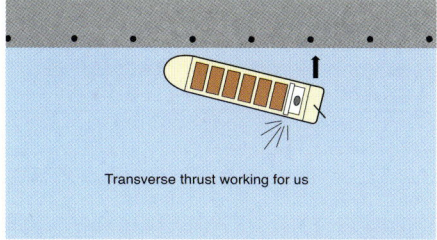

▲ Transverse thrust can act like a stern thruster and help you alongside if it is in your favour.

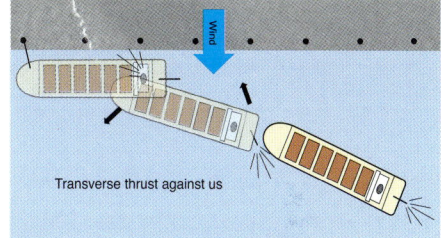

▲ Transverse thrust can also make your berthing more difficult.

Boat handling notes for berthing

Use of stream	If there is a stream, berth 'bows into' the stream for greater control. The faster the stream, the more the vessel will slide sideways. Exercise caution if getting too close to vessels moored downstream – you may slide on them. Wind direction will affect the approach angle especially in weak or no stream.
Wind parallel to the quay – on the bow	Will initially blow the bow onto the quay – on the ship's approach. Ship's way will be lost quickly. Sufficient way/bowthrusters must be used to ensure the bow does not get blown one way or the other.
Wind parallel to the quay – on the stern	Will blow the stern of the vessel away from the quay – on the ship's approach. Sufficient way is required to ensure the stern can be steered in.
Wind off the quay	Will blow the whole ship away from the berth. Way should be used to drive the ship alongside. Often an approach at 30 degrees, aiming a third to halfway along the gap, allows for the ship to be motored alongside. When approx. a boat length away, steer away from the quay to allow the vessel to come in parallel.
Wind on the quay	While initially beneficial, once the vessel starts to drift in, it is often committed so positioning is key, especially if there are nearby vessels. The bow often requires the greatest care, not to arrive too early and often rudder away from the quay is used. However, this also brings the stern in.
Using transverse thrust	On single-screw vessels, this mostly affects the stern travel to port or to starboard when coming alongside and going astern.

CRAMMER FOR DECK OFFICER ORAL EXAMS

Coming alongside, transverse helping	On a single-screw vessel, this will be affected by transverse thrust (propwalk), as well as influences of wind and stream.
	If a vessels stern walks to port when put astern, when going port side-to, the transverse thrust helps the vessel's stern come in. The approach angle may depend upon the amount of transverse thrust the vessel has, the speed of approach, thus the stopping power required. However, an approach of 30 degrees to the quay is reasonable. When a boat length from the quay, steer away from the quay and engage astern – transverse thrust will bring in the stern. Because the vessel is still moving forward, forward steerage way will still have an effect. Often the amount of RPM adjusts the amount of thrust – initially.
Coming alongside, transverse not helping	If coming alongside where the transverse thrust is not assisting, aim in about 10–20 degrees. When a boat length from the pontoon, steer away from the pontoon and go ahead to kick the stern in. Then go astern gently if possible to take off way. Alternatively with a bow thruster, crab the vessel in, by steering away from the quay and going ahead while using the bow thruster to push the bow in.

Turning

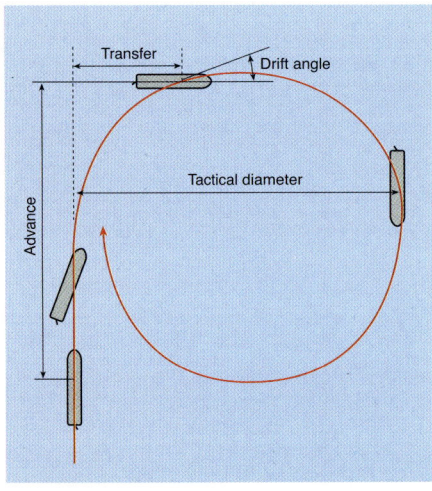

▲ When turning at speed, the vessel describes a larger turning circle and tries to 'skid' out of the turn.

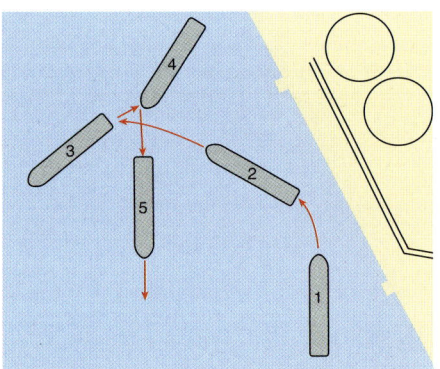

▲ A single-screw vessel will often turn better one way than the other because of transverse thrust. However, it is always useful to turn the bow through the wind as this keeps you away from the lee shore.

Turning	
Turning circles	If the rudder is put hard over when the vessel is underway going ahead and kept in this position, the ship will describe a turning circle that is not quite circular. The curvature of the path increases as the vessel turns through the first 90 degrees then remains fairly constant. The vessel also slides out of the turn, and this increases the vessel's turning circle. In close quarters, turns are started at a slow speed, so that slide is reduced and controlled.

SECTION 9

MANOEUVRING

Terms	
Advance	The distance travelled from the original heading measured from the point where helm was first applied.
Transfer	Transfer is the distance travelled measured from the original track to the point where the vessel has altered its course by 90 degrees.
Tactical diameter	Tactical diameter is the distance travelled to the left or right of the original course after a turn of 180 degrees is completed (i.e. the transfer for 180 degrees).
Drift angle	The angle between the tangent to the turning circle at any point, and the fore and aft line of the ship.
Turning in close quarters – wind and stream	
Each vessel design has its own idiosyncrasies, but all are operated using the tools of pivot points, rudder, propwash and transverse thrust/propwalk. These tools are used to counter the effects of wind and stream. Used wisely, wind and stream will make turns smaller and vessel handling easier; used unwisely, they conspire to push you on to dangers.	
Plan the manoeuvre	• Use the elements to your advantage. • Larger vessels may require tug assistance for these manoeuvres. • If the elements of wind and stream are present, always turn the bow into them to reduce the chance of being swept downwind or downstream. • Use the least possible revs. • When turning, single screws may require a short burst of power, but only when the rudder is hard over.
Turning short round – single screw – large vessel	For a left-handed propeller: 1. Wheel to port. 2. Order half ahead. 3. Once the vessel is seen to make headway, stop engine – wheel amidships. 4. Engine astern. Effect of transverse thrust will swing the bow to port and stern to starboard. Once the vessel is seen to make sternway stop the engine. 5. Wheel hard to port and engine half ahead. Vessel will continue its turn to port. 6. When the vessel has nearly completed the turn, straighten the wheel and reduce power.

Anchoring

▶ Shackles of chain joined together with painted links indicating length.

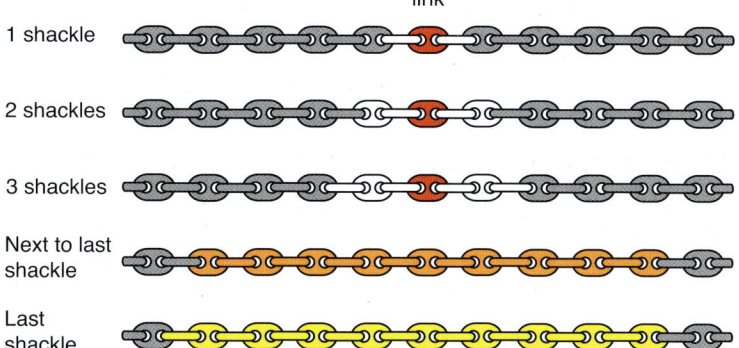

Detachable link

1 shackle

2 shackles

3 shackles

Next to last shackle

Last shackle

129

Anchoring

Types of anchors	Fisherman, Standard stockless, MK2 Stockless, CQR, Danforth, Plough, Bruce.
Chain	• Stud link – centre stud through the link to add weight and stop the chain compressing under load and kinking. • Non-stud link – used on smaller vessels – lighter than stud link for a given size.

Measurements	Metres, shackles, fathoms or feet:
	  27.5 metres = 1 shackle
	  15 fathoms = 1 shackle
	  90 feet = 1 shackle
	Large vessels use the term 'shackles of chain' – smaller vessels use other measurements dependent on the nationality of the crew and the depths stated on the charts – metres, fathoms or feet.

Chain lengths	Lengths of large vessel chain are supplied in 'shackles' (27.5m).
Joining shackles	Shackles of chain are joined by a 'kenter' or lugless joining shackle, which are designed to fit into the anchor winch gypsy.
Ganger	There is an initial short length of chain from the anchor shackle to the first 'shackle of chain' called the 'ganger'. It runs: anchor, anchor shackle, anchor swivel, short length of chain (ganger), first kenter shackle, first shackle of chain. This allows the cable to be split on deck between the stopper and the windlass.
Bitter end	The shipboard end of the anchor chain is the 'bitter end'. It will be attached so that it can be released from a position outside the chain locker in an emergency.
Markings	The kenter shackle is painted. And each successive link of chain is painted either side of the kenter shackle. 1 shackle of chain – 1 chain link painted either side. 2 shackles of chain – 2 chain links painted either side. There should also be some turns of seizing wire on the stud of the indicative link.
Spurling pipe	Chain pipe from deck/winch to chain locker.
Hawse pipe	Chain pipe from deck/winch to sea.
Devil's claw	Device that holds the chain and, in some circumstances, takes the weight of the chain off the anchor winch.
Chain stopper	Often a heavier duty pawl or physical clamp chain restraint to take the weight of the anchored ship off the winch/windlass.

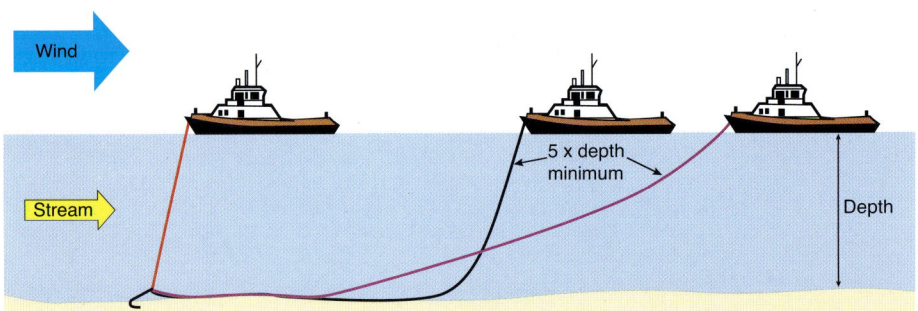

▲ Ensure enough chain (or chain and warp) is let out to ensure good holding. 5:1 chain or 6/7:1 chain and warp.

Anchor procedures

Securing for sea	<ul><li>When a ship heads to sea, the anchors must be secured.</li><li>Apply the brake on the windlass.</li><li>Apply chain stoppers, claws and use additional lashings if required.</li><li>Cover the spurling pipe to reduce water entering the chain locker. Small vessel's chain lockers tend to self-drain, if drains are free of debris.</li></ul>
Preparation for anchoring	<ul><li>Find a safe anchorage – an area sheltered from wind and possibly stream. Anchorage could be a designated anchorage that you have been told to anchor in by the port.</li><li>Ensure sufficient swinging room between you and other vessels, obstructions and channels.</li><li>Check the chart to ensure there are no hazards on the seabed, such as foul ground, cables and pipelines.</li><li>Ensure sufficient water at low water.</li></ul>
Deck preparation	<ul><li>Hold a toolbox talk. Ensure all know their roles and lines of communication.</li><li>Ensure there is effective communication between bridge and deck.</li><li>All staff to be in PPE (helmet, safety boots, gloves and goggles).</li><li>Responsible person to supervise operation.</li><li>Check the windlass brakes are on.</li><li>Establish power to windlass.</li><li>Establish communication with bridge/Master.</li><li>Clear the spurling and hawse pipe covers.</li><li>Remove lashings and stoppers.</li><li>Check windlass operates freely.</li><li>Visual check to ensure no obstructions are under the anchor at bow.</li><li>When ready, 'walk out' anchor to 1m above sea to ensure it is not jammed in the hawse pipe.</li><li>Ensure brake on and clutch off, then report 'anchor ready for letting go'.</li></ul>
Master	<ul><li>Establish communication channels with the deck crew.</li><li>Turn the vessel into the strongest element of wind or stream.</li><li>Slowly motor ahead and prepare to stop.</li><li>Stop at the designated point and lower the anchor.</li><li>Establish that the vessel is moving astern either by the elements and drift or by a short engagement of astern power.</li><li>Lower the anchor chain gradually so it lays in a line on the seabed rather than a pile of chain on top of itself.</li><li>The vessel will probably come forward to a point of rest.</li><li>Check holding by transits, fixing and note in the log.</li><li>Show anchor ball or lights.</li><li>Set measurable parameters for position and swinging circle.</li><li>Set anchor watch.</li></ul>
Anchor watch	The Master still has obligations at anchor, not least of which is the obligation to maintain a safe lookout (Rule 5). The vessel could drag into danger or collide with another vessel. Here are the normal roles associated with an anchor watch:<ul><li>Ensure Master's anchor watch instructions are understood.</li><li>Check ship's position, swinging circle and minimum depth is marked on chart.</li><li>Check the vessel's current position is within the safe value given by the Master – use transits/GPS position/echo sounder, radar to verify position.</li><li>Vibration in the anchor chain is often a sign of anchor dragging.</li><li>Length of anchor chain in use is known.</li><li>Correct lights and shapes are in use for time of day.</li><li>Oncoming visitor's identity, number and business is known (ISPS).</li><li>Stay aware – check if any oil is floating on sea around the vessel (MARPOL).</li><li>VHF receivers set to the correct working/watch channels.</li><li>Is there any ship (anchored or underway) that is likely to collide with own vessel?</li><li>Report and record necessary matters.</li><li>Check the point of vessel access is secure when not in use.</li><li>Ensure sufficient watch handover.</li><li>Master Standing Orders are usually to call during excessive wind velocity, reduced visibility or yawing angle.</li><li>Engines are available at short notice if required.</li><li>Observe the weather forecast.</li></ul>

SECTION **9**

MANOEUVRING

Emergency stop

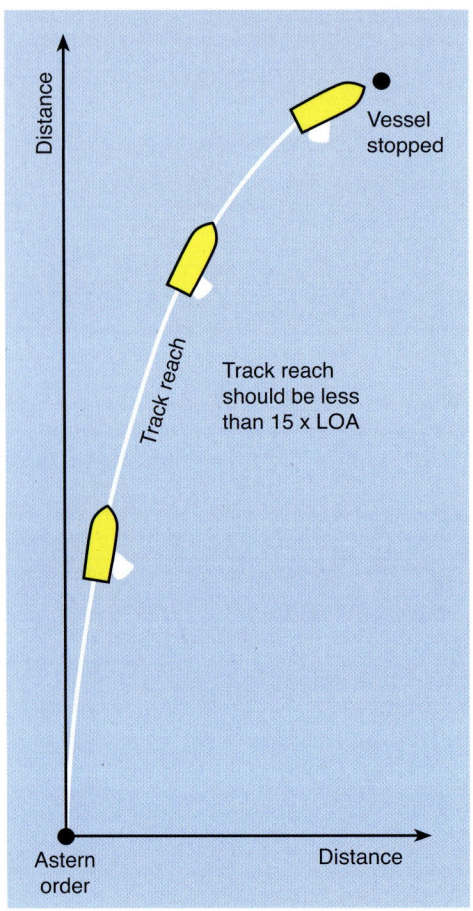

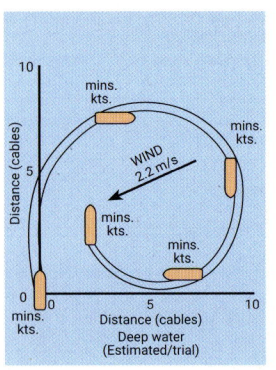

▲ It is worth establishing how quickly your vessel will stop. Single-screw vessels will often change track because of transverse thrust.

◀ Turning circles are just part of the information included on a wheelhouse poster.

Emergency stop
(Ref: IMO Resolution A. 601(15) & Bridge Procedures Guide A3)

Inertia stop	The engine is stopped/taken out of drive and the momentum is run off without astern power. • The stopping distance will depend on type and size of vessel, the direction of the wind, stream or sea state.
Crash stop	The engine is put astern to stop the vessel. • On larger vessels this can take some time because the engine has to be reversed. • On small vessels this can be carried out quickly, but caution should be taken to not 'crashing' the gearbox and rendering it useless.
Stopping distance	During a crash stop, the distance along the vessel's path measured from the position at which an order for full astern is given to the position at which the ship stops in the water is known as the '**track reach**'. • A vessel should normally be brought to rest within 15 boat lengths. • On single-screw vessels, the vessel's track when stopping will often not be straight due to the transverse thrust (propwalk) that pulls the stern to one side as reverse gear is engaged.
Rudder cycling	Can be used to reduce speed by up to 50%. • This technique cycles the rudder from port to starboard while reducing the engine speed in stages. • It can also be used when going astern or taking the engine out of gear.
Wheelhouse poster	Details of stopping distances should be available for the Master and bridge watchkeepers. This is a requirement on vessels 100m and over.

Manoeuvring information regulations

Many small vessels do not have manoeuvring cards or information and rely on information shared between Masters when handing over the ship. Any information about the boat that can be shared is very useful to an oncoming Master or pilot.

Manoeuvring information (Ref: IMO Resolution A. 601(15) & Bridge Procedures Guide A3)		
Requirement	Pilot card, wheelhouse poster and manoeuvring poster on: Ships of 100m or more. All chemical or gas carriers regardless of size. Ships that may pose a hazard due to unusual dimensions or characteristics.	
Pilot card extra requirement	IMO states: Pilot Card required on all ships to which the requirements of the 1974 SOLAS Convention apply. SOLAS V R23 Pilot Transfer Arrangements states: Ships engaged on voyages in the course of which pilots may be employed shall be provided with pilot transfer arrangements.[17] (Excerpt).	
Pilot card	Filled in by the Master. Intended to provide information to the pilot on boarding the ship. Should describe the current condition of the ship: General dimensions. General characteristics. Loading. Propulsion. Manoeuvring equipment. Other relevant equipment.	
Wheelhouse poster	Permanently displayed in the wheelhouse. Large enough to ensure ease of use. Describes the manoeuvring characteristics of the ship. Contains general particulars and detailed information: • Tonnage. • Loaded and unloaded draught. • Steering particulars.	• Anchor chain length. • Propulsion type of propeller. • Speed/pitch to RPM. • Thruster effect. • Heights, lengths, air draught. • MOB technique. • Turning circle. • Emergency stop.
Manoeuvring booklet contents	• General description. • Ship's particulars. • Characteristics of main engine. • Manoeuvring characteristics in deep water. • Course change performance. • Turning circles in deep water. • Accelerating turn. • Yaw checking tests. • Man-overboard and parallel course manoeuvres. • Lateral thruster capabilities. • Stopping and speed control characteristics in deep water. • Stopping ability.	• Deceleration performance. • Acceleration performance. • Manoeuvring characteristics in shallow water. • Turning circle in shallow water. • Squat. • Manoeuvring characteristics in wind. • Wind forces and moments. • Course-keeping limitations. • Drifting under wind influence. • Manoeuvring characteristics at low speed. • Additional information.

Towing

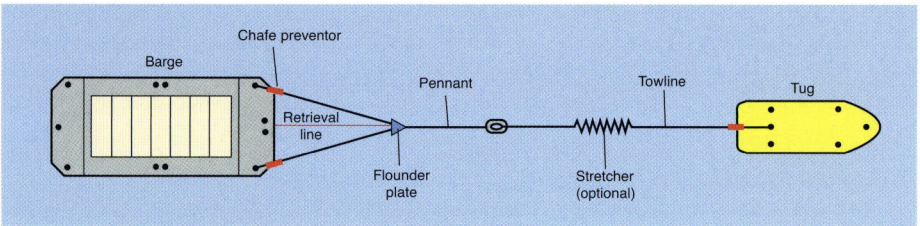

▲ An astern tow is the best option for towing at sea.

Towing	
Long tow astern will generally be connected by:	A bridle of wire or chain connecting to the vessel's strong points. Bridle connects through a (flounder) plate then on through pennants to the tow wire. Depending on conditions and duration of tow, weak links and stretchers sometimes used.
Catenary	Catenary is defined as a curve formed by a wire, rope or chain hanging freely from two points. It is very important to veer enough scope of towline to enable a catenary to form. This creates a tension in the towline that absorbs the dynamic effects of waves, wind, swell and resultant sheering by the towed vessel to each side of the towed water track.
Pre-rigging	The common arrangement is to secure a towline of the same size and strength as the main towline or bridle. This is commonly secured to alternative towing points on the vessel, e.g. spare SMIT bracket or deck bollards. • The end is secured to a messenger line that is then led outside of guardrails (secured by weak links) to the stern of the vessel. • The messenger is coiled on deck and secured to a strop connected to a buoy. • The buoy is streamed astern and thereby provides an accessible recovery point should the emergency towline be required.
Emergency towing	Emergency towlines should be rigged on the towed vessel before departure. This enables the tug to re-establish a towline in the event of the primary towline parting or being ditched. This is arranged so that it can be recovered without having to board the towed vessel at sea. ▶ Emergency towlines rigged up just in case the main towline fails.

Section 10
Bridge equipment

When looking down this list it will be apparent that smaller vessels do not necessarily require what you would think they require to go to sea. However, smaller vessels tend to carry a lot more equipment than is laid down here. On small commercial vessels, their equipment is laid down in the Small Vessel Codes of Practice.

SOLAS V R19 bridge equipment

Equipment Reg 19 SOLAS V (general requirements)

It should be noted that vessels will need to apply all those requirements under their tonnage as well as those applicable to their tonnage.

	All ships	150 GT+	300 GT+	500 GT+	3000 GT+	10000 GT+	50000 GT+	Notes
Magnetic compass	Y							
Pelorus or bearing device	Y							
Charts and publications	Y							
GNSS	Y							
Radar reflector	Y							Under 150GT.
Sound receiver	Y							When the bridge is totally enclosed so the OOW can hear sound signals.
Comms to emergency steering	Y							Telephone or means from bridge to emergency steering position.
Spare magnetic compass		Y						
Day/night signal lamp		Y						
BNWAS		Y						And passenger ships irrespective of size. Exemptions possible for older ships.
Echo sounder			Y					
Radar (9GHz)			Y					
Electronic Plotting Aid			Y					Electronic plotting of at least 10 targets, but without automatic tracking (ships 300–500GT).
Speed and distance measure (log)			Y					

SECTION 10

BRIDGE EQUIPMENT

	All ships	150 GT +	300 GT +	500 GT +	3000 GT +	10000 GT +	50000 GT +	Notes
Transmitting heading device			Y					To transmit information to radar, ARPA, speed etc.
AIS			Y					300GT and over on international voyages plus all domestic passenger ships, plus domestic cargo over 500GT.
Gyro for helm				Y				
Em. steering Gyro repeater				Y				
Gyro repeater for bearings				Y				Ships less than 1600GT fitted 'as far as possible'.
Rudder, prop, thrust, pitch indicators				Y				
ATA Automatic Tracking Aid				Y				
ECDIS				Y				Passenger ships.
ECDIS					Y			Tankers and cargo ships.
Radar 3GHz					Y			
2nd ATA					Y			
ATA					Y			Tracking at least 20 targets.
Automatic heading system					Y			
ARPA						Y		
Heading or track control						Y		
Rate of turn indicator							Y	
Speed and distance device (SOG)							Y	Forward and athwartship movement.

137

Small vessel bridge equipment

Small vessel codes – Navigational/Misc equipment S18–19 (see codes for detail)

Equipment	MGN 280	Workboat code Ed2
Charts and Nautical Publications	Corrected or Type approved Mini ECDIS system.	
Official logbook	Not mentioned in code.	Over 25GT, carry and complete.
Compass	Adjusted with card. Ability to take bearings.	
Electronic compass	Can be used instead of compass (with back-up power).	
Echo sounder	Yes.	
GNSS	Yes.	
Log	Yes or can be the GNSS.	
Class A AIS		Recommended.
Radar X Band	Not mentioned in code.	Yes, If ARPA fitted then also an (TMHD) electronic compass.
Electronic chart system		High-speed vessels recommended fit.
Signalling lamp	Yes.	
Radar reflector	Yes. Cat 6 should not put to sea in fog.	Yes. Passive or active. Cat 6 should not put to sea in fog.
Barometer	Yes.	Yes in area Cat 0–3 or Navtex.
Searchlight	Yes, for search and recovery.	
Sailing monohull	Anemometer and inclinometer.	Not mentioned but required through having to also comply with equivalent standards (WBC Ed2 S.25.11).
Sailing multihull	Anemometer.	
Sailing vessels	Wire/rig cutters.	

Compass requirements

The compass is quite rightly the number one piece of bridge equipment. It is worth noting that the requirement for transmitting heading device comes in at the same point as radar, so that an effective target tracking system can be in place.

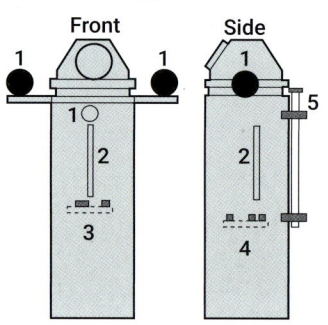

◀ Parts that would be used to adjust the compass.

1. Spheres (quadrantal soft iron correctors).
2. Heeling error magnet bar/tube.
3. Athwartship magnets.
4. Fore and aft magnets.
5. Flinders bar.

Other parts: light dimmer, clinometer, night shade.

Compass

Requirement	SOLAS Chapter V Reg 19
All ships irrespective of size	A properly adjusted magnetic compass, independent of a power supply and displaying the reading at the main steering position. A pelorus or compass bearing device, independent of any power supply to take bearings over an arc of the horizon of 360°. Means of correcting heading and bearings to True at all times.
150GT and over	A spare magnetic compass interchangeable with the magnetic compass.
300GT and over	A properly adjusted transmitting heading device, or other means to transmit heading information for input to the radar, plotting aid etc.
500GT and over	A gyro compass, or other means, to determine and display their heading by shipborne non-magnetic means, being clearly readable by the helmsperson at the main steering position. These means shall also transmit heading information for input to the radar, plotting aid etc., plus: gyro compass heading repeater, or other means, to supply heading information visually at the emergency steering position if provided, plus: gyro compass bearing repeater, or other means, to take bearings, over an arc of the horizon of 360°, using the gyro compass or other means.
Responsibility	Owner and Master to ensure that compasses on their ships are maintained in good working order. Compass fitted on the centreline of the ship.
Adjustment when:	a. First installed. b. They become unreliable. c. Following structural repairs. d. Electrical equipment close to the compass is added or removed. e. Two years have elapsed since the last adjustment. f. At any time the Master considers it necessary.
Masters to check the magnetic compasses after:	a. Carrying cargoes that have magnetic properties. b. Using electromagnetic lifting appliances to load or discharge. c. If the ship has been subject to severe contact or electrical charges. d. The ship has been laid up or has been lying idle, even a short period of idleness can lead to serious deviations, especially for small vessels.
Compass performance monitoring	Monitored frequently. Recording deviations in the compass deviation book. Check compass error after every large alteration of course. Record error at least every watch. Checking deviation may show need for repair or adjustment. In addition, compasses should be inspected occasionally by a competent officer or compass adjuster.
Operational checks	Gimbal is free. Card is clear and floating freely, level and without friction. No bubbles in liquid. No leaks around bowl. Lighting works. Free of portable magnetic influence (phones).
Portable equipment	Phones, radios and electrical equipment can affect the compass so keep them clear.

Adjusters	In the UK, all adjustments should be made by a compass adjuster who holds a Certificate of Competency as Compass Adjuster issued by the UK Government. If a qualified compass adjuster is unavailable and the Master considers it necessary then adjustments may be made by a person holding a Certificate of Competency (Deck Officer) Class 1 (Master Mariner). The compass must be readjusted by a qualified compass adjuster at the next available opportunity.
Emergency steering	Ships over 150GT shall have communication with emergency steering position for relaying heading information. Ships over 500GT shall have visual compass readings at the emergency steering position.
Azimuth ring or circle	This is placed over a compass and rotates to measure bearings of terrestrial and celestial points. An azimuth circle is fitted with a prism that reflects down to read the compass card when the observer sights the object through the sighting vanes. Reflector mirrors and shades can be used when taking bearings of celestial objects. ▲ Azimuth circle: useful for collision avoidance and taking bearings.

Gyro compass

Master compass	Maintains True North using the gyroscope.
Repeater compasses	Receive True direction from the master compass.
Course recorder	Continuous record of the ship's manoeuvres and headings.
Siting	• The master compass shall be installed with its fore-and-aft datum line parallel to the ship's fore-and-aft datum line to within ±0.5 degrees. • The compass card of the master compass, or a repeater of the heading information, is sited so it is clearly readable by the helmsman when steering the ship. • Repeaters used for taking visual bearing shall be installed with their fore-and-aft datum lines parallel to the ship's fore-and-aft datum line to within ±0.5 degrees. • Master compass sited to avoid excessive errors caused to gyro compass installation due to the ship rolling, pitching or yawing.
Operational checks	• Gyro compass is running and settled in sufficient time for use. • Repeaters synchronised with 'main gyro' once per watch. • Gyro alarm checked daily. • Check between magnetic and gyro compass daily. • Compass errors ascertained each watch. • All repeaters to be within 0.5 degrees of the gyro compass when underway, corrections for latitude and speed error.

SECTION 10

Gyro compass possible interfaces	• Master compass • Repeater compass • Autopilot • Course recorder • Rate of turn indicator	• Radar • GNSS • Voyage data recorder • ECDIS • Emergency steering compass

Voyage data recorders

Voyage data recorders

A voyage data recorder (VDR) or a simplified voyage data recorder (S-VDR) stores critical vessel information, in a secure and retrievable form, similar to a 'black box'. This information is for use during any investigation to identify the cause(s) of an incident.

Vessels (on international voyages)	S – VDR	VDR
Passenger ships		X
Ro-ro passenger ships		X
Ships other than passenger ships of 3000GT or more		X
Cargo ships of 3000GT or more	X	
Input		
Time and date	X	X
Vessel position	X	X
Speed	X	X
Heading	X	X
Echo sounder		X
Wind (Speed and direction)		X
Audio (Bridge)	X	X
Audio (Comms)	X	X
Radar	X	X
Hull stresses		X
Engine order		X
Rudder order		X
Hull openings (doors etc.)		X
Alarms (Mandatory bridge alarms)		X
Fire and watertight doors		X

Requirements:
Be accessible following an incident but secure against tampering;
Maximise the probability of survival/recovery of final recorded data after an incident;
Be of a highly visible colour and marked with retro-reflective materials;
Be fitted with an appropriate device to aid location;
Have dedicated reserve power source so that in the event of power outage during an incident it records the next two hours;
Data should be easily downloadable via industry standard interfaces (USB/Ethernet etc.);
Record information for a minimum of the last 12 hours of the voyage (preferably longer).

BRIDGE EQUIPMENT

141

Automatic Identification System (AIS)

While AIS is compulsory on large vessels, many small vessels fit the system to be able to 'see and be seen'. It should be remembered that while AIS is good, it only picks up those other vessels with functioning AIS, whereas radar has a greater probability of picking up all targets.

Automatic Identification System (AIS)

Requirement	SOLAS Regulation V/19.2.4 requires all vessels of 300GT and above engaged on international voyages and all passenger ships irrespective of size to carry AIS on board.	
AIS Types Class A:	Mandated for all vessels 300GT and above engaged on international voyages as well as all passenger ships.	
Class B:	Provides limited functionality and intended for non-SOLAS vessels. Primarily used for pleasure craft and small commercial vessels.	
Data	The AIS information transmitted by a ship is of three different types:	
	Static information	Information about the vessel, entered into the AIS on installation. Information only changed if ship changes name, MMSI, location of GNSS antenna or changes class.
	Dynamic information	Navigational status information, is automatically updated from the ship sensors connected to AIS (speed, position, COG, etc.).
	Voyage-related information	Information that might need to be manually entered and updated during the voyage (draught, hazardous cargo, ETA and destination).

Information item	Information generation, type and quality of information
Static	
MMSI (Maritime Mobile Service Identity)	Set on installation. Note that this might need amending if the ship changes ownership.
Callsign and name	Set on installation. Note that this might need amending if the ship changes ownership.
IMO Number	Set on installation.
Length and beam	Set on installation or if changed.
Type of ship	Select from pre-installed list.
Location of position-fixing antenna	Set on installation or may be changed for bi-directional vessels or those fitted with multiple antennae.

SECTION 10

BRIDGE EQUIPMENT

Dynamic	
Ship's position with accuracy indication and integrity status	Automatically updated from the position sensor connected to AIS. Accuracy indication is approximately +/-10m.
Position Time stamp (UTC)	Automatically updated from ship's GNSS connected to AIS.
Course over ground (COG)	Automatically updated from ship's GNSS connected to AIS. This information might not be available.
Speed over ground (SOG)	Automatically updated from the position sensor connected to AIS. This information might not be available.
Heading	Automatically updated from the ship's heading sensor connected to AIS.
Navigational status	Navigational status information has to be manually entered by the OOW and changed as necessary, for example: • underway using engines • at anchor • not under command (NUC) • restricted in ability to manoeuvre (RIATM) • moored • constrained by draught – aground • engaged in fishing • underway by sail. As these relate to ColRegs, any AIS change required could be undertaken at the same time lights or shapes were changed.
Rate of turn (ROT)	Automatically updated from the ship's ROT sensor or derived from the gyro. This information might not be available.
Voyage-related – all manually entered at the start of the voyage or during if changed.	
Ship's draught	Maximum draught for the voyage and amended as required.
Hazardous cargo type (if carried)	DG (Dangerous goods). HS (Harmful substances). MP (Marine pollutants). Indications of quantities are not required.
Destination and ETA	Kept up to date as necessary.
Route plan (waypoints)	At the discretion of the Master and updated when required.
Safety related	
Free format short text messages would be manually entered, addressed to either a specific addressee or broadcast to all ships and shore stations.	

CLASS A AIS reporting intervals

Type of ship	General reporting interval
Ship at anchor/moored and not moving faster than 3 knots	3 mins
Ship at anchored/moored and moving faster than 3 knots	10 secs
Ship 0–14 knots	10 secs
Ship 0–14 knots and changing course	$3^{1}/_{3}$ secs
Ship 14–23 knots	6 secs

continued ⇨

Type of ship	General reporting interval
Ship 14–23 knots and changing course	2 secs
Ship >23 knots	2 secs
Ship >23 knots and changing course	2 secs

Craft not subject to SOLAS (CLASS B) reporting intervals	
Type of ship	**General reporting interval**
Class B 'SO' shipborne equipment not moving faster than 2 knots	3 mins
Class B 'SO' shipborne equipment moving 2–14 knots	30 secs
Class B 'SO' shipborne equipment moving 14–23 knots	15 secs
Class B 'SO' shipborne equipment moving > 23 knots	5 secs
Class B 'CS' shipborne equipment not moving faster than 2 knots	3 mins
Class B 'CS' shipborne equipment moving faster than 2 knots	30 secs
SO (Self Organised) transmissions reporting intervals are similar to those of Class A, whereas the CS (Carrier Sense) possibly transmits less frequently.	

Section 11
Watchkeeping

Regulations on watchkeeping come straight from STCW Chapter VIII. While much of STCW is about the standards of training, Chapter VIII is about the standards of watchkeeping. When reading about the watchkeeping and lookout, it is worth having a copy of the ColRegs to hand (especially Part B, Section 1) as they overlap and reading both together can aid greater understanding. A Bridge is not normally complete without a copy of the Bridge Procedures Guide (BPG), which is an everyday translation of STCW Chapter VIII with added best practice.

Watchkeeping and Master's authority

Preparation for sea	
Pre-sailing operational checks	Prior to departure, it is the Master's responsibility to ensure that the vessel is fit and secured for sea. While the Master may delegate many of these tasks, the responsibility stays with the Master. A log entry should be made to state the checks have been completed.
Watertight integrity	• Close watertight doors below decks and between cargo holds. • Close weathertight doors on exposed decks and vessel entry points. • Close hatches leading to deck, cargo holds or tanks. • Ensure emergency escape hatches can be opened from below. • Close windows and portlights liable to water ingress. • Close applicable ventilators and breather pipes where seawater can enter. • Close cargo hold fan dampers, except when ventilating. • Close sounding and free space pipes. • Regular checks to ensure that all self-closing devices and non-return valves are operating correctly. • In-port discharge covers removed so that outlets can be used once again. • Ensure movable or vulnerable equipment is secured and the vessel is safe and ready for the passage.
Ship's business	• Briefings/communications. • The following should take place before each departure: • Crew advised of departure time. • New crew inductions carried out. • Safety briefing carried out. • Pre-departure brief to crew on mooring operations.
General	• Is everyone on board and are their names/numbers recorded? • Are shore workers back on shore? • Have replenishments taken place: fuel, water, lubricants, stores and spares? • Cargo or passenger manifests complete. • Galley and below decks secured, so that loose items will not fall when underway. • Stowaway search completed.
Safety checks	• Engine checks completed and forward and reverse gear operable. • Steering checks complete. • Lifejackets and appropriate PPE issued. • Life Saving Appliances checked. • Fire doors closed.
Deck checks	• Gangways removed and stowed. • Cranes, hoists and davits are housed for sea and secured. • Windlasses, mooring winches, hawsers and deck gear ready for use. • Shoreside hook-ups to power or water disconnected and made safe. • Items on deck, inside accommodation areas, including passageways are secured.

SECTION 11

Bridge induction checklist

Bridge induction checklist	
Compass and heading devices	**Radar and plotting aids**
GNSS	GMDSS
Echo sounder	Speed/distance Logs
Bridge equipment – logs, binos, wipers etc.	Internal communications
Navigation lights	Sound, shape and light signals
Voyage Data Recorder	BNWAS
Propulsion systems	Steering systems
AIS	ECDIS
Charts and publications	Bridge procedures and Master's orders
Emergency alarm panels	Watertight door indicators

Watchkeeping responsibilities

Watchkeeping responsibilities (Ref: STCW VIII, MGN 315)	
Master must ensure	Watchkeeping arrangements are adequate for maintaining a safe navigational or cargo watch.
Officer Of the Watch	• The Officer Of the Watch (OOW) is the Master's representative when the Master is not on the Bridge. • IMO states: Under the Master's general direction, the officers/crew of the navigational watch are responsible for navigating the ship safely during their periods of duty. They are particularly concerned with avoiding collision and stranding.[18] (Excerpt). • The lead OOW may oversee other officers on the bridge.
Chief Engineer	Ensures that watchkeeping arrangements are adequate to maintain a safe engineering watch.
Lookouts	Required to report back to the OOW or Master. Extra lookouts may be required because of vessel type, area of operation and visibility.
Watch arrangements The make-up of a navigational watch will take into account:	• Appropriately qualified and experienced personnel. • At no time shall the bridge be left unattended. • Weather conditions, visibility and daylight or darkness. • Proximity of navigational hazards. • Use and operational condition of navigational aids. IMO states: • Whether the ship is fitted with automatic steering. • Whether there are radio duties to be performed. • Unmanned machinery space controls, alarms/indicators on the bridge. • Any demands on the watch due to special operational circumstances.[19] (Excerpt).

CRAMMER FOR DECK OFFICER ORAL EXAMS

Handing and taking over a watch

Handing over the watch	Do not hand over the watch if: • The relief watch is not capable of carrying out their duties. In this event, notify the Master. • A manoeuvre such as course alteration is taking place.
Taking over the watch	Before taking over the watch the relieving officer shall ensure: 1. The relieving watch are capable of performing their duties. 2. Their vision is fully adjusted to the light conditions. 3. Appropriate instructions and information have been given to watchkeepers and lookouts. 4. Master's standing orders with reference to safe navigation are understood. 5. Position, course, speed and draught of the ship. 6. Effect of tides, currents, weather, visibility upon course and speed. 7. Procedures for the use of main engines to manoeuvre. 8. Navigational situation, such as: • condition and limitations of bridge and safety equipment; • the errors of compasses; • the presence and movement of ships in the vicinity; • the conditions and hazards likely to be encountered; • effects of heel, trim, water density, squat on under-keel clearance. 9. Status of fire detector and other alarm systems.

▲ Lookout: one of the most important parts of being on the bridge.

SECTION 11

Responsibilities of lookout

Lookout	IMO states: The lookout has three main duties: 1. Maintaining a continuous state of vigilance by sight and hearing, as well as by all other available means. 2. Fully appraising the situation and the risk of collision, stranding and other dangers to navigation. 3. Detecting ships or aircraft in distress, shipwrecked persons, wrecks, debris and other hazards to safe navigation. • A lookout should not be assigned or undertake anything that could interfere with lookout. • The duties of the lookout and helmsperson are separate. • A helmsperson shall not be considered to be the lookout while steering, except in small ships where an unobstructed all-round view is provided at the steering position.[20] (Excerpt).
To ensure an adequate lookout is maintained, the Master should consider the following:	1. Visibility, state of weather and sea. 2. Traffic density. 3. Required attention when near traffic separation schemes or busy channels. 4. Additional workload caused by the ship's functions, operating requirements and manoeuvres. 5. Crew member fitness for duty – on call or assigned to the watch. 6. Knowledge and confidence in officers and crew competence. 7. Officer experience and their familiarity with ship equipment, procedures and manoeuvring. 8. Availability of bridge assistance to be summoned when necessary. 9. The operational status of instrumentation, controls and alarms. 10. The size of vessel and field of vision available. 11. Bridge layout, which might inhibit detection of external developments.

Sole lookout	IMO states: The OOW may be the sole lookout in daylight provided that, on each occasion:
	1. The situation has been carefully assessed and it has been established without doubt that it is safe to do so.
	2. Full account has been taken of:
	    state of weather
	    visibility
	    traffic density
	    proximity of dangers to navigation
	    the attention necessary when in or near TSS.
	3. Assistance is immediately available to be summoned when required.
	[21] (Excerpt).

MCA and sole lookout	The MCA considers it dangerous and irresponsible for the OOW to act as sole lookout during periods of darkness or restricted visibility.

Performing the radio watch

The radio operator performing the duties shall:	Ensure the watch is maintained on the appropriate channels. • Check the operation of the radio equipment and energy sources. • Report any failures of equipment to the Master.
Record the following in the radio/GMDSS log	• Summary of distress, urgency and safety working. • Important incidents relating to the radio. • The ship's position daily. • Condition of the radio equipment and sources of energy.
Records inspected by	Ship's Master or authorised official

WATCHKEEPING

Deck Watch in Port requirement

Master's decision	• Master decides the composition of the deck watch, depending on the mooring, ship type and duties. If necessary, a qualified officer shall be in charge. • The Master and the Chief Engineer shall decide the composition of a safe engineering watch. Officers in charge of the engineering watch shall not be distracted by other duties when supervising the ship's machinery.
A deck watch shall be kept to:	• Ensure safety of life, the ship, the port, the environment and the safe operation of machinery and loading or unloading of cargo. • Observe international, national and port rules and regulations. • Maintain order on the ship.

Taking over the deck watch in port

Prior to taking over the deck watch, the relieving officer shall be informed by the officer in charge	• The depth of water at the berth. • Draught and time of High and Low Water. • Securing of moorings. • Arrangements of anchors and scope of chain. • State of main engines and availability for emergency use. • Work to be performed on the ship; status of cargo loading. • Levels of water in the bilge. • Signals/lights shown. • Crew members on board and other personnel. • State of fire-fighting appliances. • Any special port regulations. • Master's standing and special orders. • Lines of communication ashore, port, port operations etc. • Any pollution prevention reporting requirements.
The relieving officer shall verify	• Security of moorings and anchor scope. • Correct signals shown. • Fire and LSA measures are adequate. • Awareness of hazardous or dangerous cargo being loaded and action to take. • Environmental conditions likely to affect the ship.

Performing the deck watch

The Officer in charge of the deck watch shall:	Make rounds at appropriate intervals and check: • Gangway, anchor chain and moorings – especially on the turn of the tide and where there is a large tidal range. • Draught and UKC. • Weather and sea state. • Observance of safety and fire protection. • Water level in bilges. • Persons on board – especially those in Permits to Work Ops. • Exhibiting correct signals.
Generally	• In bad weather – take measures to protect the ship. • Prevent pollution. • In an emergency – sound the alarm, inform Master and take all measures to reduce damage to persons, cargo or ship. • Offer assistance to those in distress. • Take precautions if propellers are turning. • Keep relevant logbook entries.

SECTION 11

Code flags

Code flags

Letter	Phonetic	Flag	Morse	Meaning
A	Alpha		*-	I have a diver down – keep clear.
B	Bravo		-***	I am taking in, discharging or carrying dangerous cargo.
C	Charlie		-*-*	Yes.
D	Delta		-**	I am manoeuvring with difficulty.
E	Echo		*	Turning to starboard.
F	Foxtrot		**-*	I am disabled. Communicate with me.
G	Golf		_ _*	I require a pilot.
H	Hotel		****	I have a pilot on board.
I	India		**	I am turning to port.
J	Juliet		*---	I am on fire and am carrying dangerous cargo; keep clear.
K	Kilo		-*-	I wish to communicate with you.
L	Lima		*-**	Stop your vessel immediately.
M	Mike		--	My vessel is stopped; making no way.
N	November		-*	No.
O	Oscar		---	Man overboard.
P	Papa		*--*	Return to ship; proceeding to sea.
Q	Quebec		--*-	Request Customs clearance.
R	Romeo		*-*	No meaning.
S	Sierra		***	I am operating astern propulsion.
T	Tango		-	Keep clear of me.
U	Uniform		**-	You are running into danger.
V	Victor		***-	I require assistance.
W	Whisky		*--	I require medical assistance.
X	X-ray		-**-	Stop carrying out your intentions; watch for my signals.
Y	Yankee		-*--	I am dragging my anchor.
Z	Zulu		--**	I require a tug.

WATCHKEEPING

CRAMMER FOR DECK OFFICER ORAL EXAMS

Flag aide-memoire

B	Carrying, loading or unloading dangerous cargo	B for Bang
D	Manoeuvring with difficulty Morse same sound signal one long and two short = tow, sail, RAM, NUC, Fish etc	D for difficulty
H	Pilot on board – white red, same as lights Morse 4 short same as sound signal	
J	I am on Fire	J for Juliet (my heart is on fire – *Romeo and Juliet*)
K	I wish to communicate	Flag is two halves – half a Kilo
M	My vessel is stopped	Morse 2 long blasts Underway, not making way
O	Person Overboard – Sound signal for person overboard same as Morse	3 long blasts
U	You are running into danger	U for You
W	I require medical assistance	Red dot in middle is similar to red nose after a drinking session
X	Stop your vessel and WATCH (specs) for my intentions. Morse _.._	Looks like pair of x-ray specs (glasses)

Section 12
Meteorology

A useful way to learn weather is to look at the synoptic chart each day and make your own forecast of wind direction and the type of weather for a particular sea area. Then read the actual forecast for that sea area and see if you are close. Every day you have the ideal opportunity to test yourself and get the answers to your self test.

Weather instruments

Weather instruments	
Anemometer	Measures wind speed – rotating arrangement of cups.
Wind vane	Measures wind direction.
Barometers	Barometers or barograph, measures air pressure.
Thermometer	Measures temperature.
Hygrometer	Measures the relative humidity (moisture in the air). Most common type of Hygrometer is a wet and dry bulb thermometer. One thermometer is measuring air temperature, the other has a muslin or cloth on its bulb, led into a small tub of water (therefore wet). The difference of the two temperatures gives an idea of the humidity and dew point. See the table in the Mariner's Handbook to determine dew point.

Hygrometer use			
Humidity	Evaporation	Temperature difference	Outcome
High	Weak	Dry and wet bulbs read almost the same	Dew, fog, rain etc.
Low	Intense	Dry bulb reads much higher than wet bulb	Hot and dry weather

Stevenson screen on a vessel
Meteorological vented shelter housing a hygrometer. The most common type is a portable Stevenson screen and this is positioned so that it is not overly affected by other sources of the ship's heat. The shelter protects the contents from direct sunlight, wind and rain.

Scales and terminology

World Meteorological Organisation (WMO) Sea State Code		
WMO Sea State Code	Wave height	Characteristics
0	0 metres	Calm (glassy)
1	0 to 0.1 metres	Calm (rippled)
2	0.1 to 0.5 metres	Smooth (wavelets)
3	0.5 to 1.25 metres	Slight
4	1.25 to 2.5 metres	Moderate
5	2.5 to 4 metres	Rough
6	4 to 6 metres	Very rough
7	6 to 9 metres	High
8	9 to 14 metres	Very high
9	Over 14 metres	Phenomenal

Beaufort Scale

Beaufort number	Term	Knots	Observations in open sea
0	Calm	<1	Sea like a mirror.
1	Light air	1–3	Ripples with the appearance of scales are formed, but without foam crests.
2	Light breeze	4–6	Small wavelets, still short but more pronounced; crests have a glassy appearance and do not break.
3	Gentle breeze	7–10	Large wavelets; crests begin to break; foam of glassy appearance; perhaps scattered white horses.
4	Moderate breeze	11–16	Small waves, becoming longer; fairly frequent white horses.
5	Fresh breeze	17–21	Moderate waves, taking a more pronounced long form; many white horses are formed (chance of some spray).
6	Strong breeze	22–27	Large waves begin to form; the white foam crests are more extensive everywhere (probably some spray).
7	Near gale	28–33	Sea heaps up and white foam from breaking waves begins to be blown in streaks along the direction of the wind.
8	Gale	34–40	Moderately high waves; dense streaks of foam along the direction of the wind; crests of waves begin to topple, tumble and roll over; spray may affect visibility.
9	Strong gale	41–47	High waves; dense streaks of foam along the direction of the wind; crests of waves begin to topple, tumble and roll over; spray may affect visibility.
10	Storm	48–55	Very high waves with long, overhanging crests; the resulting foam, in great patches, is blown in dense white streaks along the direction of the wind; on the whole, the surface of the sea takes a white appearance; the tumbling of the sea becomes heavy and shock-like; visibility affected.
11	Violent storm	56–63	Exceptionally high waves (small and medium-sized ships might be for a time lost to view behind the waves); the sea is completely covered with long white patches of foam flying along the direction of the wind; everywhere the edges of the wave crests are blown into froth; visibility affected.
12	Hurricane	64 and over	The air is filled with foam and spray; sea completely white with driving spray; visibility very seriously affected.

Timings

Imminent	Within 6 hours
Soon	Within 6 to 12 hours
Later	More than 12 hours

Visibility

Very poor	Less than 1,000m
Poor	1,000m–2NM
Moderate	2–5NM
Good	More than 5NM

Movement of systems

Slowly	Less than 15 knots
Steadily	15 to 25 knots
Rather quickly	25 to 35 knots
Rapidly	35 to 45 knots
Very rapidly	More than 45 knots

Barometric pressure

Mb or hPa	Pressure is measured in millibars (mb) or hectopascals (hPa). These equal the same (1hPa = 1mb), but are alternative units used.
Standard pressure	Standard barometric pressure at sea level is approximately 1013hPa. Extremes in high and low pressures can range between 1050 (high) to 950 (low).
High and Low	The centre of a high or low pressure is marked with a cross and the pressure stated next to it.
Isobars	Isobars on a weather map (synoptic chart) are lines of equal pressure, often spaced at 4hPa intervals. Close lines equal greater wind speed. Isobars surround centres of high or low pressure.

Barometric tendency
The rate of change of pressure indicates the speed of an approaching weather system, the increased chance of worsening weather and the greater the wind speed. Normally, slow pressure change is good – fast pressure change is bad.

Rising/falling slowly	Change of 0.1 to 1.5hPa in 3 hours
Rising/falling	Change of 1.6 to 3.5hPa in 3 hours
Rising/falling quickly	Change of 3.6 to 6.0hPa in 3 hours
Rising/falling very rapidly	Change of more than 6.0hPa in 3 hours

SECTION 12

METEOROLOGY

▶ When the wind changes from one direction to another it is termed backing or veering, depending on whether it is clockwise or anticlockwise.

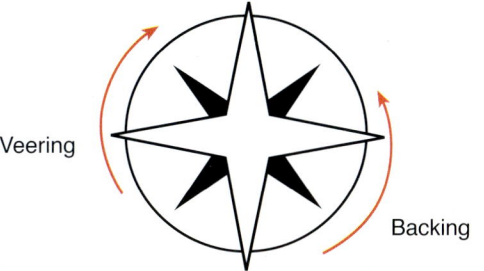

Wind		
Wind direction	Direction from which the wind is blowing. For example, Westerly Force 3: wind blowing from the west to the east at Beaufort Force 3 (7–10 kts).	
Isobar relationship	Wind direction generally follows the isobars. Wind blows roughly 15 degrees into a low pressure and 15 degrees out of a high pressure.	
Hemisphere	**Low**	**High**
North	Blows anticlockwise	Blows clockwise
	Blowing slightly inwards to the centre of the low by 10–20 degrees.	Blows slightly out of the isobars by 10–20 degrees.
South	Blows clockwise	Blows anticlockwise
	Blowing slightly inwards to the centre of the low by 10–20 degrees.	Blows slightly out of the isobars by 10–20 degrees.
Backing and veering	As a high or low pressure system passes over us, the wind changes direction either clockwise or anticlockwise. The forecast term for either change is backing and veering.	
Backing	Change of the wind direction anticlockwise (W to SW)	
Veering	Change of the wind direction clockwise (SW to W)	
Buys Ballot's law	Identifies the approximate position of the centre of a low pressure. Northern hemisphere – face the wind and the centre of the low will be 90–135 degrees on your right-hand side. Southern hemisphere – face the wind and the centre of the low will be 90–135 degrees on your left-hand side.	

Tropical revolving storms

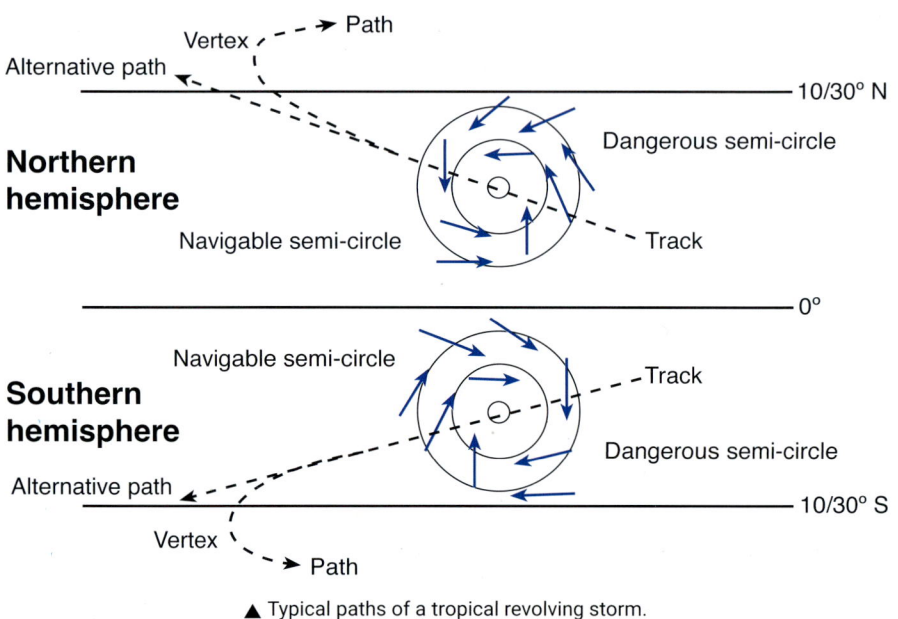

▲ Typical paths of a tropical revolving storm.

Tropical revolving storms (TRS)	
Where	Originate in latitudes between 5 and 20 degrees. Somewhere along their track, they curve away from the equator.
Winds	Gale-force winds likely up to 100NM from the eye of the storm. Gusts 30–50% higher than mean wind speeds. Heavy swell to mountainous seas.
When	Most frequent – late summer to early autumn, depending on hemisphere.
Travel – N hemisphere	W and WNW in the northern hemisphere at a speed of about 12 knots, then curve to N and then travel NE.
Travel – S hemisphere	W and WSW in the southern hemisphere at a speed of about 12 knots, then curve to S and then travel to SE.
Track	The route the TRS has already passed.
Path	Predicted route where the TRS may pass in the near future.
Vertex	Westernmost point of the TRS, when recurving takes place.
Dangerous semicircle	The side of a tropical cyclone where the storm has the strongest winds and heavy seas. The vessel is blown into the path of the TRS. To the right of the path in the northern hemisphere. To the left of the path in the southern hemisphere.
Navigable semicircle	The vessel is blown away from path of the TRS. The side of a tropical cyclone where winds are weaker/seas smaller, although all parts of TRS are dangerous. To the left of the path in the northern hemisphere. To the right of the path in the southern hemisphere.

SECTION 12

TRS signs	Long, slow swell coming from the approximate centre of the TRS. barometric reading 3hPa or more below the mean expected for the time as shown in the Admiralty Sailing Directions. An appreciable change in wind direction and strength. Cirrus cloud, then altostratus, then broken cumulus or fracto-stratus.
Strategy	Try to establish: 1. the position of the storm (eye) (use Buys Ballot's law) 2. the path of the storm. If you are on the path of the storm – remember the navigable quadrant is normally the side towards the equator. Also consider the storm tracks back on itself. It travels at 10–12 knots – so with early indication you may be able to get to a better position with less wind.

Categories		
Category	Wind Speed (knots	Damage to landfall
1	64–82	Minimal
2	83–95	Moderate
3	96–112	Extensive
4	113–135	Extreme
5	136 or higher	Catastrophic

Fog

Fog is simply cloud at sea level. There are two types: advection or radiation fog.

Fog	
Sea or advection fog	Caused by warm, moist air moving over cold water. Cold water cools the lowest layer of air so that water vapour in the air condenses to form water droplets.
When	Common when warm moist air mass moves over cold water.
How it clears	Slow to clear without change of temperature of the sea (heading inshore or offshore) or change of wind direction changing humidity.
Land or radiation fog	Without cloud cover heat radiates upwards and is lost in the atmosphere. As the ground cools, the air above it cools. If the air temperature falls below the dew point, fog is formed. Although this is a land fog, it drifts down rivers and estuaries and finds its way over coastal waters.
When	Formed during clear nights under high pressure. Often worse in the autumn and winter, especially if there is no or little sun. The coldest part of the night is around dawn, therefore the hour after dawn can see the worst radiation fog.
How it clears	Heating by the sun will quickly burn off the fog and a strong wind will rapidly disperse it.

Low-pressure systems

It is quite normal to be asked to interpret a synoptic chart during an exam. Look at the synoptic charts for a week or so before your exam to build up a picture of what is happening and to remind yourself of the various symbology.

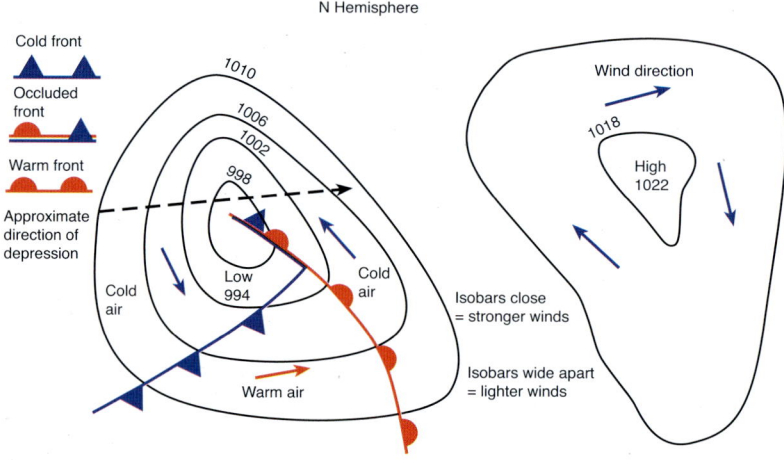

▲ Common terms in a northern hemisphere low and high pressure system.

Low-pressure

Low-pressure areas are formed where cold and warm air masses meet. Cold dry air comes from the poles. Warm moist air comes from the tropics and picks up moisture from the sea along the way. Sometimes the warm and cold air temperatures are gradual and have little effect on our weather. Sometimes the temperature and humidity is more abrupt and creates deeper depressions. As the warm, moist air from the Atlantic rises over the colder, denser air from the poles the resulting change causes the barometric pressure to drop.

Warm front	Boundary of warm, moist air. Signified on a weather chart by a line with semi-circles.
Warm sector	Area of warm, moist air wedged between the warm front and cold front, with cold air ahead and behind.
Cold front	Boundary of cold air. Signified on a weather chart by a line with triangles.
Occluded front	Where the warm and cold fronts have joined. Signified on a weather chart by a line with both semi-circles and triangles.
Trough	Isolated lines that have no semi-circles or triangles are areas where there is unstable air, often resulting in cloud and showers. Sometimes they are a dead/dying occluded front.
Isobar	Line of equal pressure shown on a weather chart. Wind roughly flows along the line of isobars – therefore direction is deduced. The closer the isobars, the greater the wind speed.

SECTION 12

METEOROLOGY

Cycle of a depression or low pressure system	When the pressure drops this is the creation of a low-pressure system. A cold front travels faster than a warm front. The clash of temperatures allows the pressure to continue to fall. The cold front chases and catch up with the warm front and when it succeeds, the fronts occlude. Once the front is fully occluded the low-pressure system starts to dissipate.	
Approach of a warm front (northern hemisphere)	Wind	Backs to SW or S. Increases.
	Cloud	Cirrus, cirrostratus, nimbostratus. Starts high and wispy, then layers up and gets lower. Often a halo effect around the sun or moon at the start.
	Weather	Rain or drizzle, moderate to heavy around the front.
	Barometer	Increased rate of fall.
	Temperature	Often rises.
	Visibility	Reduces in rain and low cloud.
In the warm sector	Wind	Veers and may increase.
	Cloud	Low level cloud with breaks to higher level cloud.
	Weather	Drizzle, occasional fog if sea and dew point similar temperature.
	Barometer	Often steady/slight fall.
	Temperature	Increase.
	Visibility	Decrease in visibility due to drizzle or fog.
On the cold front	Wind	Wind veers, freshens in squalls.
	Cloud	More chance of higher level cloud, then large cumulonimbus.
	Weather	Possible showers, sometimes with hail, snow etc.
	Barometer	Sharp rise in pressure.
	Temperature	Reduces.
	Visibility	Increase except in showers.
Behind the cold front	Wind	Often slowly starts to reduce.
	Cloud	Cumulus, although cumulonimbus may still be present.
	Weather	Occasional showers in cumulonimbus, clearing up.
	Barometer	Increases.
	Temperature	Decrease.
	Visibility	Increases.

Section 13
Navigation

Charts and nautical publications will come up in an exam at a few possible times, be it passage planning or being asked to demonstrate a particular technique. Be fully aware of the carriage requirements for publications and the methods of updating paper and electronic charts.

Charts and nautical publications

Charts and nautical publications (SOLAS Ch V 19.2.1.4 and 27)	
Chart requirements	IMO states: SOLAS V Regulation 19.2.1.4 nautical charts and nautical publications to plan and display the ship's route for the intended voyage and to plot and monitor positions throughout the voyage. An electronic chart display and information system (ECDIS) is also accepted as meeting the chart carriage requirements.[22] (Excerpt).
Up to date	IMO states: SOLAS V Regulation 27 nautical charts and nautical publications: Nautical charts and nautical publications, such as sailing directions, lists of lights, notices to mariners, tide tables and all other nautical publications necessary for the intended voyage, shall be adequate and up to date.[23] (Excerpt).
Chart Folio NP 131	Charts and nautical publications catalogue: details all charts and nautical publications either online or in paper format. Useful for overview of which charts and publications are required for a passage. Coverage worldwide.
Main types of chart projection	
Mercator	This is the standard type of chart projection as it portrays north and south in up/down positions all across the chart. However, it stretches the size of areas away from the equator, increasing in distortional effect towards the poles. Rhumb line courses are plotted on Mercator charts and the angle will be the same as it crosses each meridian, so they appear as straight lines. Passages up to 500 miles are often plotted on a Mercator chart.
Gnomonic	Often used for ocean passages or very detailed harbour plans. Meridians converge and lines of latitude curve on a gnomonic chart. This is very obvious on a passage chart, but unnoticeable on a harbour plan. Small scale gnomonic charts are used when planning ocean crossings as Great Circle courses appear as straight lines; thus the shortest route can be easily found, and intersections of the GC course with the meridians can then be plotted onto the suitable Mercator charts.

Chart types

Navigation charts come in different formats		Paper charts distributed by a hydrographic office. Official Nautical Paper Charts.
		Paper charts distributed by third-party companies. Can be official or unofficial paper charts.
		Electronic charts distributed by a hydrographic office ENCs and RNCs.
		Electronic charts distributed by third-party companies. Unofficial ENCs and RNCs.
		The only official electronic chart that can be used on a vessel is an ENC distributed by a hydrographic office, complying with stringent standards.
Standards		Official hydrographic paper and electronic charts must comply with standards set by the International Hydrographic Organisation and International Maritime Organization. The standards cover regularity for chart updating, the format in which the updates will be given and the conformity of symbology on the chart.
Commercial vessels		Only 'Official Nautical Charts' from a hydrographic office or chart maker approved by the flag can be used on commercial vessels.
Chart and system acronyms		**ENC** – Electronic Navigational Chart
		RNC – Raster Navigational Chart
		ECS – Electronic Chart System ECS are often used on small vessels and known as chartplotters. They can only be used for situational awareness and not as a stand-alone device. Updated official paper nautical charts must be used with ECS.
		ECDIS – Electronic Chart Display and Information System ECDIS can be used to portray ENCs as a standalone system without paper charts. However, a back-up system must be in place of either a second ECDIS or an appropriate set of updated paper charts.
Paper		Paper charts are issued by a National Hydrographic Office or through approved chart agents. • They are accurate when first published but require regular updating. • Colours and symbols on official charts are mostly standardised. • A folio or series of charts are required to navigate from berth to berth. • Always use the largest chart scale for the job. • It is good practice to identify all charts required for a passage, then put them in order of use in a chart holder/passage folio.
Electronic charts		When charts are displayed electronically on a screen, they are either Raster Navigational Charts (**RNCs**) or Electronic Navigational Charts (**ENCs**).
Raster (RNC)		Raster navigational charts are a scanned image of the paper chart. On a screen the vessel's position can be overlayed. However, the chart is non-interactive, therefore the chart does not allow any alarms to be set for crossing a shallow depth contour or nearing a navigational hazard.
ENC (Electronic Navigational Chart)		ENCs are also known as vector charts and are an electronic database of digitised chart data, which can be displayed as a seamless chart. On vector charts the data is 'layered', enabling the user to: • Deselect certain categories of data, such as textual descriptions. • Select or deselect spot soundings, nature of seabed, cables etc. • Election of a depth contour to an alarm providing an electronic safety contour. **Caution:** Deselect data should be used with extreme caution as it is possible to remove data essential for safe navigation.

SECTION 13

Chart scale

Small scale	Small detail
Large scale	Large detail

ENC chart usage bands

- Official ENCs are allocated to a purpose band based upon the compilation scale of the ENC. This is analogous to a series of paper charts covering the same area, ranging from small scale charts to large scale plans.
- The prefix number denotes the chart scale. For example, US 58907 would be: US Chart – (5) Harbour Chart – 8907 Chart number.

Prefix	Name	Scale
1	Overview	<1:1 499 999
2	General	1: 350000 – 1:1 499999
3	Coastal	1: 90000 – 1: 349999
4	Approach	1: 22000 – 1:89000
5	Harbour	1: 4000 – 1: 21999
6	Berthing	> 1: 4000

Electronic navigation charts specifications and standards

These specifications define how hydrographic offices construct an ENC to ensure that all electronic charts contain all the chart information necessary for safe navigation.

S-57	Data Transfer Standards: The S-57 protocol is to standardise the transfer of digital hydrographic data between national hydrographic offices, manufacturers, mariners and data users.
S-58	Standard of validation checks hydrographic offices must perform on ENCs before they are issued to mariners. Checks include: ENC issues that may cause an ECDIS to malfunction. Land objects appearing in open water or depths plotted on land.
S-63	Encryption Standards: S-63 data reduces the risk of inaccurate (unofficial ENC) data and the risk of bugs introduced to a ship's system. S-63 covers: Authentication – assurance that the ENC data is from an approved source. Selective access – restricting ENC access to those cells licensed to a customer. Piracy protection – encrypted ENC info to prevent unauthorised use of data.
S-52	Presentation Library: S-52 is a standard that determines how ENC data is displayed on an ECDIS/ECS screen through symbols, line styles and colours etc. Therefore, the symbols and abbreviations should be the same across all ENCs in a similar ethos to those used around the world on paper charts. Symbols and abbreviations for ENCs are contained in NP5012, which conforms to S-52.

NAVIGATION

165

The UKHO website has a very good chart update area listing all the updates and electronic versions of the types of updates that can be applied. Visiting this UKHO site can give you a very good understanding of how the updates are portrayed.

1376   ENGLAND - South Coast - Buoy.
Source: Dart Harbour Authority

Chart 2253 (INT 1723) [*previous update 1240/22*] ETRS89 DATUM

Insert	⚓ B (seasonal)		50° 19' ·980N., 3° 33' ·660W.
Delete	former B (seasonal) buoy		50° 19' ·850N., 3° 33' ·660W.

▲ Example of a weekly Notice to Mariners. Correction 1376 would be applied to chart 2253.

Chart and nautical publications updates
SOLAS requires charts and nautical publications to be 'adequate and up to date'.

Updates available	UKHO website	Weekly Notices to Mariners (NM)	Cumulative	Annual
	Chart QR Code	(ENC) Admiralty Vector Chart Service	(ENC) Admiralty Information Overlay	Regional ENC co-ordination centres
Weekly notices	I. Explanatory notes II. Updates to nautical charts – including permanent, temporary and preliminary (T&Ps) III. Reprints of Navarea 1 Navigation warnings IV. Updates to Admiralty Sailing Directions V. Admiralty List of Lights and Fog Signals VI. Updates to Admiralty List of Radio Signals VII. Updates to Miscellaneous Admiralty Nautical Publications VIII. Updates to Admiralty Digital Services			
Cumulative List NP 234 (A) (B) (Year)	Issued every six months, January (Part A) and July (Part B). Contains information about which corrections have been applied to a chart over the last two years. From this, the weekly NMs can be consulted to get the detail to apply. Also contains a list of the current editions in force of nautical publications.			
Cumulative example	**Chart No.**	**Edition**	**Notices to Mariners**	
	155	July 2017	**2019 (3)** 419 **(9)** 1026 **(17)** 2095 2021 **(42)** 4152 (Bold indicates year and week number)	
Annual Summary of Admiralty Notices to Mariners (NP 247) Parts 1&2	Issued annually (late December). **Part 1 contains two sections. Notices to Mariners 1–26.** S. 2 Temporary and Preliminary Notices still in force.			
	Annual Notices			
	Admiralty tide tables		Suppliers of Admiralty charts	
	Firing practice and exercise areas		Safety of British Merchant Ships in periods of peace, tension or conflict	

SECTION 13

	Mine laying and mine countermeasure areas	National claims to Maritime Jurisdiction
	GNSS positions, horizontal datums and position shifts	Mandatory expanded inspections EU Directive 2009/16/EC
	Canadian charts and nautical publications regulations	US Navigation safety regs relating to navigation, chart publications
	High-speed craft	Marine environmental high-risk areas
	Part 2 used to check Sailing Directions and Nautical Publications are in date. **Section 1** Current editions of Admiralty sailing directions **Section 2** Sailing directions updates in force **Section 3** Current editions of Admiralty miscellaneous nautical publications **Section 4** Miscellaneous nautical publications updates in force	
QR code	Admiralty Charts have a QR code in the bottom left-hand corner. Scanning the code identifies corrections to be applied to that chart number.	
Application of chart corrections	Permanent correction numbers are noted in the bottom left-hand corner of the chart. Magenta/violet ink pen with a 0.18 or 0.25 nib. If a year date is added, it should be underlined. Update noted in chart correction book.	
	Temporary and preliminary corrections are applied in pencil and a record kept in the chart correction book or the front cover of the chart in question.	
ENC Updates	Electronic Navigation Charts updated by weekly Notices to Mariners by: Hydrographic Offices or Regional ENC co-ordination centres (RENC). Received on board by email/data file AVCS – Admiralty Vector Chart Service ECDIS/ENC chart database updating is either automatic or by the user.	
The AIO (Admiralty Information Overlay)	A worldwide digital dataset designed to be displayed over ENCs in ECDIS and other display systems to provide additional information during passage planning. AIO is refreshed every week as part of the Admiralty Vector Chart service. Admiralty AIO also contains T and P corrections and identifies areas where there are differences between ENCs and paper charts.	

▶ Extract from Cumulative Notices to Mariners Jan 23.

Chart No.	Edition	Notice to Mariners
54	Jan. 2020	2020 **(16)** 1976 **(19)** 2364 **(52)** 6249 **(53)** 6317 **2021 (21)** 2107 **(46)** 4758 **(50)** 5170 **2022 (11)** 997 **(19)** 1770

Chart information

Describing a chart	Number of the chart	Title	Date of printing
	Date of publication	Date last new edition	Last correction

References

CD	Chart Datum often the same or based on LAT
LAT	Lowest Astronomical Tide (often the same as CD) is defined as the lowest tide level that can be predicted to occur under average meteorological conditions and under any combination of astronomical conditions.
HAT	Highest Astronomical Tide (HAT) is defined as the highest tide level which can be predicted to occur under average meteorological conditions and under any combination of astronomical conditions.

MHWS	Mean High Water Springs
MLWS	Mean Low Water Springs
MHWN	Mean High Water Neaps
MLMN	Mean Low Water Neaps
Range	Difference between a Low and High Water height
MSL	Mean Sea Level
CATZOC	**Category Zone of Confidence** The table below identifies the position accuracy, depth accuracy and seafloor coverage in each area shown on a chart. CatZoc is used extensively on ENCs (electronic navigational charts) and becoming more prevalent on paper charts. It corresponds to values given in the source data diagram on a paper chart or when an area of an ENC is interrogated.

Category Zone of Confidence (CATZOC) table

ZOC	Position Accuracy	Depth Accuracy		Seafloor Coverage	Typical Survey Characteristics
A1	± 5m + 5% depth	= 0.50 + 1%d		Full area search undertaken. Significant seafloor features detected and depths measured	Controlled, systemic survey high position and depth accuracy achieved using DGPS or a minimum three high quality lines of position (LOP) and a multibeam, channel or mechanical sweep system
		Depth	Accuracy		
		10m	± 0.6m		
		30m	± 0.8m		
		100m	± 1.5m		
		1000m	± 10.15m		
A2	± 20m	= 1.00 + 2%d		Full area search undertaken. Significant seafloor features detected and depths measured	Controlled, systemic survey achieving position and depth accuracy less than ZOC A1 and using a modern survey echosounder and a sonar or mechanical sweep system
		Depth	Accuracy		
		10m	± 1.2m		
		30m	± 1.6m		
		100m	± 3.0m		
		1000m	± 21.00m		
B	± 50m	= 1.00 + 2%d		Full area search not achieved, uncharted features, hazardous to surface navigation are not expected but may exist	Controlled, systemic survey achieving similar depth but lesser position accuracies than ZOC A2, using a modern survey echosounder, but no sonar or mechanical sweep system
		Depth	Accuracy		
		10m	± 1.2m		
		30m	± 1.6m		
		100m	± 3.0m		
		1000m	± 21.00m		
C	± 500m	= 2.00 + 5%d		Full area search not achieved, depth anomalies may be expected	Low accuracy survey or data collected on an opportunity basis such as soundings on passage
		Depth	Accuracy		
		10m	± 2.5m		
		30m	± 3.5m		
		100m	± 7.0m		
		1000m	± 52.00m		
D	Worse than ZOC C	Worse than ZOC C		Full area search not achieved, large depth anomalies expected	Poor quality data or data that cannot be quality assessed due to lack of information
U	Unassessed – The quality of the bathymetric data has yet to be assessed				

SECTION 13

Navigational records – SOLAS V R28 and IMO Res. A916 (22)

IMO states: All ships engaged on international voyages shall keep on board a record of navigational activities and incidents:
- Which are of importance to safety of navigation.
- Which must contain sufficient detail to restore a complete record of the voyage.[24] (Excerpt).

Before the voyage	Data relating to the general condition of the ship	Steering, navigational and communication inspections
	Manning and provisioning	Draught
	Cargo aboard	Result of stability/stress checks
During the voyage	Courses steered and distances sailed	Entry and compliance with ship routeing or reporting systems
	Position fixes	Weather and sea conditions
	Changes to the voyage plan	Pilots' embarkation/disembarkation
On special events	Death and injuries among crew and passengers	Malfunctions of shipboard equipment and aids to navigation
	Hazardous situations and emergency	Distress messages received
At anchor or in port	Operational or administrative matters, safety and security of the ship should be recorded.	
Method of recording	Methods of recording should be permanent and may be handwritten, electronic or mechanical. If not recorded in the ship's logbook, should be approved by the administration.	
Preservation of records	<ul><li>Pages of the ship's logbook should be numbered.</li><li>Do not erase or remove handwritten records needing correction, but strike through with a single line and rewrite correctly.</li><li>Times used should be synchronised by using a common clock.</li><li>Electronically or mechanically input records should be protected to prevent deletion, destruction or overwriting.</li><li>Logs kept for one year minimum or as long as the Administration requires.</li></ul>	

Ships of 500 gross tonnage and above on international voyages exceeding 48 hours, shall:
- Submit a daily report to its company.

The company shall:
- Retain it and all subsequent daily reports for the duration of the voyage.

The report shall contain the following:
- Ship's position.
- Ship's course and speed.
- External or internal conditions affecting the ship's voyage or its normal safe operation.

NAVIGATION

Nautical publications

If you are able to open up these books, either at your college or on the ship's bridge, it is much easier to remember what is included within them. They will form part of the publications that would be consulted during the appraisal and planning part of a passage plan. Many are area specific and a number of publications will make up world coverage on a particular subject. The rear cover of the NP often highlights the part of the world it covers.

Nautical publications	
Admiralty Sailing Directions (NP 1 to 72)	Waterways directions. Port facilities. Directions for port entry. Navigational hazards. Buoyage. Climate information. Diagrams and photographs of ports and day marks.
Admiralty Tide Tables (NP 201 to 208)	Worldwide tide times for standard ports and secondary port differences. Times and height differences at secondary port. Supplementary tables including land levelling to chart datum connections where known.
Admiralty List of Lights and Fog signals (NP 74 to 88)	Fifteen regional volumes provide comprehensive details and world-wide coverage of all fixed lights, fog signals and some lit floating marks. Range tables and diagrams. Light characteristics and co-located aids to navigation. Abbreviations and glossary. List of lights and fog signals.
Admiralty List of Radio Signals Volume 1 (NP 281)	Maritime Radio Stations (Parts 1 and 2). Global Maritime Communications. Satellite Communication Services. Coastguard Communications. Maritime TeleMedical Assistance Service (TMAS). Radio Quarantine and Pollution reports. Anti-Piracy Contact Table.
Admiralty List of Radio Signals Volume 2 (NP 282)	Radio Aids to Navigation, Sat Nav Systems, Differential GPS (DGPS), Legal Time, Radio Time Signals & Electronic Position Fixing Systems Parts 1 and 2. Listing of VHF Radio Direction-Finding Stations. Worldwide listing of Racons and Ramarks (AIS) Aids to Navigation (AtoN). Worldwide listing of Radio beacons transmitting DGPS corrections. International Standard and Daylight Saving Times and Dates. International Radio Time Signal Broadcast details.
Admiralty List of Radio Signals Volume 3 (NP 283)	Maritime Safety Information Services (Parts 1 and 2). Maritime Weather Services. Safety Information broadcasts. Worldwide Navtex and SafetyNET information. Submarine and Gunnery Warning details (Subfacts and Gunfacts). Radio-Facsimile Stations, frequencies and weather map areas.
Admiralty List of Radio Signals Volume 4 (NP 284)	Meteorological Observation Stations. All met observation stations listed worldwide.

SECTION 13

Admiralty List of Radio Signals Volume 5 (NP 285)	Worldwide requirements for GMDSS. Distress communications and operational procedures. SOLAS regulations. Extracts from ITU Regulations. Navtex and Maritime Safety Information. Distress and SAR (incorporating MRCC and MRSC contacts). Worldwide Operational DSC ranges and Search and Rescue (SAR) regions.
Admiralty List of Radio Signals Volume 6 (NP286)	Pilot Services, Vessel Traffic Services, and Port Operations (Parts 1–8). Pilot information, contact details and procedures. Vessel Traffic Service information, contact details and procedures. National and International Ship Reporting Systems. Port information, contact details and procedures.
Ocean Passages for the World (NP 136, 2 vols.)	Details of weather, currents, trade routes and ice hazards for worldwide oceanic voyage planning. Detailing weather, climate, wind, swell, ice hazards for each ocean.
The Nautical Almanac (NP 314)	Essential for routine and emergency astronavigation, and the calculation of daylight hours and mandatory gyro checks. Times of sunrise and sunset, twilight and moonrise and set. Standard times for countries around the world. Sight reduction tables and sight reduction forms.
Admiralty Mariner's Handbook (NP 100)	Information on nautical charts, their use, regulation and survey. Tides and currents. Characteristics of the sea. Basic meteorology. Navigation in ice. Hazards and restrictions to navigation.
IALA Buoyage System (NP 735)	Provides identification and meaning information on the Cardinal. and Lateral Buoyage systems for IALA A and B.
Admiralty Distance Tables (NP 350, 3 vols.)	Global coverage of the shortest navigable distances between key positions.
Admiralty Guide to symbols and abbreviations used on paper charts (NP 5011)	A quick reference guide containing comprehensive information on the symbols and abbreviations used on paper charts.
Admiralty Guide to ENC symbols used in ECDIS (NP 5012)	A quick reference guide containing comprehensive information on the symbols and graphics used on Electronic Navigational Charts.
Annual summary Admiralty Notices to Mariners (NP 247)	Published annually every January in two parts. Part one contains Annual NMs and reprint of all Admiralty. Temporary and Preliminary Notices that are in force from 1 January. Part two lists the current editions of Sailing Directions and amendments that have been published in the weekly editions of Admiralty NMs that are in force from 1 January.
Other publications	
International Code of Signals (ICS) (SOLAS V/21 MGN 610)	Contains single and dual flag meanings for general signalling and medical signals. Also covers signals by light, semaphore and radio telephone procedures. The requirement to carry ICS is given in SOLAS V/21. UK guidance states that this does not apply to vessels under 150GT engaged on any voyage.

IAMSAR Manual Vol III (SOLAS V/21 MGN 610)	Volume III, Mobile Facilities, is intended to be carried aboard rescue units, aircraft and vessels to help with performance of a search, rescue or on-scene co-ordinator function, and with aspects of SAR that pertain to their own emergencies. UK SOLAS V Guidance allows that carriage of Volume III of the IAMSAR manual need not apply to: Ships below 150GT engaged on any voyage; ships below 500GT not engaged on international voyages; fishing vessels. Flag administration to decide (SOLAS V/1.4).
	Contents: Section 1: Overview Section 2: Rendering Assistance Section 3: On-Scene Co-ordination Section 4: On-Board Emergencies Appendices Regulation V/33 of SOLAS Masters obligations to distress messages Search Action Message Factors Affecting Observer Effectiveness Standard Format for Search and Rescue Situation Report (SITREP) SAR Briefing and Debriefing Form

Publications

The following publications are considered by the MCA to satisfy the basic requirements of SOLAS Carriage requirements SOLAS Ch V 19.2.1.4
(Ref: MS (Carriage of Nautical Publications) Regulations, 1998) (SI 1998/2647)

International Code of Signals (IMO)
IAMSAR Manual Vol III
Mariner's Handbook (UKHO)
Merchant Shipping Notices, Marine Guidance Notes and Marine Information Notes (MCA)
Notices to Mariners (UKHO)
Notices to Mariners Annual Summary (UKHO)
Lists of Radio Signals (UKHO)
Lists of Lights (UKHO)
Sailing Directions (UKHO)
Nautical Almanac
Navigational Tables
Tide Tables
Tidal Stream Atlases
Operating and Maintenance Instructions for Navigational Aids carried by the Ship

Passage planning

Requirements for passage/voyage planning

SOLAS Chapter V, Regulation 34	IMO states: Safe navigation and avoidance of dangerous situations
	1. Prior to proceeding to sea, the Master shall ensure that the intended voyage has been planned using the appropriate nautical charts and nautical publications for the area concerned, taking into account the guidelines and recommendations developed by the organization (IMO).
	2. The voyage plan shall identify a route that:
	   1. takes into account any relevant ships' routeing systems;
	   2. ensures sufficient sea room for the safe passage of the ship throughout the voyage;
	   3. anticipates all known navigational hazards and adverse weather conditions; and
	   4. takes into account the marine environmental protection measures that apply, and avoids as far as possible actions and activities that could cause damage to the environment.[25] (Excerpt).

IMO guidelines for voyage planning	IMO states: The need for voyage and passage planning applies to all vessels. There are several factors that may impede the safe navigation of all vessels and additional factors that may impede the navigation of large vessels or vessels carrying hazardous cargoes. These factors will need to be taken into account in the preparation of the plan and in the subsequent monitoring of the execution of the plan.[26] (Excerpt).
A.P.E.M.	Appraise, Plan, Execute and Monitor are the four stages of passage planning identified by IMO Res. A.893.(21).

Voyage planning – Appraise Plan Execute Monitor (APEM)

Appraisal

All information relevant to the contemplated voyage or passage should be considered. Its aim is to provide a clear indication of: areas of danger, areas to navigate safely, existing routeing or reporting systems, vessel traffic services areas where marine environmental protection considerations apply. Using the following information, an overall appraisal of the intended voyage or passage is made.

Condition of the vessel	Stability	Equipment	Operational limits
	Manoeuvring data	Draught	Air draught
Cargo	Distribution	Stowage	Securing on board
Crew	Competent	Well-rested crew	Inducted
Certificates	Crew	Vessel	
	Equipment	Passengers and or cargo	
Charts and publications	Appropriate scale	Up-to-date charts and publications	Permanent, preliminary or temporary NMs
	Sailing directions	Lists of lights	Routeing guides
	Lists of radio aids to navigation	Passage planning charts	Tidal atlases and tide tables

Conditions	Weather routeing	Port information	Volume of traffic
	Pilot pick up/drop off	Ships' routeing	Ship reporting systems
	Shorebased emergency response arrangements	Vessel traffic services	Marine environmental protection measures

Planning
Once a full appraisal is made, a detailed passage or voyage plan should be prepared. The plan should be berth to berth, including areas where a pilot is used. Containing:

Plotting the route on the chart	True direction of route indicated on chart	Manoeuvring characteristics of the vessel
Method and frequency of fixing – primary and secondary options	Course alteration points and effect of turning circle and stream	Draught on routes and in channels with critical clearances
Safe speeds	Vessel Traffic Services Area	Ships' reporting and routing
All areas of danger marked	Contingency plans for deep water or port of refuge	Use of routing and reporting systems
Speed limitations due to squat, hazards, proximity of nav hazards on route	The plan should be: 1) recorded, 2) marked on charts and in a passage record book or file 3) agreed and signed by the Master.	

Execution
Execute the voyage in accordance with the plan.
Leave on time taking into account tidal considerations and passage times. Consider…

Should you depart?	Conditions suitable?	Meteorological conditions	Day or night passing of danger points
ETA at critical points tide heights – flow	Reliability/status of nav equipment	Traffic conditions at high-risk areas	

Monitor
The plan and vessel's position should be constantly monitored. Progress along the track should be recorded and position updated regularly. Plan changes should be recorded.

Parallel indexing	GNSS	Transits	Leading lines
Spot depths	3-point fixes	Estimated positions	Fix by ranges

Position logged regularly. Fix frequency will depend on proximity to hazards.
Rule of thumb: Frequency of fixes should be at half the time it will take to reach the nearest navigational danger at the current speed.

SECTION 13

Ships' routeing

Ships' routeing and Traffic Separation Schemes

The purpose of ships' routeing is to improve the safety of navigation in converging areas and in areas where the density of traffic is great or where freedom of movement of shipping is inhibited by restricted sea room, the existence of obstructions to navigation, limited depths or unfavourable meteorological conditions (IMO Res 576).

These areas may include:	Reducing the chance of head-on encounters. Reducing collisions between crossing traffic and shipping in traffic lanes. Simplifying traffic flow in converging areas. Organising traffic in concentrated offshore exploration/exploitation areas. Organising traffic flow for certain dangerous/undesirable ship classes. Reducing grounding risks in areas where water depths are critical. Organisation of traffic through or clear of fishing grounds.

Terms used

Traffic Separation Scheme (TSS)	A routeing system controlling opposing traffic by using traffic lanes.
Traffic lane	Lanes designated with arrows on the chart showing one-way traffic and separated by zones, lines and occasionally natural features.
Separation line or zone	A line or zone separating traffic lanes from another traffic lane, route, sea area or inshore traffic zone.
Inshore traffic zone	A designated area between the landward boundary of a TSS and the coast. Referenced in rule 10(d) of ColRegs.
Roundabout	A circular separation zone or point and traffic lane where traffic moves in a counter-clockwise direction around the roundabout.
Two-way route	A defined route where two-way traffic aims to provide safe passage through waters where navigation is difficult or dangerous.
Recommended route	A route for the convenience of ships that is often marked by centreline buoys.
Recommended track	An examined route to provide, 'so far as possible', one that it is free of dangers and along which ships are advised to navigate.
Deep-water route	A surveyed route more suitable for deep-draught vessels.
Precautionary area	An area where ships must navigate with particular caution.
Area to be avoided	An area where navigation is particularly hazardous or it is exceptionally important to avoid casualties and which should be avoided by all ships, or certain classes of ship.
Established direction of traffic flow	A traffic flow pattern indicating the directional movement of traffic as established within a traffic separation scheme.
Non-compliance in TSS	Observed vessel in a TSS that appears not to be complying with the scheme should be notified by the best available means. If the TSS is within a Vessel Traffic Service (VTS) area, the VTS should be notified.
Flag YG	The international code signal YG, 'you appear not to be complying with the TSS', can be used. A Master receiving this signal by whatever means should immediately take action to rectify the situation.

175

Marine safety information

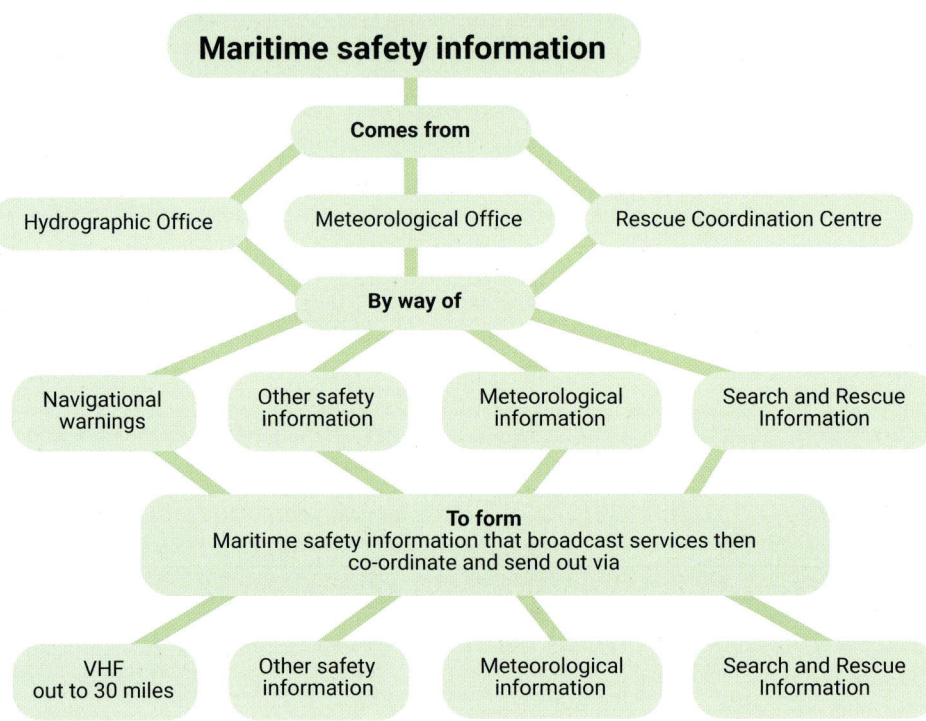

Lights

It is important to be able to describe the difference between an isophase, occulting, fixed, flashing, quick flash and long flash, both at sea and during an exam. Review different charts and be able to interpret and discuss what the light abbreviations mean, including the height of light, range and sectors.

Light characteristics		
Lights are on or off for a total period denoted in seconds (s). Therefore, all of the light sequence happens within this time period.		

Abbreviation	Characteristic	Description	Example
F	Fixed	Always on	2 FG (Vert) 2 Fixed Green Lights vertically

SECTION 13

Abbreviation	Characteristic	Description	Example
Fl	Flashing	Regular repeating light flash Rate less than 50 flashes per minute	Fl G Flashing green light
L.Fl	Long Flash	Single long flash not less than 2s duration	LFl 10s – long flash in a 10s period
Fl(2)	Group Flash	Flashing light with a group of flashes per period	FL(2) 5s – 2 grouped flashes in a 5s period
Fl(2+1)	Composite Group Flash	Flashing light with successive groups of flashes per period	Fl R(2+1) 8s – 2 red flashes followed by 1 red flash in an 8s period
F.Fl	Fixed and Flashing	A fixed light with pulses of a higher intensity flashing light	F.Fl G 5s – Fixed light with a regular high intensity pulse within a 5s period
Q	Quick	Continuous flashing 50–79 flashes per minute	Q – Quick flashing light (white)
Q (3)	Group Quick	Group of quick flashes followed by a period of darkness	Q(3) 5s – Quick 3 flash in a 5s period
IQ	Interrupted Quick	Quick flashing light with period (interruption) of darkness	IQ
VQ	Very Quick	Continuous flashing 80–158 flashes per minute	VQ – Quick Flashing light (white)
VQ(9)	Group Very Quick	Group of very quick flashes followed by a period of darkness	VQ (9) 10s – Very Quick 9 flash in a 10s period
IVQ	Interrupted Very Quick	Quick flashing light with period (interruption) of darkness	IVQ
UQ	Ultra Quick Lights	Continuous flashing more than 160 flashes per minute	UQ
Mo (U)	Morse	Light with durations that appear as dots/dash denoting Morse letter	Mo(U)R 15s – Morse U Red (..-) in a period of 15s
Iso	Isophase	Equal durations of light and dark within a period	Iso R 6s – Red light 3s on and 3s off
Oc	Occulting	Light that is on more than it is off within a period	Oc G 6s – Green light on for 4 or 5s and off for 1 or 2s
Gp Oc	Group Occulting	Light sequence that is on more than it is off within a period	Oc (2) 8s – Sequence of two lights that are on for longer than off. Often a longer period of light followed by a shorter period of light

NAVIGATION

177

Abbreviation	Characteristic	Description	Example
Dir or Dir Lt	Directional Light	Lights that shine in particular arcs or sectors	DIR WRG – White Red Green lights all shining in separate areas from the same light
(vert)	Vertical	Lights positioned one above the other	4FG(vert). 4 fixed lights vertically arranged
(hor)	Horizontal	Lights positioned side by side	2 FR(hor). 2 fixed lights horizontally arranged
Occas	Occasional	Light that is used or switched on when required (e.g. for a ferry coming in)	
In fog	Fog Light	Light that is only used when visibility reduces	In fog Fl W 5s
Al	Alternating Light	Often found with directional lights when in between two sectors	e.g. Al WG (alternating White Green)
Intens	Intensive Light	Very intense light	F Bu (Intens)
Lts in line	Lights in Line	Transit of lights	Lts in line (071). Lights in line at 071 degrees True

Sounds

Abbreviation	Characteristic	Description	Example
Dia	Diaphone	Compressed air low pitched	Dia 20s. Diaphone sounded in a period of 20s
Horn	Horn	Air or electric horn	Horn 30s. Horn blown within a period of 30s
Siren		Compressed air siren	
Reed		Compressed air weaker reed signal	Reed(2) 30s. Two blasts in succession in a period of 30s
Explosive		Firing explosive charges	
Bell		Erratic sounding if by wave action or regular if ashore	Bell (1) 5s
Gong		Erratic sounding if by wave action or regular if ashore	
Whistle		Erratic sounding if by wave action or regular if ashore	
Morse Code		Characters of Morse Code sounded by horn normally	Horn Mo (U) 30s

Colours

Abbreviation	Characteristic	Description		Example	
G	Green	W		White	Bu	Blue
R	Red	Y		Yellow	Vi	Violet

Other

Abbreviation	Characteristic	Description	Example		
M	Miles	m	metres		

SECTION 13

Light characteristics aide-memoire

Cardinal buoys	Black stripes indicate where the cones point (apex) Lights similar to a clockface except N	
Isolated danger	Black red black Light characteristic 2 flash	Similar to Dennis the Menace's jumper ...Go...Away...or Keep... Clear

Lights and ranges

Light range is influenced by:	• The height of the light above the horizon. • The intensity of the light. • The meteorological visibility (amount of water droplets in the atmosphere). • The height of the observer.
Nominal range	The range of the light stated on the chart. Nominal range is stated for 'clear visibility' (meteorological visibility of 10 miles). A light may be seen further or less than this range depending on the meteorological visibility and its intensity.
Luminous range	Light's maximum distance seen – determined by visibility and light intensity. Does not take into account – height of light, observer or Earth's curvature. Luminous range is calculated using the luminous scale chart in Admiralty list of lights. It requires the height of the light and current visibility to be entered to deduce the actual luminous range in the actual conditions.
Geographical range	Distance the light can be seen taking into account the height of the light and the height of the eye of the observer. This is calculated using dipping tables, which require the height of the light and the height of the observer's eye to get the range at which the light first shines above the horizon.
Light loom	Before seeing the actual light break over the horizon, it is possible to see the loom of the light first. This is like a halo or flashing glow as the light 'dips' or 'breaks' on the horizon. This becomes the geographical range and could be used to help establish a position line as it will give a distance and if used in conjunction with a bearing would give a basic fix.

NAVIGATION

IALA buoyage

Often a candidate will think they know buoyage, but the level of detail required is often higher than they think. You should be able to line up a set of buoys in a straight line and be able to name the top mark, light characteristic, letters underneath and what side to pass. Anything less will be a fail.

Buoyage

Safe Water Mark Fairway buoy	Not always present but marks the start or finish of pilotage into the harbour. Colour: Red White vertical stripes. Top mark: Red ball. Light: White Morse A, Isophase, Occulting or Long flash 10s. Letters underneath on chart: RW. Action: Can pass either side, however preference may be to pass to port so vessel on reciprocal course has a clear side to pass.	▲ Fairway buoy
Isolated Danger marks	Placed on top of the danger they are marking. Colour: Black Red horizontal stripes. Top mark: Two black balls. Light: White – Group flash 2. Letters underneath on chart: BRB. Action: Review chart and traffic to establish best side to pass.	▲ Isolated danger mark
Emergency Wreck Marking Buoy	Placed close to a new wreck or as multiples surrounding the wreck. Buoy is in position until permanent marking of the wreck has been carried out or the wreck removed. Colour: Blue and Yellow vertical strip. Top mark: Vertical cross on top. Light: Alternating Occulting Blue & Yellow, 3s; fl.1s, ec.0.5s, fl.1s, ec.0.5s. Racon: if fitted recommended Morse D Letters underneath on chart: probably none as it is temporary (but 'BuY' if any). Action: Stay well clear. Consult MSI to see if there is any further navigational information.	▲ Emergency wreck marking buoy
Special marks	Special marks – are used to identify designated areas, such as a safe swimming area off a beach, guard zones or used for semi-permanent yacht racing marks. Often the chart will state their purpose. If they are a pole or sphere, they are a normal special mark. If they take on the shape of a lateral mark, then they become a lateral and special mark. **Colour:** Yellow with a diagonal cross on top. **Lights:** Yellow lights. Any rhythm not used for white lights. **Letters underneath on chart:** Y. **Action:** Consult the chart.	▲ Special mark

SECTION 13

NAVIGATION

Cardinals

Mark a danger. Positioned north, east, south or west of the hazard.

Cardinals identified by the direction of cones and the yellow and black stripes. Cones point towards the black stripes on the buoy.

When seeing a cardinal, a mariner should consult the compass to check where north is.

White lights on a cardinal are quick or very quick and are remembered by thinking of a clock face:
3 – 6 – 9 – or continuous (12).

North Cardinal:	**East Cardinal:**
Colour: Black Yellow	Colour: Black Yellow Black
Light: Quick or very quick Continuous	Light: Quick or very quick 3, 10s or 5s
Top mark: 2 cones pointing up	Top mark: 2 cones, apexes apart
Letters underneath: BY	Letters underneath: BYB
Action: Pass to the north.	Action: Pass to the east.
South Cardinal:	**West Cardinal:**
Colour: Yellow Black	Colour: Yellow Black Yellow
Light: Quick or very quick 6 + 1 long flash, 15s or 10s	Light: Quick or very quick 9, 15s or 10s
Top mark: 2 cones pointing down	Top mark: 2 cones, apexes together
Letters underneath: YB	Letters underneath: YBY
Action: Pass to the south.	Action: Pass to the west.

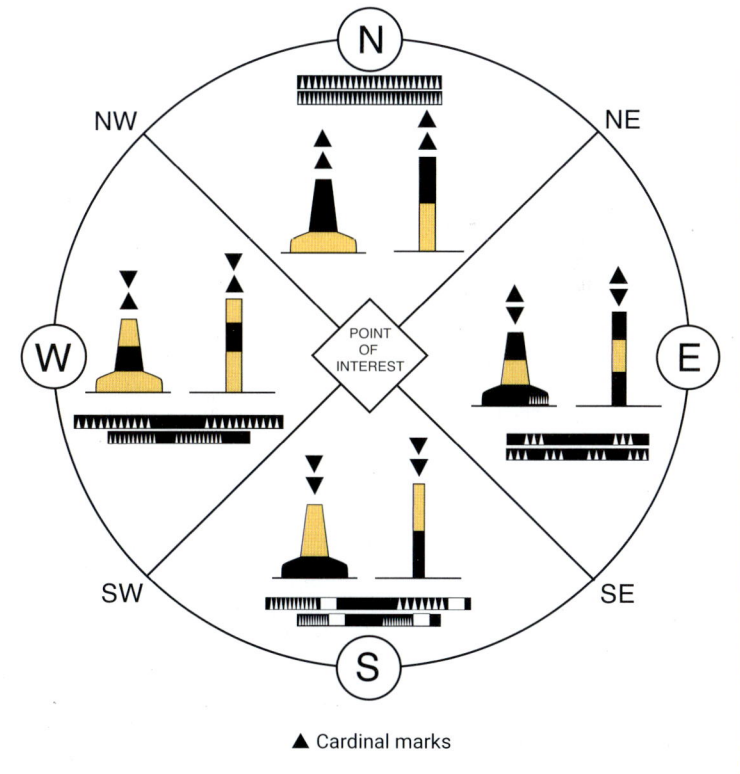

▲ Cardinal marks

Lateral marks IALA A
Lateral marks show the edge of a navigable channel. They are coloured red or green and are a particular shape.

Starboard lateral	Green (cone) marks the starboard side of the channel on entry. Colour: Green. Light: Green. Any rhythm except 2+1. Top mark: Green cone, apex up. Letters underneath: G. Action: Leave it on your starboard side on entry.	▲ Starboard lateral (IALA A)
Port lateral	Red (can) marks the port side of the channel on entry. Colour: Red. Light: Red. Any rhythm except 2+1. Top mark: Red can. Letters underneath: R. Action: Leave it on your port side on entry.	▲ Port lateral (IALA A)

Preferred channel marks
Placed at the point where a channel divides, when proceeding in the 'conventional direction of buoyage', a preferred channel may be indicated by a modified port or starboard lateral mark.

Preferred channel to starboard	Colour: Red Green Red. Light: Red 2+1. Top mark: Red can. Letters underneath: RGR. Action: Leave it on your port side on entry if following the preferred channel.	▲ Preferred channel to starboard (IALA A)
Preferred channel to port	Colour: Green Red Green. Light: Green 2+1. Top mark: Green cone, apex up. Letters underneath: GRG. Action: Leave it on your starboard side on entry if following the preferred channel.	▲ Preferred channel to port (IALA A)

Lateral marks IALA B

Starboard lateral	**Red** (cone) marks the starboard side of the channel on entry. Colour: Red. Light: Red. Any rhythm except 2+1. Top mark: Red cone, apex up. Letters underneath: R. Action: Leave it on your starboard side on entry.	▲ Starboard lateral (IALA B)
Port lateral	**Green** (can) marks the port side of the channel on entry. Colour: Green. Light: Green. Any rhythm except 2+1. Top mark: Green can. Letters underneath: G. Action: Leave it on your port side on entry.	▲ Port lateral (IALA B)

SECTION 13

Preferred channel to starboard	Colour: Green Red Green Light: Green 2+1. Top mark: Green can. Letters underneath: GRG. Action: Leave it on your port side on entry if following the preferred channel.	▲ Preferred channel to starboard (IALA B)
Preferred channel to port	Colour: Red Green Red Light: Red 2+1. Top mark: Red cone, apex up. Letters underneath: RGR. Action: Leave it on your starboard side on entry if following the preferred channel.	▲ Preferred channel to port (IALA B)

ColRegs aide-memoire

Rule 6a safe speed	Visibility Density Manoeuvrability Lights back scatter Wind/weather Draught	Visibly Dense Man Scatters Hazards Deep
Rule 6b safe speed	Characteristics Range Weather Ice Number Exact	C R W I N E
Rule 6b safe speed	Characteristics … Constraints … Effect on … Possibility that … Number … More exact assessment …	Charlie's Cats Eat Pies No More
Rule 18 priorities	Not under command Restricted in her ability to manoeuvre Constrained by draught Engaged in fishing Sailing Power-driven Seaplane	New Rods Catch Fish So Purchase Some
Pilot boat	White over red	White hat over a red face – pilot wearing a white hat after climbing up the ladder
Constrained by draught	Red Red Red	Rudder Rubbing Rocks
Not under command	Red over Red	Captain is dead
Towing	Yellow over white	Towline's tight
RAM	Balls and diamonds	Diamonds are our best friend
Sounds	Turn to starboard or port	Clockface – aiming at 12 to starboard (1) one blast to port (11) two blasts

NAVIGATION

Terminology

Navigation often gets overlooked by a keen student eager to fill their heads with vessel stability, MARPOL and Business and Law, only to fall down on calculating compass error, plotting a position or forgetting how to label a course to steer. Therefore ensure you revisit the basics. Know your paper and electronic charts – especially rocks, wrecks and the nature of the seabed.

Navigational terminology		
DR	Dead Reckoning	
EP	Estimated Position	
CTS	Course to Steer	
Stream		
Course over ground		
Water track		
Fix		
Waypoint		
Fix by bearings		
Fix by ranges		
COG	Course Over Ground	BTW	Bearing to Waypoint
SOG	Speed Over Ground	XTD	Cross Track Distance
WPT	Waypoint	XTE	Cross Track Error
All fixes, EPs, DRs to be noted with time and log reading. Only True courses applied to the chart			

Compass

Useful mnemonics

Compass	True Variation Magnetic Deviation Compass Add West	Tiny Vans Make Daily Calls At Work
Compass	CADET	Compass ADd East for True

Magnetic Compass

360 degrees	32 compass points	1 compass point = 11 ¼ degrees	4 compass points = 45 degrees

Variation	<ul><li>Difference in degrees/minutes between True and Magnetic North changes annually. Charts show True North. Magnetic compass points to Magnetic North.</li><li>Shown on chart on compass rose or in the legend. Variation: 5° 10' West 2020 (5'E).</li><li>Calculation to establish the variation in that area and adjusted to the bearing.</li><li>Turns a True (T) bearing into a Magnetic (M) bearing.</li></ul>
Compass deviation	<ul><li>Effect of ferrous objects and electromagnetic interference on a magnetic compass.</li><li>A compass is 'swung' to eliminate or reduce errors of deviation, and a deviation card is then issued by a compass adjuster noting any errors or not.</li><li>A deviation card is required to be renewed every two years.</li><li>Frequent compass checks by comparing headings on transits are required.</li></ul>
Total compass error	<ul><li>Is the sum of variation and deviation.</li><li>If an azimuth circle/ring is used to take bearings on the main compass then a total compass error can be applied to all bearings taken while on that particular heading.</li><li>This is because: The deviation is for the course the ship is steering and any bearings using that same compass would be affected by the same deviation. Variation noted on the compass rose stays the same while the vessel is in the area.</li></ul>

Calculation for applying corrections

	+ West		− East	
True (T)	Variation	Magnetic (M)	Deviation	Compass (C)
	− West		+ East	
Example	320(T) with 6W Variation and 2 E Deviation = 320 + 6 − 2 = 324(C) To go the other way from 010(C) +2 −6 =006(T).			

Examples of a deviation card and a compass showing 32 compass points

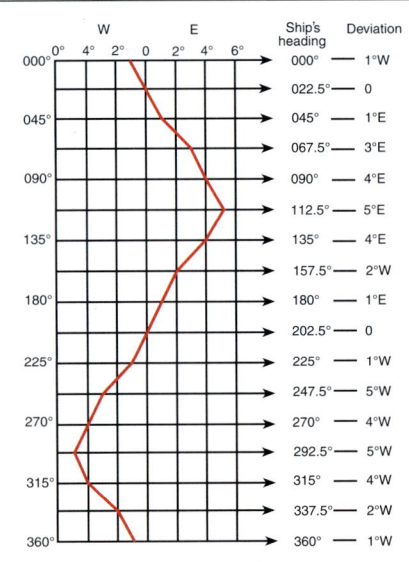

▲ Sample deviation card from a compass adjuster after the compass is 'swung'.

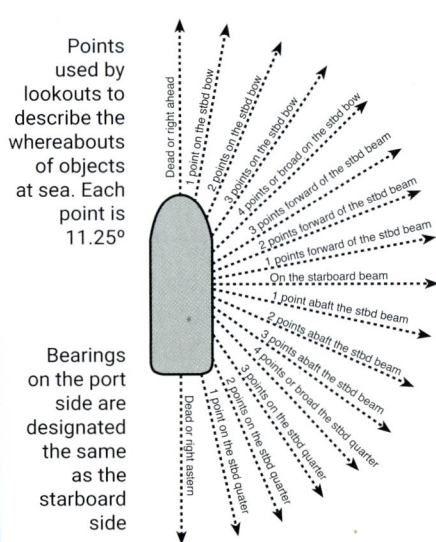

Points used by lookouts to describe the whereabouts of objects at sea. Each point is 11.25°

Bearings on the port side are designated the same as the starboard side

▲ Identifying points during lookout duties.

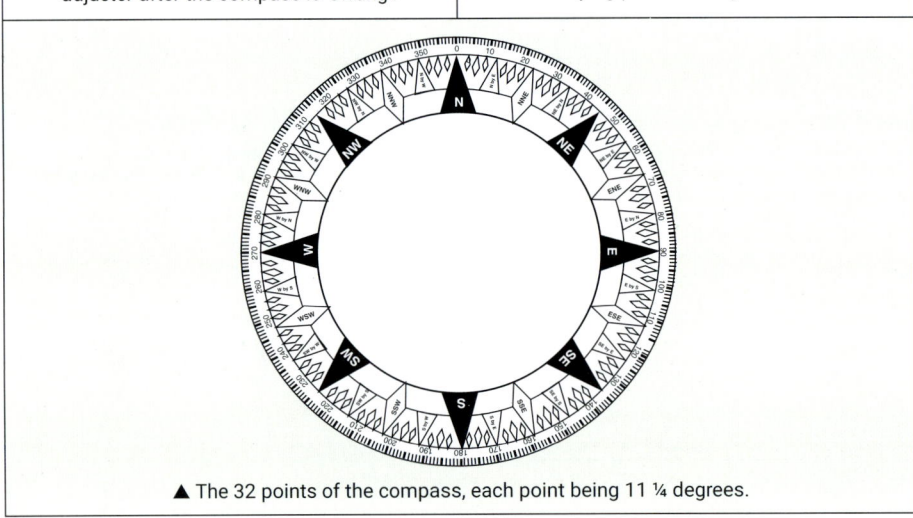

▲ The 32 points of the compass, each point being 11 ¼ degrees.

SECTION 13

Techniques

Illustrated techniques

▶ Dead Reckoning – the simplest form of tracking our progress.

Dead Reckoning (DR)

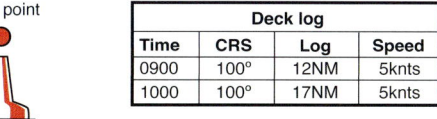

▼ Estimated Position – very useful for double checking GNSS position when out of sight of land.

Estimated Position (EP)

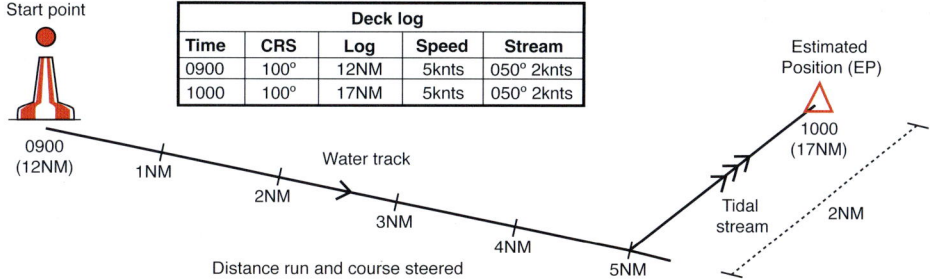

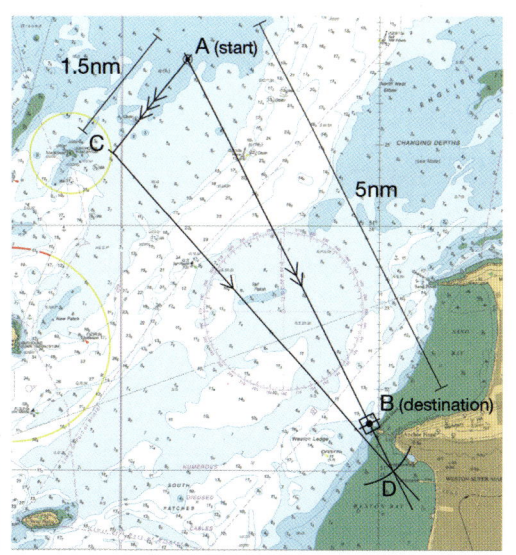

◀ Course to steer – to predict our vessel's heading to achieve a destination.

▼ Running fix – still asked in exams but rarely used in anger.

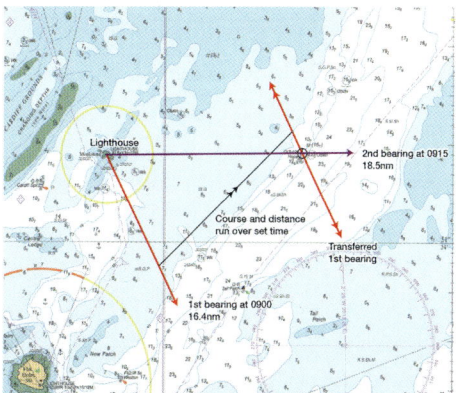

Navigational techniques	
Dead Reckoning	Distance run and course steered over a period of time.
Estimated Position	Distance run, course steered and effects of tide and wind applied over a period of time. A true EP is historical and can be used to check the vessel's position when out of sight of land and comparing it to other sources of information such as GNSS.
A projected EP	Used to establish where the vessel will be at a particular time, such as if crossing a TSS at right angles, a Projected EP will show where the vessel will come out of the TSS.
Course to Steer	This is used to predict what the vessel should steer, often to stay on a ground track or to give the shortest or safest route. A CTS takes into account predicted vessel speed, distance, stream and wind.
Running Fix	If there is only one charted object on which to take a bearing, it is possible to take a running fix. 1. Take the first bearing and note the vessel's heading and log reading. 2. Plot the bearing on the chart. After a set time (usually 15, 20 or 30 minutes) take another bearing and note the log reading. 3. Plot the heading, distance run and any stream over the period, from anywhere along the first bearing line. This is the 'run line'. 4. Plot the second bearing on the chart. 5. To find the position, the first bearing is transferred parallel through the end of the run line until it crosses the second bearing. 6. This is the approximate position. **Note:** the length of time chosen between bearings is usually a quarter, third or half an hour as it simplifies equations if a percentage of tidal stream is applied.

GNSS

While it is fair to say that Global Navigation Satellite Systems (GNSS) could be termed as our primary navigational source, it is always wise to remember that prudent navigators always back up their position by another means; for example, estimated position, fix, radar, transit etc. It is also wise to be aware of the sources of error that can occur with both GNSS and radar.

Global Navigation Satellite Systems (GNSS)		
GPS	Global Positioning System	
GLONASS	Globalnaya Navigazionnaya Sputnikovaya Sistema	Fully operational Russian GNSS system
Galileo		Near fully operational European GNSS System
BDS	BeiDou	Fully operational Chinese GNSS system

SECTION 13

NAVIGATION

GNSS corrective systems		
DGPS	Differential Global Positioning System	Corrective system for GPS using ground-based fixed reference points then transmitting the differential/corrective data to GBAS or SBAS. DGPS now discontinued around UK coast.
GBAS	Ground-based Augmentation System	Ground-based receivers and transmitters that broadcast corrective GNSS data regionally.
SBAS	Space-based Augmentation System	Similar to DGPS but corrective signals are transmitted over a wider area using satellites.

Key horizontal datums		
WGS 84	World Geodetic Survey 1984	Datum used by GNSS systems
ETRS 89	European Terrestrial Reference Survey 1989	Datum in Europe compatible with WGS 84
NAD 83	North American Datum 1938	Datum in N. America compatible with WGS 84
PZ-90	Parametry Zemli 1990 goda	Russian GLONASS datum compatible with WGS 84

Types of SBAS				
WAAS	(US) Wide Area Augmentation System		EGNOS	European Geostationary Navigation Overlay Service (Europe)
GAGAN	Indian Augmentation System		MSAS	Japanese Augmentation System
CDGPS	Canadian Augmentation System		SNAS	Chinese Augmentation System

GNSS Errors and limitations	
Incorrect data inputted by user	Incorrect datum used
Solar activity in ionosphere	Receiver errors
Errors in satellite orbit	Satellite clock errors
Weather (changes in pressure, density, temperature and humidity) in the troposphere	Multipath errors – where signals bounce off nearby objects on the way to the receiver increasing the timing signal length.

Systems primarily using GNSS		
ECDIS	Electronic Chart Display Information System	Mandatory electronic chart display system on large vessels.
ECS	Electronic Chart System	Optional chart display system on small vessels.
AIS	Automatic Identification System	VHF/GPS system that transmits and receives vessel positional data and displays on a screen.

ECDIS

ECDIS alarms and indicators
(Ref: IMO Res. A.232(82) ECDIS Performance Standards)

Alarm	An alarm or alarm system that announces by audible means, or audible and visual means, a condition requiring attention.
Indicator	Visual indication giving information on the condition of a system or equipment.

Crossing safety contour	**Alarm**
Area with special conditions	**Alarm or indication**
Deviation from route	**Alarm**
Positioning system failure	**Alarm**
Approach to critical point	**Alarm**
Different geodetic datum	**Alarm**
Malfunction of ECDIS	**Alarm or indication**
Default safety contour	**Indication**
Information over scale	**Indication**
Large scale ENC available	**Indication**
Different reference system	**Indication**
No ENC available	**Indication**
Customised display	**Indication**
Route planning across safety contour	**Indication**
Route planning across specified area	**Indication**
Crossing a danger in route monitoring mode	**Indication**
System test failure	**Indication**

Radar

▶ Radar, with parallel index lines to aid monitoring position and course.

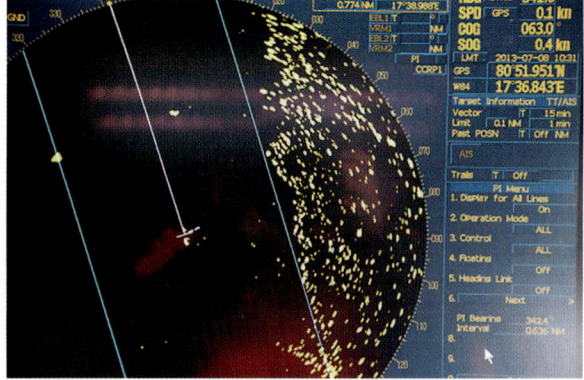

… SECTION **13**

NAVIGATION

Radar

RADAR	Radio Aid to Detection And Ranging.
X Band, 3cm, 9GHz	9GHz All mandatory fit over 300GT and any small craft will use X band radar.
Pros and cons	**Pro:** Picks up SARTS and better in fair weather. **Con:** Not so good for longer range detection.
S Band, 10cm, 3GHz	3GHz Radar as required on vessels over 3000GT.
Pros and cons	**Pros:** Better long-range detection. Better penetration through rain. **Cons:** Higher power; bigger scanner.
Performance monitoring	Every watch Test transmission and receiving performance of the radar. Keep a record from new: will assist in monitoring deterioration of magnetron.
Operational checks	• Check heading alignment of radar with fixed objects on the bow. • Check heading alignment with compass. • Be aware of the ship's blind sectors – ensure a poster informs OOWs. • Check VRM, EBL and ring accuracy with overlays. • Check compass alignment and heading alignment with chart overlay. • Stabilisation for ColRegs good practice is sea stabilised, by log.
Brilliance	Brightness of the display. Could also be called contrast etc.
Gain	Changes the amplitude or sensitivity of the returning radar pulses.
Range	Adjusts the distance the radar sees. Range is sometimes tied into adjusting the radar pulse length and repetition rate.
Tune	Tunes the receiver module to the transmitted frequency and ensures all detected targets are displayed on the PPI.
PPI	Plan Position Indicator – Centre of the screen on a conventional radar display.
PI	Parallel Indexing – Position monitoring technique using a prepositioned line on the radar screen giving a distance off a known point.
Sea clutter	Clutter caused by waves and disturbances close to the vessel, removed locally by use of the sea clutter control. Often known as STC Sensitivity Time Control, reducing the sensitivity from faster returning targets (those closer to the vessel).
Rain clutter	Clutter control that reduces noise from rain clouds. Can help with better range discrimination on land as noise is reduced.
EBL	Electronic Bearing Line – used to gain bearings to an object.
VRM	Variable Range Marker – variable range ring for establishing distances.
ARPA	Automatic Radar Plotting Aid – Automatic tracking device of radar contacts.
MARPA	Mini-Automatic Radar Plotting Aid – Manual acquisition tracking device of radar contacts.
ARPA aim	1. Reduce the workload of observers by enabling them automatically to obtain information about plotted targets, so that they can perform as well with several separate targets as they can by manually plotting a single target. 2. Provide continuous, accurate and rapid situation evaluation.

ARPA requirement	<ul><li>Automatically track 20 targets</li><li>Be available on 3, 6 and 12 mile displays</li><li>Display both True and Relative vectors of targets</li><li>Indicate when a target is getting close, a target is lost</li><li>Present range of the target</li><li>Present bearing of the target</li><li>Predicted target range at the closest point of approach (CPA)</li><li>Predicted time to CPA (TCPA)</li><li>Calculated True course of the target</li><li>Calculated True speed of the target</li><li>Allow both sea and ground stabilisation</li></ul>

ARPA performance requirements
(Ref: IMO Res. A.823(19) ARPA Performance Standards)

In 1 min with 95% probability give	<ul><li>Relative course (degrees)</li><li>Relative speed (knots)</li><li>CPA (nautical miles)</li></ul>
In 3 min with 95% probability give	<ul><li>Relative course (degrees)</li><li>Relative speed (knots)</li><li>CPA (nautical miles)</li><li>TCPA (min)</li><li>True course (degrees)</li><li>True speed (knots)</li></ul>

Key radar (Ref: ColRegs). IMO states:

Rule 5	Every vessel shall at all times maintain a proper lookout by sight and hearing as well as by all available means appropriate in the prevailing circumstances and conditions so as to make a full appraisal of the situation and of the risk of collision.
Rule 6	Every vessel shall at all times proceed at a safe speed so that she can take proper and effective action to avoid collision and be stopped within a distance appropriate to the prevailing circumstances and conditions. In determining a safe speed the following factors shall be among those taken into account: b. Additionally, by vessels with operational radar: i. the characteristics, efficiency and limitations of the radar equipment; ii. any constraints imposed by the radar range scale in use; iii. the effect on radar detection of the sea state, weather and other sources of interference; iv. the possibility that small vessels, ice and other floating objects may not be detected by radar at an adequate range; v. the number, location and movement of vessels detected by radar; vi. the more exact assessment of the visibility that may be possible when radar is used to determine the range of vessels or other objects in the vicinity.[27] (Excerpt).
Rule 7	a. Every vessel shall use all available means appropriate to the prevailing circumstances and conditions to determine if risk of collision exists. If there is any doubt such risk shall be deemed to exist. b. Proper use shall be made of radar equipment if fitted and operational, including long-range scanning to obtain early warning of risk of collision and radar plotting or equivalent systematic observation of detected objects. c. Assumptions shall not be made on the basis of scanty information, especially scanty radar information.
Rule 8	b. Any alteration of course and/or speed to avoid collision shall, if the circumstances of the case admit, be large enough to be readily apparent to another vessel observing visually or by radar; a succession of small alterations of course and/or speed should be avoided.[28] (Excerpt).

SECTION 13

Rule 19	

	c. Every vessel shall have due regard to the prevailing circumstances and conditions of restricted visibility when complying with the Rules of Section I of this Part.
	d. A vessel that detects by radar alone the presence of another vessel shall determine if a close-quarters situation is developing and/or risk of collision exists. If so, she shall take avoiding action in ample time, provided that when such action consists of an alteration of course, so far as possible the following shall be avoided:
	  i. an alteration of course to port for a vessel forward of the beam, other than for a vessel being overtaken;
	  ii. an alteration of course towards a vessel abeam or abaft the beam.[29] (Excerpt).

Radar checks and limitations

Performance monitoring	Every watch Tests transmission and receiving performance of the radar
Operational checks	• Check heading alignment of radar with fixed objects on the bow. • Check heading alignment with compass. • Be aware of the ship's blind sectors – ensure a poster informs OOWs. • Check VRM, EBL and ring accuracy with overlays. • Check compass alignment and heading alignment with chart overlay. • Stabilisation for ColRegs good practice is sea stabilised, by log.
Errors	• Heading alignment of scanner to that of the head of the ship. • Input of heading sensor to radar. • Heading input to tracking aids – ATA, MARPA, ARPA. • Speed input to tracking aids – ATA, MARPA, ARPA. • Belt/cog slip in scanner – making display jumpy.
Limitations	Needs to be viewed • Not all vessels' radar have ARPA. • Small objects may not be seen. • Blind sectors on own ship. • Sea conditions or sea clutter control too high, obscuring targets. • Range scales should be changed to increase situational awareness. • Heading sensor required for stabilised display. • Characteristics, efficiency and limitations of the radar equipment. • Scanty information – for instance not enough plots taken of a target.

NAVIGATION

Radar use

	Heading sensor	View	Benefits	Problems
Head up	Does not require input from heading sensor therefore non-stabilised display.	Top of the radar screen points to vessel's head.	What you see on the radar is what you see out of the window.	When the vessel turns, the whole radar picture turns in the opposite direction and makes it unreadable during the turn. Difficult to read bearings as they are relative to the vessel's heading.
North up	Requires a heading sensor input.	North stays at the top of the screen.	Screen same orientation as chart. Stabilised display, so when vessel turns, screen remains the same and only heading line moves around the screen. Compass bearings can be read directly from the radar.	Can take practice to know whether targets are to port or starboard. Can take practice when travelling south and the heading line opposes the orientation of the screen.
Course up	Requires a heading sensor input.	Course stays at the top of the screen.	Stabilised display, but showing similar view to head-up.	Course up is often only utilised when on autopilot and on a heading for a while. If a course change happens then the course-up function is reset when a vessel changes course.
Relative motion	Our vessel fixed in the centre of the screen.			
True motion	Our vessel off centred and then progressively moves across the screen.			
Basic stabilisation	Heading sensor input to radar. This allows a North-up display, stabilising the radar.			
Sea stabilised	Heading, plus speed input from log. This is the recommended set up for collision avoidance. Fixed objects have a course and speed equal to the reverse course and speed of our own vessel. The movement of our vessels and other vessels is their movement through the water and this is what we base ColRegs actions upon.			
Ground stabilised	Heading, plus speed input from GPS (therefore SOG). This shows fixed objects as fixed and displays moving objects as their course over ground and not their course through the water. This could be problematic for collision avoidance. However, it is good for navigation.			
Fixing	Electronic Bearing Lines (EBL) and Variable Range Markers (VRM) are used for fixing position. Better accuracy is had with ranges; however, caution should be used with gently shelving coastlines, which may give a poor echo return.			
Parallel indexing	Position monitoring technique using a prepositioned line on the radar screen, giving a distance off a known point.			

SECTION **13**

Navtex

Navtex

Navtex is an acronym for Navigational Telex. It uses a chain of base stations to broadcast Maritime Safety Information to a receiver on the vessel, this receiver stores the information so that it is viewable when required.

Nav areas	Navtex system divides the world into 21 'nav areas', the UK is NAVAREA I. Northern Europe and the Mediterranean are in NAVAREA II & III.
Frequencies	MF on a standard frequency of 518kHz in English, some units have a supplementary 490kHz channel to receive national Navtex messages in the local language. 518kHz provides the Shipping Forecast and Navigation Warnings, whereas 490kHz provides inshore waters forecasts and outlooks.
Broadcasts	Broadcast intervals are 4 hours on 518kHz and twice daily on 490kHz. Gale warnings and SAR information is transmitted upon receipt and repeated in the next routine broadcast. Range 300–400 miles.
Information provided	By Hydrographic and Meteorological Office and Rescue Coordination Centre. - Navigational warnings - Meteorological information - Other safety-related information - Search and Rescue information
Station identities	To allow the user to choose the messages most relevant to their area of operation, broadcasting base stations have an ID code that is entered into the vessel's Navtex. For instance: Niton = (E). A full list of times and stations are given in Admiralty List of Radio Signals Vols 2 & 5 and a small craft almanac.

UK Navtex I.D. example	E Niton	G Cullercoats	O Portpatrick	Q Malin Head	W Valentia

Message categories	The system can receive many categories of information, this too can be tailored to suit the user needs. Information types are given an ID letter so any unwanted letters/information can be programmed out. E.g. A Navigation warning B Meteorological warning C Ice report D Search and Rescue E Meteorological forecast F Pilot Service message G AIS message H Loran J Satnav info K Other electronic navaid info L Navigational warnings – Submarine and Gunnery info Letters A, B and D (BAD) cannot be programmed out for safety reasons.
Deciphering Navtex information	Navtex data has start and finish text, before the actual message, such as: ZCZC GB22 Date NNNN ZCZC All messages start with this code G ID letter of the transmitting station (G = Cullercoats) B ID letter of the type of warning (B = Meteorological) 22 ID number of the message (numbered 01 – 99) Actual text of message NNNN End of the message.

Sextant

Sextant errors	
Adjustable errors	
(P) Perpendicular Error – (1st Error)	Perpendicular error – is when the (Index) mirror is not perpendicular to the plane of the instrument.
(S) Side Error – (2nd Error)	Side Error – is when the (Horizon) glass is not perpendicular to the plane of the instrument.
(I) Index Error – (3rd error)	Index Error – is when the (Horizon) glass and the (Index) mirror are not parallel to each other.
Correcting adjustable errors	
Correcting (P) Perpendicular Error – (1st Error)	**(1st Error)** Set the Index bar between 30 and 40 degrees, hold the sextant horizontally with the arc furthest away from you, look into the index mirror with the sextant tilted to a small angle, check if the true and reflected arcs are in line. If they are not in line then adjust the screw on the index mirror (the index mirror has only one screw).
Correcting (S) Side Error – (2nd Error)	**(2nd Error)** Set the index bar at zero, hold the sextant nearly horizontal, look into the eye piece at the horizon and see if the true and reflected images are in line. If they are not in line then adjust the screw nearest the plane of the instrument on the horizon glass (there are two screws on the horizon glass, use the one nearest the base of the sextant).
Correcting (I) Index Error – (3rd error)	**(3rd Error)** Set the index bar to zero, hold the sextant vertically, look into the eye piece at the horizon to see if the true and reflected images are in line. If they are not in line then adjust it with the screw furthest away from the base of the sextant on the horizon mirror or adjust the vernier wheel. If it's ON the ARC then subtract it from your observed altitude. If it's OFF the ARC then add it to your observed altitude.
Non-adjustable errors – often age/wear related or through manufacture	
Wear on the micrometre rack	This would cause a lack of grip between the frame 'arc' and the index arm, due to wear. This would cause inconsistent errors.

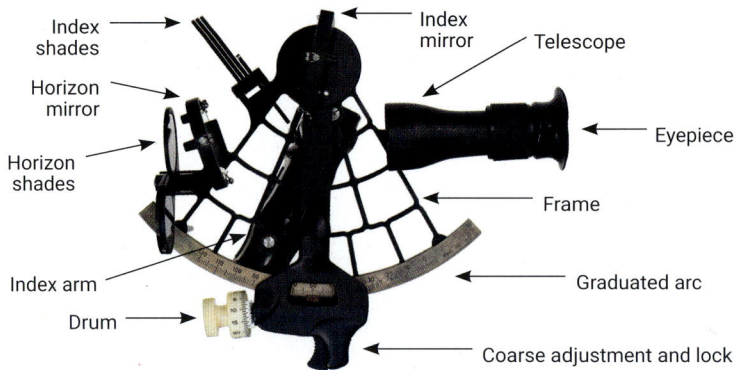

▶ Parts of a sextant. Often an examiner will ask about correcting adjustable errors.

Index shades, Horizon mirror, Horizon shades, Index arm, Drum, Index mirror, Telescope, Eyepiece, Frame, Graduated arc, Coarse adjustment and lock

SECTION 13

Graduation error	Inaccurate measurement of scale markings and/or the vernier
Shade error	Surfaces of the shades not being parallel to each other
Optical errors	Scratches, prismatic errors on the telescope lens or mirror
Centring error	Pivot of the index bar not centred with the arc (possibly worn pivot)
Collimation Error	The optical axis of the telescope is not parallel to the plane of the instrument.

Useful measurements

Useful measurements and numbers			
1 metre	3.281 feet	0.547 fathom	
1 foot	0.305 metre		
1 fathom	6 feet	1.826 metres	
1 nautical mile	6080 feet	1852 metres	
1 cable	608 feet	185.2 metres	
10 cables	1 nautical mile	1 minute of arc of the equator	
100 fathoms	600 feet	182.88 metres	
1 kilometre	3280.8 feet	546.8 fathoms	
1 knot	1 nautical mile per hour	1852 metres per hour	
Compass 360 degrees	32 compass points		
1 compass point	11 ¼ degrees		
4 compass points	45 degrees		
1 Shackle	90 feet	27.5 metres	15 fathoms
Fresh water density 1000kg/m^3	Sea water density 1025kg/m^3		

Questions and answers

Below are sample exam questions, but it's important to note that the actual questions asked will depend on the specific exam and qualification you are taking. Therefore, it's crucial to prepare by studying a wide range of subjects, not just those covered in these samples. While topics like ColRegs, buoyage and safety are always important, the types of questions will differ depending on the vessel you operate, whether it's a 23m code vessel, a 23m passenger vessel in inland waters or a 230000GT super tanker. Make sure you understand the rules and regulations that apply to your last vessel and the syllabus of the exam you are taking. Good luck!

GENERAL

	Questions	Answers
1	Assigned as Master to a vessel: What are you looking for as you approach the vessel?	• General condition – rust, paintwork, plating, scuppers • Mooring lines – condition, tended, sufficient. Fendering • At sea level – draught marks and load lines legible, trim, list, no visible pollution, no oil streaks from scuppers • Access – general condition, correctly rigged, markings, ancillary equipment in place, adequately lit, security in place • Crew – working safely, correct PPE, safe movement provisions

2	When taking over as Master, what documents and information would you expect to receive in your handover?	• Bridge equipment and vessel defects and actions to rectify
		• Charter party and voyage orders
		• Passage plan
		• Logbooks (Deck, OLB, ORB, GMDSS, Garbage, Ballast, Sulphur etc)
		• All trading and equipment certification
		• Stability information booklet
		• Survey schedule – anything outstanding or upcoming
		• Any crew issues – disciplinaries, warnings, reliefs due etc
		• Safe keys and/or combination with contents:
		  ○ ships Security Plan (if ISPS compliant)
		  ○ controlled drugs and register
		  ○ cash
		• Computer passwords
		• Latest M-Notices, safety flashes, company SMS amendments etc. received
		• Latest Safety Committee, ISPS, Ship Management and SMS Review meetings, and anything outstanding from them

QUESTIONS AND ANSWERS

	Questions	Answers
3	What pre-sailing checks would you be doing?	• Watertight integrity • Hatches, portholes, vents, sounding pipes and other weathertight openings secure • Deck scuppers clear • Cargo, stores and loose items secure, IMDG manifest landed ashore, cargo paperwork completed • All crew on board, crew list landed ashore, new crew inductions completed • Steering gear checks (SOLAS V/26) • Engine controls and back-ups checked and ready • Full check of all bridge gear • Services and gangways disconnected • Cranes/derricks etc. secure for sea • Safety briefing to pax • LSA checked; PPE issued as necessary • Mooring crew briefed; equipment powered up and ready for use • Port authorities, pilot and agent informed; Customs clearance received.

SAFETY AND RESPONSE TO EMERGENCIES

	Questions	Answers
4	What are your obligations on receipt of distress (SOLAS V/33)? a. Who do you inform? b. Who takes primary responsibility? c. Casualties retrieved from raft; condition deteriorates. Actions?	To proceed with all despatch to the assistance of those in distress: a. Coastguard and all other ships in the vicinity. Broadcast MAYDAY RELAY if necessary. b. Normally, the first ship to arrive at the casualty will assume the role of on-scene commander; MRCC will take on co-ordination of assets. c. Request help or lifeboat medevac ASAP; proceed with all speed to Emergency Rendezvous Point (RVP).
5	Which publication requires us to be prepared for emergencies? a. List some of the emergency scenarios for which we should have contingency plans. b. How often should you carry out various drills?	• ISM/DSM code *(see table below)*

a.	b.
Fire	Monthly (weekly on pax. V/Ls)
Abandon ship	Monthly (weekly on pax. V/Ls)
Man overboard/rescue boat	Monthly
DLR/MES	Monthly
Enclosed space rescue	2-monthly
Damage control	3-monthly (pax. V/Ls only)
Emergency steering	3-monthly
Pollution	3-monthly
ISPS/security	3-monthly
Lifeboat launch	3-monthly
DLR demo and inflation	4-monthly
Freefall lifeboat to water	6-monthly
Security and SAR ship/shore	Annually
MES demo and deployment	3-yearly
Collision	As necessary and as stipulated in company drill matrix
Grounding	
Flooding	
Cargo/medical incidents	
Failure of critical equipment	
Blackout	

	Questions	Answers

6	What information should be shown on the Muster List?	- Emergency alarm signals
		- Crew muster locations
		- Duties of each crewmember at General Emergency and Abandon Ship situations w.r.t:
		  - prepping and deploying survival craft
		  - closing of water/firetight doors
		  - use of communications
		  - equipping of survival craft
		- Crew evacuation locations and assigned life-saving appliances (LSA)
		- Responsibility for maintenance of fire-fighting equipment (FFE) and LSA
		- Responsibility for release of fixed FFE
		- Responsibility for care of disabled and casualties
		- List of substitutes

7	In addition to the Muster List, what other safety information should be available to you on board?	- Fire and safety control plan - LSA plan - Training Manual - Code of Safe Working Practice (COSWP) - Stability Information Booklet (possibly) - Security plan (possibly) - Shipboard Oil Pollution Emergency Plan (SOPEP) (possibly)

8	What were the LSA arrangements on your last vessel?
	a. How often should they be inspected? Serviced? Deployed?
	b. Who is responsible for their maintenance?
	c. Would this information be displayed anywhere?
	d. Have you ever been with MES? DLR?
	  i. How often deployed?
	  ii. What ancillary equipment?
	  iii. How often training for designated crew?
	e. Describe precautions prior to lifeboat launch drill.
	f. MFRs inspection and service: How often? What gear?
	g. How often renew falls? End-for end?
		Ensure you know the arrangements on your last vessel
		a. Weekly, Annually, dependent upon type of LSA. See above
		b. Generally the C/O who may delegate to a Junior Officer
		c. Yes – on the Muster List
		d. Yes/No
		  i. MES – 6-yearly alternate systems; DLR – 4-monthly
		  ii. Manufacturers' training aids should be on board
		  iii. Monthly
		e. Fall preventer devices fitted; no-one on board for first lowering and raising to/from water
		f. Annual inspection and service of On-Load release gear and winch brake systems
		g. 4-yearly; 2-yearly

9	Actions on abandoning to a liferaft?	- **Cut** painter, **stream** sea anchor, **close** covers, **maintain**; inflate floor, dry out, group up, set lookouts, issue seasickness pills
10	You are faced with a medical emergency on board. From what or whom can you get advice and assistance?	- Ship captain's medical guide - International Maritime Dangerous Goods (IMDG) Code Medical First Aid Guide (MFAG) - MGN 623 (M+F) Telemedical advice - Initial contact through Coastguard; PAN PAN if necessary

QUESTIONS AND ANSWERS

	Questions	Answers
11	Fire-fighting equipment: a. Service and inspection schedules? b. Hydraulic testing intervals? c. What equipment is included in a 'fireman's outfit'? d. Fire tetrahedron and classes of fire? e. Precautions prior to release of E/R CO_2? f. Why are electrical fires no longer classed as Class E fires?	a. Weekly visual inspection; annual basic service by competent person; 5-yearly test discharge b. 10-yearly c. SCBA, fire-retardant protective clothing, rubber insulating boots, helmet, safety lantern, insulated hand axe, 30m lifeline d. Heat, Air, Fuel, Chain Reaction. The Classes of fire are based on the fuel involved: | A	Carbonaceous | |---|---| | B | Flammable liquids | | C | Flammable gases | | D | Flammable metals | | F | Unsaturated cooking fats | e. Ensure full muster; ensure all vent systems and doors secure; fuel supply to engines shut-off; boundary cooling in place f. Because electricity is not a fuel, but a source of heat
12	Master's obligatory reports (SOLAS V/31)?	• Dangerous derelict or direct danger to navigation • Dangerous ice • Gale-force winds, sub-zero temps causing severe ice accretion • Storm-force winds, for which no warning received • Tropical storm • Pollution or potential pollution • Daily report if international voyage > 48 hrs (SOLAS V/28.2)
13	Upon what is a permit to work based? a. What does it contain? b. How long is it valid? c. Who is named on it?	Risk assessment a. The nature and location of the work to be done The nature and results of any preliminary tests Machinery and equipment to be used A checklist of all the control measures identified in the RA b. Signatures of Authorising Office and Authorised Workers Close-out section c. Maximum 24 hours d. Authorising Office
14	Define hazard and risk	• Hazard – anything with the potential to cause harm • Risk – the product of the likelihood and severity of the consequences of the hazard occurring
15	What level of risk should we be trying to achieve with our control measures?	• As low as reasonably practicable (ALARP)
16	Enclosed space: precautions prior to entry? a. Minimum O_2 concentration? b. Maximum flammable gas? c. CO and H_2S limits? d. Drill frequency?	24 hours ventilation, test atmosphere, a. At least 20% b. 1% LEL in conjunction with 20% O2 c. |	CO	H_2S | |---|---|---| | STEL – 15 mins max | 100 ppm | 10 ppm | | Time weighted – 8 hrs max | 20 ppm | 5 ppm | d. 2-monthly

	Questions	Answers
17	Give me some examples of marine casualties. a. What are the Master's responsibilities with regard to these? b. When? c. Who else should report? Who else should the Master report to? d. What need not be reported?	• The death of, or serious injury to a person • The loss of a person from a ship • The loss, presumed loss or abandonment of a ship • Material damage to a ship • The ship being unfit to proceed, or requires flag state approval or a condition of class before it may proceed • At sea, a breakdown of the ship, requiring towage • The stranding or disabling of a ship, or collision • Material damage to marine infrastructure that could seriously endanger the safety of the ship, another ship or any individual • Pollution, caused by damage to a ship or ships a. Must report to MAIB b. As soon as practicable, by the quickest means c. Ship owner (unless sure the Master has reported), harbour and IW authorities; MCA officials d. Deliberate acts; defects and detentions; accidents to passengers not associated with operation of v/l; accidents/injuries ashore

17	e. What would you do on board post-incident?
	f. What sort of things are classed as marine incidents?
		e. Preserve evidence, take statements, take photographs, inform DPA, commence investigation (i.a.w safety officer), record in OLB, download VDR
		f. Near misses! Examples of marine incidents include:
		  i. Close-quarters situations where urgent action was required to avoid collision
		  ii. Any event that had the potential to result in a serious injury
		  iii. A fire that did not result in material damage
		  iv. An unintended temporary grounding on soft mud, where there was no risk of stranding or material damage
		  v. A person overboard who was recovered without serious injury
		  vi. Snagging of fishing gear causing dangerous heel

18	What would be your actions in the event of engine failure?	• NUC lights and shapes
		• Assess proximity of traffic and navigation hazards – potentially 'SECURITÉ' message
		• Assess weather conditions: can a jury-rigged sea anchor be streamed?
		• Assess drift
		• Prepare and drop anchor if possible
		• Liaise with engineer regarding timescale and possibility of repair
		• Keep passengers informed of the situation
		• Inform DPA and prepare to enter towage contract (Lloyd's Open Form?)
		• Prepare for worst-case scenario, ie:
		  ◦ emergency muster of crew
		  ◦ prepare LSA
		  ◦ prepare for possible abandonment
		  ◦ prepare GMDSS distress message

19	Man overboard: actions?
	a. Describe a Williamson turn
	b. Where would you find information of search patterns?
		a. i. Wheel hard over towards the casualty
		  ii. When 60° off original course, wheel hard over to the other side
		  iii. Steady up on reciprocal course
		b. IAMSAR Manual Volume III

QUESTIONS AND ANSWERS

	Questions	Answers
20	What are the different classes of fire?	A – Carbonaceous B – Flammable Liquids C – Flammable Gases D – Flammable metals F – Unsaturated cooking oils
21	a. What is the fire triangle (quadrilateral?) b. How would you extinguish a Class D fire? c. And a Class F? d. Why are electrical fires no longer thought of as a Class of fire?	a. Heat, air, fuel (chain reaction) b. Specific Class D dry powder c. Wet chemical d. Because electricity is the source of the heat, not the fuel
22	List the distress signals. a. When might you use them?	• Gun/explosive signal 1 min • Red stars • RT 'MAYDAY' • Square flag and ball • Red parachute/hand flare • Raising and lowering arms • Inmarsat distress alert • EPIRB/SART signals • Continuous fog signal • Morse SOS – any method • InterCo 'NC' • Flames • Orange smoke signal • DSC VHF Ch. 70 • DSC on MF/HF frequencies • Dye marker • Orange canvas with black square and circle a. When a person, ship, aircraft or vehicle is in grave and imminent danger and requires immediate assistance.
23	Blackout: What would your actions be?	Same as for engine failure (see Question 18), plus: • Change to manual or emergency steering • Cancel all alarms • Establish which systems, if any, still have power • Check cargo decks for movement of cargo if safe to do so • Check galley staff warned and everything secured • Keep passengers informed
MARPOL		
24	What pollutants are covered under MARPOL?	Annex I: Oil Annex II: Noxious liquids in bulk Annex III: Hazardous substances in packaged form Annex IV: Sewage Annex V: Garbage Annex VI: Emissions
25	Where are the Annex I and V special areas?	• Mediterranean Sea area • Baltic Sea area • Black Sea area • Red Sea area • 'Gulfs area', including the Gulf of Oman • North Sea area • Antarctic area S of 60°S • Wider Caribbean Region, including the Gulf of Mexico and the Caribbean Sea
26	Who must carry a SOPEP Plan?	• Tankers ≥ 150GT • Other ships ≥ 400GT

	Questions	Answers
27	What are the contents of a SOPEP Plan?	• Instructions to Master in the event of a spill • Duties of crew • Inventory of clean-up equipment on board and location of locker(s) • List of coast state contacts • GA, pipeline and other relevant plans • Procedures for testing the plan
28	What other pollutants might a ship deposit that are not covered by MARPOL?	• Anti-fouling and ballast
29	Which vessels require garbage management plan? a. What does it contain? b. What additional records would you keep? c. What else is required under Annex V?	a. V/Ls ≥ 100GT or ≥ 15 persons b. Procedures for collecting, processing storage and disposal of garbage. Designation of a 'garbage' officer. c. V/Ls ≥ 400GT should keep a Garbage Record Book d. Placards and shore reception facilities
30	Which vessels require a Garbage Record Book?	V/Ls ≥ 400GT or ≥ 15 persons on international voyages
31	Which vessels must display garbage disposal placards?	V/Ls ≥ 12m length
32	What entries should be made in the Oil Record Book, Part I?	• Ballasting or cleaning of oil fuel tanks • Discharge of dirty ballast or cleaning water from oil fuel tanks • Collection, transfer and disposal of oil residues (sludge) • Non-automatic starting of discharge overboard, transfer or disposal otherwise of bilge water that has accumulated in machinery spaces • Automatic starting of discharge overboard, transfer or disposal otherwise of bilge water that has accumulated in machinery spaces • Condition of the oil filtering equipment • Accidental or other exceptional discharges of oil • Bunkering of fuel or bulk lubricating oil
33	What precautions will you take prior to undertaking bunkering operations?	• V/L(s) securely moored • Safe access between vessel(s) • Grade, quantity, sulphur content and pumping rate(s) agreed • MSDS exchanged, and sampling procedures agreed • Correct pipeline line-up checked and all superfluous connections blanked • Hose in good condition, properly rigged and fully bolted • Tank ullage sufficient and verified • Tank lids closed and vents clear • Communications and emergency stop procedures agreed • Correct lights and signals shown • Fire and spill kit available • Scuppers plugged • Watchkeepers at manifold and tank gauging stations • Accommodation doors and ports closed. No smoking regs in place

QUESTIONS AND ANSWERS

	SHIPBOARD OPERATIONS	
	Questions	**Answers**
34	How would you define seaworthiness?	• V/L has watertight integrity • C/L meets the minimum required stability criteria • V/L fully complies with all rules, regulations, conventions and codes

35	What checks are required with regard to steering gear?	SOLAS V/26 requires:
		• Full test of steering gear within 12 hours of departure to include:
		  ◦ main and auxiliary steering gear
		  ◦ remote steering gear control systems
		  ◦ steering positions located on the navigation bridge
		  ◦ emergency power supply
		  ◦ rudder angle indicators showing the actual position of the rudder
		  ◦ remote steering gear control system power failure alarms
		  ◦ the steering gear power unit failure alarms
		  ◦ automatic isolating arrangements and other automatic equipment
		• Checks and tests shall include:
		  ◦ full movement of the rudder
		  ◦ a visual inspection of all moving parts
		  ◦ communications between the bridge and steering gear compartment
		  ◦ alignment of compass repeater at emergency steering position

36	What regular maintenance would you carry out on the magnetic compass?	• Light oil on gimbals • Check for bubbles • Check error every watch, after magnetic cargoes and after structural changes • Adjust every two years
37	Precautions when sending somebody aloft?	• Risk assessment, taking special account of weather conditions • All equipment inspected, fit for purpose and certified under LOLER and PUWER regulations • Only competent and experienced crew to work aloft • Proper safety harness with lifeline or fall arrestor • Safety net rigged if possible/practicable • If overside – working lifejacket, supervisor on deck with lifebuoy, light, line and quoit; rope ladder to waterline • Lockout tagout whistles, radars, aerials; reduce emissions • Tools on lanyards, carried aloft in bucket on heaving line • Cordon-off deck area below • Issue PtW
38	What checks and precautions would you take prior to loading cargo?	a. The deck area for their stowage is clean, dry and free from oil and grease b. The cargo, cargo transport unit or vehicle, appears to be in suitable condition for transport, and can be effectively secured c. All necessary cargo securing equipment (including dunnage) is on board and in good working condition d. Cargo in or on cargo transport units and vehicles is properly stowed and secured on to the unit or vehicle

	Questions	Answers
39	a. How many classes of IMDG Hazardous Cargoes are there? b. What information regarding a dangerous good (DG) must be stated on the Dangerous Goods Note? c. What other information should be stated? d. What other documentation must you have on board prior to loading a consignment of DG?	a. Nine b. UN number; PSN; Class; Packing Group; Emergency Procedures. Shipper's Declaration and Container/Vehicle Packing Certificate must be signed c. Shipping marks, gross and net mass, and/or cube; details of shipper and consignee; ports of loading and discharge; details of CTU, haulier and customs seal d. The Document of Compliance for the Carriage of Dangerous Goods Dangerous Good manifest and stowage plan MSDS and/or IMDG Code Volume 3 – the Supplement

40	What precautions and procedures should you put in place for the bunkering of potable fresh water?	• Designated fresh water hose
		• Hoses should be durable, with a smooth, impervious lining, and equipped with fittings, including adapters, to permit connection to the shore potable water hydrants and filling connections to prevent their use for loading other liquids.
		• Hoses should be:
		  ◦ clearly marked (generally coloured blue)
		  ◦ stowed in a locker clear of the deck
		  ◦ drained and capped at both ends after use
		  ◦ flushed through and discharged to waste before loading

41	Safe access: a. Which V/Ls require gangways and accommodation ladders? b. Max angles c. Testing and certification d. Pilot ladder details of construction?	a. V/Ls ≥ 30 m and ≥ 120m respectively b. 30° and 55° respectively c. Tested, certified and inspected under LOLER regulations d. As per IMO Resolution A. 1045(27) and SOLAS V/23

42	a. Which ships must carry and complete an Official Log Book (OLB)?
	b. What entries should be made in the OLB?
	c. Give some examples of narrative entries?
		a. All vessels ≥25GT
		b. List of crew
		  i. births and deaths
		  ii. musters, drills and training
		  iii. steering gear tests
		  iv. inspections of crew accommodation
		  v. inspections of food and water
		  vi. load line details
		  vii. record of draughts and freeboards
		  viii. narrative section
		c. Narrative entries:
		  • changes of Master
		  • appointment of SO and SSO, and Safety Committee
		  • official working language of the ship
		  • signing on/off crewlist
		  • disciplinaries
		  • medical incidents
		  • deviations
		  • any other 'out-of-the-ordinary' incidents

QUESTIONS AND ANSWERS

	Questions	Answers
43	Taking over the deck watch in port, what information will you want from the Officer you are relieving?	• The depth of water at the berth • Draught and time of High and Low Water • Securing of moorings • Arrangements of anchors and scope of chain • State of main engines and availability for emergency use • Work to be performed on the ship; status of cargo loading • Levels of water in bilge • Signals/lights shown • Crewmembers and other personnel on board • State of firefighting appliances • Any special port regulations • Masters standing and special orders • Lines of communication ashore, port, port operations etc • Any pollution prevention reporting requirements

44	Inspection of galley and stores. What are you looking for?	• General cleanliness in, on, under, behind
		• Cleanliness and personal hygiene of galley staff
		  • Signs of illness or cuts/abrasions
		  • Blue plasters
		• Cleanliness of filters and uptakes
		• PPE – chemical stations, bacon slicer, pot-wash
		• Dedicated hand-wash with nail-brush and paper towels
		• Signage
		• Fridge seals and proper segregation within
		• Food stored correctly – separated, with sufficient air flow around
		• Fridge temperatures
		• No ice build-up in freezers
		• Dry stores stowed at correct levels – heavy items waist height
		• Cleaning chemicals properly segregated
		• FFE not blocked, and emergency shut-downs signed
		• Check crew emergency procedures knowledge

45	What do you understand by the terms KB, KM, KG, GM and GZ?	a. KB – vertical distance from keel to centre of buoyancy b. KM – vertical distance from keel to transverse metacentre c. KG – vertical distance from keel to centre of gravity d. GM – metacentric height: vertical distance between centre of gravity and metacentre e. GZ – righting lever: perpendicular distance between verticals through the centres of buoyancy and gravity
46	What might be an indication of the vessel having poor stability?	A long, slow roll period, with possibly a 'hang' at the extent of each roll, indicating a small metacentric height (GM)

	Questions	Answers
47	Explain the difference between stiff and tender ships? a. What might be the disadvantages of an overly stiff ship? b. How might you correct for it?	Stiffness and tenderness of the ship is dependent upon the magnitude of the metacentric height (GM): the greater the GM, the stiffer the ship, the faster the roll period; the smaller the GM, the more tender the ship, the slower the roll period a. Very uncomfortable to work on – increased potential for personal injury due to violent ship movement Extra stain put on cargo lashings due to accelerations and thus greater potential for cargo shift b. Move weights to a higher position in the ship, if possible; discharge ballast from low down in the ship
48	What effect on stability do slack tanks have?	• The free surface effect of slack tanks causes a virtual rise in the centre of gravity (G) of the ship, thus reducing the metacentric height, and hence reducing the stability of the vessel.

NAVIGATION

	Questions	Answers
49	The forecast for German Bight is: South-west 5 to 7, increasing gale 8 at times, perhaps severe gale 9 for a time later Slight or moderate becoming moderate or rough Showers Good, occasionally poor a. What actions will you take? b. When will you expect the severe gale 9 to hit? c. What does 'poor' mean?	a. Try to avoid if possible; if not prepare for heavy weather (see Question 50) b. Sometime after 12 hours from the time of issue c. Misty – visibility between 1000m and 2NM
50	What preparations will you make when warned of the approach of 'heavy weather'?	Ensure: • All cargo and stores properly secure; no loose items on deck • Hatches fully battened down and secured; deadlights fitted • Vent flaps, booby hatches and all other potential downflooding points fully secure • Deck scuppers and freeing ports clear • Slack tanks either pressed-up or emptied; swimming pools emptied; bilges dry; free surface reduced to a minimum • Shifting boards installed in holds with free-flowing cargoes • Warn all HoDs and crew; chefs prepare cold food only • Restrict access to outer decks; rig jackstays and lifelines and instigate PtW system if work outside is needed • Attempt to divert to avoid the worst of the weather • Log weather conditions frequently

QUESTIONS AND ANSWERS

	Questions	Answers
51	State Buys-ballot's law.	• Face the wind, and the centre of the low pressure area will lie 8 to 10 points on your right in the Northern hemisphere, or to your left in the Southern hemisphere

52	a. What are the dimensions of the Plimsoll Mark?
	b. What is the distance between the S and the F load lines known as? Where will you find it?
	c. Are you ever allowed to leave the berth with your relevant load line submerged?
		a. A circle with diameter 300mm intersected by a line 450mm long with its upper edge passing through the centre of the circle. Both circle and line are 25mm thick.
		b. The Fresh Water Allowance. It will be found on the load line certificate. It can also be calculated from the formula
		$FWA = \dfrac{Displacement}{4 \times TPC}$ at the summer draught
		c. Yes: allowance can be made for:
		  i. density of dock water, calculated as a proportion of the FWA
		  i. stores, fuel and water that may be consumed on pilotage between berth and sea

53	Explain the passage planning process and the necessity for a plan, including statutory requirements.	A berth-to-berth passage plan is required under SOLAS V/34, which complies with the guidelines contained in IMO Resolution A.893(21). Passage planning is generally considered to be a 4-stage process; briefly: • A – Appraisal: All information relevant to the contemplated voyage or passage should be considered with the aim of providing a clear indication of, among other things, areas of danger, areas to navigate safely, existing routeing or reporting systems, vessel traffic services areas where marine environmental protection considerations apply • P – Planning: Plotting the route on the charts, with courses, distances, planned speeds, margins of safety and contingency plans • E – Execution: Execute the voyage in accordance with the plan • M – Monitoring: The plan and vessel's position should be constantly monitored. Progress along the track should be recorded and position updated regularly
54	State six factors to be taken into account at the Appraisal stage of the passage plan.	• Optimum economical route • Min UKC, draught and squat • Tidal streams and current • Weather routing and forecasts • Reliability of charts ENCs • Prohibited/areas to be avoided • Adequate bunkers, water, stores • Time zones • Reporting requirements – ALRS • Reliability of A to N – ALL • ETA • Areas of high traffic density • Berth-to-berth plan • Air draught • GC RL route • Application of ColRegs (TSS) • Watch schedules / Bridge manning • Proximity of nav dangers (eg ice) • Abort and anchoring positions • Pilotage points and areas • Reliability of nav equipment • Ocean currents

	Questions	Answers
55	State five factors that would influence the margin of safety when undertaking the planning stage of a voyage plan.	<ul><li>Tides</li><li>Weather</li><li>Proximity of navigation dangers</li><li>Available depth of water</li><li>Traffic density</li><li>Navigation warnings</li><li>Chart source data/ CATZOC</li><li>Environmental restrictions</li><li>Manoeuvring characteristics</li></ul>
56	Carriage of nautical publications: what are they?	<ul><li>Mariners' Handbook</li><li>Merchant Shipping Notices, Marine Guidance Notes and Marine Information Notes</li><li>Notices to Mariners</li><li>Lists of Radio Signals</li><li>Lists of Lights</li><li>Sailing Directions</li><li>Nautical Almanac</li><li>Navigational Tables</li><li>Tide Tables</li><li>Tidal Stream Atlases</li><li>Operating and Maintenance Instructions for Navigational Aids Carried by the Ship</li><li>IAMSAR Vol III</li><li>International Code of Signals</li></ul>
57	As Master, what factors will you take into account when deciding whether a single watchkeeper is sufficient to keep a safe lookout?	<ul><li>The situation has been carefully assessed and it has been established without doubt that it is safe to do so</li><li>Full account has been taken of:<ul><li>state of weather</li><li>visibility</li><li>traffic density</li><li>proximity of dangers to navigation</li><li>the attention necessary when in or near TSS</li><li>design and layout of the bridge</li><li>arcs of visibility</li><li>radar equipment fitted and their limitations with respect to navigation</li></ul></li><li>Other duties that the officer may have to engage in and which could be a distraction from the keeping of a proper lookout such as:<ul><li>operation of GMDSS and other communications equipment such as cell phones and email systems</li><li>navigational maintenance such as completion of logs and other record-keeping and correction of charts and publications</li><li>routine testing and maintenance of bridge equipment</li></ul></li><li>Assistance is immediately available to be summoned when required</li></ul>
58	What subjects are covered in the six volumes of the Admiralty List of Radio Signals?	Vol 1: Coast Radio Stations Vol 2: Radio Aids to Navigation Vol 3: Maritime Safety Information Vol 4: Meteorological Observation Stations Vol 5: GMDSS Vol 6: Port, Pilotage and VTS services
59	What additional considerations would you, as navigator, take when at the Appraisal stage of planning a passage using ECDIS?	<ul><li>Full ENC coverage at appropriate scale? If not, what?<ul><li>order RNCs c/w permits</li><li>order paper charts for back-up</li><li>check RCDS allowed</li></ul></li><li>All permits for ENCs</li><li>Permits remain valid for duration of voyage</li></ul>

QUESTIONS AND ANSWERS

	Questions	Answers
60	How would you check that your position shown on the ECDIS is accurate?	• Cross-check by independent means: radar overlay, manual position fix, V-AIS overlay
61	What are the five mandatory alarms in ECDIS?	• Crossing the safety contour • Change of geodetic datum • Deviation from route (exceeding XTD) • Approach to a critical point • Positioning system failure
62	What does CATZOC mean, and how would it influence the passage plan?	• Category Zone of Confidence: rates the reliability and accuracy of data presented in ENCs and, latterly, is the system adopted on paper charts within the source data diagram. ZOCs divided into 6 categories: A1, A2, B, C, D and U • By reference to the depth and position accuracies associated with each CATZOC, suitable margins of safety may be applied during the planning stage of the passage to ensure charted features are passed at a safe distance

63	What do you understand by the term WOA triangle?	This is the vector triangle used to resolve a radar plot:
		  • WO is the vector showing the direction and magnitude of Own Ship over the time of the plot
		  • OA is the relative approach track of the target vessel, and is, effectively, the resultant of the vector triangle. If projected past the origin of the plot, CPA and TCPA may be easily determined
		Given the above two vectors, the direction and magnitude of the target v/ls vector can be determined, and thus her course, speed and, more importantly, her aspect

64	Explain limitations of ARPA to a new cadet.	• Limited number of targets that can be tracked simultaneously – check the manual; but minimum of 20 • Automatic acquisition is not infallible – do not rely upon it • Similarly, do not rely on CPA and TCPA alarms – they will not sound if the target has not been acquired • Takes time to calculate and re-calculate target data after either own ship or target changes course and/or speed – up to three minutes • There may be 'target swap' if two targets get close to one another – beware • ARPA may only be available on a limited number of ranges – 3, 6 and 12NM • Need to check indications for relative or true vectors and trails, and time scales – may not always be immediately obvious • Ensure displayed target data is from the ARPA and not the AIS feature – do not use AIS data for collision avoidance. • ARPA data may be affected if COG and SOG are used instead of HDG and STW • The displayed accuracy of the target data depends upon the target aspect and relative speed and position w.r.t. own ship – CPA may be up to 0.7NM in error, and true course and speed may be up to 7.4° and 1.2 kts respectively

	Questions	Answers
65	Why is determination of the target V/Ls aspect important?	• So that we can determine our obligations under ColRegs, and also, perhaps, gain an idea of what action the target V/L might take
66	a. What is the order of setting up the radar? b. What do the rain and sea clutter controls do?	a. Brilliance: Adjusts the brightness of the display and graphics Gain: Adjusts the sensitivity of the radar receiver module Range: Select an appropriate range for your area of operation Tuning: Tunes the receiver module to the transmitted frequency b. Rain clutter suppresses the trailing edge of the returning pulse, allowing discrimination of legitimate targets which might otherwise be obscured within rain showers. Rain clutter works over the entire screen Sea clutter modifies the gain, and hence the sensitivity, of the receiver close to the ship, and serves to suppress echoes returned from the surface of the sea. Allows discrimination of legitimate targets that might otherwise be obscured within the echoes returned from the sea
67	Joining a new ship, what initial checks would you make on your radar system?	• HL and compass alignment • Pulse synchronisation • Shadow sectors • Initial Performance Monitor reading • Radar logbook, especially the records of the Performance Monitor and running hours. • VRM and EBL accuracy
68	a. What might cause errors in the GNSS position solution? b. What do you understand by these acronyms? i. RAIM. ii. G/SBAS. iii. WAAS/EGNOS.	a. i. satellite clocks ii. orbit errors iii. ionospheric/tropospheric delay iv. receiver noise v. multipath error vi. solar flare activity vii. paper and e-chart inaccuracies b. i. RAIM: Receiver Autonomous Integrity Monitoring. A means of determining whether the resulting position estimate is safe to use through an algorithm within the receiver, ie whether the position solution is safe to use ii. G/SBAS: Ground and satellite-based augmentation systems. Basically, differential GNSS using either ground stations (now discontinued in UK) or a separate satellite system iii. WAAS: Wide Area Augmentation System. The North American SBAS EGNOS: European Geostationary Overlay Service. The European SBAS

QUESTIONS AND ANSWERS

	Questions	Answers

69	Handing over the watch. How?	**Do not hand over the watch if:**
		• The relief watch is not capable of carrying out their duties. In this event, notify the Master
		• A manoeuvre such as course alteration is taking place
		Before taking over the watch the relieving officer shall ensure:
		• The relieving watch can perform their duties
		• Their vision is fully adjusted to the light conditions
		• Appropriate instructions and information have been given to watchkeepers and lookouts
		• Master's standing orders with reference to safe navigation
		• Position, course, speed and draught of the ship
		• Effect of tides, currents, weather, visibility upon course and speed
		• Procedures for the use of main engines to manoeuvre
		• Navigational situation, such as:
		  ◦ condition and limitations of bridge and safety equipment
		  ◦ the errors of compasses
		  ◦ the presence and movement of ships in the vicinity
		  ◦ the conditions and hazards likely to be encountered
		  ◦ effects of heel, trim, water density, squat on under-keel clearance

70	Methods of checking compass error?	• Transits of chart-identifiable objects • Celestial observation of the azimuth of either sun, moon, planets or stars, and then calculation using almanac and nautical tables • By amplitude of the sun sunrise or sunset, and then calculation either using almanac and tables or by scientific calculator using the formula sin *Amplitude* = sin *Declination*. sec *Latitude*
71	Purpose of taking compass errors?	• Primarily to determine the deviation of the magnetic compass on the current heading, and maintain a record of the same. • As a consequence, we may also obtain the error in the gyro
72	How will you know if your charts are up to date?	• First, check you have the latest chart edition by reference to NP234 – The Cumulative List of N to M published twice yearly, and updated weekly at https://msi.admiralty.co.uk/NoticesToMariners/Weekly. Follow the link to NP234WkXX-YY • Using that same publication, check all corrections as listed have been applied to the chart and noted in the bottom left-hand corner • N.B. Scanning the QR code will give you all the corrections for the latest edition of the chart, but not the latest edition date, which might be misleading • Refer also to the Part 1 of the Annual Summary of N to M and the monthly list of T and P Notices in force to check these have also been applied

	Questions	Answers

73	What is the 'normal' projection of Admiralty charts? Are you aware of any other projections and their uses?	• **Mercator projection or transverse Mercator**
		  ○ the chart is 'orthomorphic'; ie, the land is shown in its correct shape
		  ○ rhumb lines are shown as straight lines
		  ○ distance can be measured directly off the chart
		  ○ used for general and coastal navigation
		• **Gnomonic projection:**
		  ○ Chart is not orthomorphic; bearings and distances cannot be measured directly
		  ○ The appearance of the chart will vary depending upon the tangent point on the earth upon which the chart is constructed
		  ○ Great circles appear as straight lines, and their selected co-ordinates may then be transferred to a Mercator chart
		  ○ Used for passage planning an ocean crossing – the great circle is the shortest distance between two points on the surface of the earth.

74	Where would you find details of horizontal and vertical datums on the chart in use?	• Within the chart's general information section at or near the title. If horizontal datum is WGS 84, then that might well be printed in magenta around the border of the chart.

LEGISLATION, BUSINESS AND LAW

	Questions	Answers
75	a. What do you understand by International Conventions and Codes? b. Who publishes them? c. How are they enacted into UK law?	a. International Conventions are drafted by various agencies of the UN and provide a framework for nation states to formulate their own legislation and thus form 'International Law'. The Codes add detail and specifications to the provisions of the Conventions b. Agencies of the UN. In the marine industry, they are published by the IMO c. By means of Secondary Legislation Regulations (drafted by the MCA) enacted by the Secretary of State under powers bestowed on him by the Primary Legislation – the Merchant Shipping Act 1995
76	How does the application of UNCLOS, SOLAS and the Merchant Shipping Act 1995 differ?	• UNCLOS applies to 'States Parties' and all users of the seas • SOLAS applies to ships, generally those over 500GT engaged on international voyages • The MS Act 1995 is the primary legislation for UK-registered vessels and applies to all UK-registered ships, wherever they might be trading. May also apply to ships registered in UK overseas territories and possessions
77	What do you understand by the term 'the four pillars of maritime safety', and which publications do they include?	• SOLAS, MARPOL, STCW published by the IMO, and MLC jointly published by IMO and ILO
78	Which body is the UK's Flag State Administration?	• The Maritime and Coastguard Agency (MCA)

QUESTIONS AND ANSWERS

	Questions	Answers

79	a. Who issues MSNs, MGNs and MINs, and what are they for?
	b. What do the abbreviations M and F mean?
	c. What about Notices to Mariners, the Annual Summary and Cumulative Lists?
		a. The MCA issue:
		  i. Merchant Shipping Notices: stating, or integral to, aspects of the law
		  ii. Marine Guidance Notes: guidelines on application of, and MCA's interpretation of, the law
		  iii. Marine Information Notes: time- or audience-limited information for the marine industry
		b. M means applicable to Merchant ships; F means applicable to Fishing Vessels.
		c. N to M are issued/published by the Admiralty and UK Hydrographic Office and contain corrections to charts and nautical publications

80	What is the purpose of the ISM Code?	• To provide an international standard for the safe management of ships and for pollution prevention
81	Explain the purpose of the coding system.	• To allow owners of 'small' vessels (<24 m load-line length) to opt out of some aspects of Merchant Shipping legislation, which may be too onerous, or impractical or irrelevant to those small vessels providing that the vessels comply with the relevant Code of Practice (Red, Blue, Yellow, Brown, SCV or WB2) issued by the MCA and comprising more appropriate equivalent standards
82	What certification would you expect on a Cat 1 workboat? a. Anything additional if > 15 persons on an international voyage? b. And if carrying DG? c. And if ISM compliant?	• Certificate of Registry (if registered) • SCV/WBC Certificate, including SCV/WBC 2 and 'Licence' Disc • Insurance certification • Radio certification a. International Sewage Pollution Prevention Certificate; MLC Certificate, c/w DMLC Parts 1 and 2 b. Document of Compliance for the Carriage of DG Evidence of crew training in DG c. A copy of the Company's ISM DoC, plus the vessel's original Safety Management Certificate
83	Who publishes CoSWP and which ships must carry it?	• The MCA in conjunction with industry experts. All UK ships must carry at least one copy. All crew members must have access to it. It may be on a computer server, with LAN to Crew Areas
84	When should a safety officer (SO) and committee be appointed? a. Who appoints the SO? b. Who appoints the safety reps? c. Who chairs the safety committee	If five or more workers are employed on board a ship a. The Company appoints the SO – usually by rank b. The ship's crew will elect safety representatives to sit on the Safety Committee c. The Master

	Questions	Answers

85	What is the ISPS Code, and what is its purpose?
	a. To whom does it apply?
	b. What are its main requirements?
	c. Where would you find the SSP?
	d. How is the SSP formulated?
	e. Who conducts the SSA?
		The International Ship and Port Facility Security Code: its purpose is to provide an international framework involving governments, local administrations and the shipping and port industries to detect security threats and take preventive measures against them.
		a. Passenger V/Ls, cargo V/s ≥500GT, MODUs on international voyages; plus ports servicing such v/ls.
		b.
		  i. assess threats; exchange info inter-government
		  ii. maintain communications between ships and ports
		  iii. prevent unauthorised access to ships and ports
		  iv. prevent introduction of weapons, explosives and incendiaries to ships and ports
		  v. provide means of raising alarm
		  vi. ship and port security plans be drawn up
		  vii. training, drills and exercises
		c. Under lock and key in the custody of the Master
		d. Based upon the findings of the Ship Security Assessment
		e. A recognised security organisation

86	What are the duties of individual seafarers under health and safety legislation?	• Take reasonable care for their own health and safety and that of others on board who may be affected by their acts or omissions • Co-operate with anyone else carrying out health and safety duties – including compliance with control measures identified during the employer's or company's evaluation of risk • Report any identified serious hazards or deficiencies immediately to the appropriate officer or other authorised person • Make proper use of plant and machinery and treat any hazard to health or safety (such as a dangerous substance) with due caution • Under the regulations, it is also an offence for any person intentionally or recklessly to interfere with or misuse anything provided in the interests of health and safety
87	a. What do you understand by the term LOF? b. And the SCOPIC Clause?	a. Lloyd's Open Form – the simplest form of Salvage Agreement: No Cure No Pay b. Special Compensation P&I Clause – allows for a salvor to claim reasonable expenses, even if the property is not salved; used, generally, for anti-pollution cases

88	a. What are the hours of work and rest regulations?
	b. Crewmember complaining of fatigue: your actions?
		a. The minimum hours of rest shall be not less than:
		  i. ten hours rest in any 24-hour period; and
		  ii. 77 hours rest in any seven-day period
		  iii. daily hours of rest cannot be divided into more than two periods, one period must be at least six hours. The two periods must provide at least ten hours' rest.
		  iv. schedule of duties for each crewmember posted, detailing the daily schedule of duties at sea and in port
		  v. Records maintained and signed
		b. Determine reasons, adjust watches/work pattern to allow compensatory rest and replace with another crewmember.

QUESTIONS AND ANSWERS

	Questions	Answers

89	MLC:
	a. What is its purpose?
	b. To whom does it apply?
	c. What are the main provisions of MLC?
		a.
		  i. every seafarer has the right to a safe and secure workplace that complies with safety standards
		  ii. every seafarer has a right to fair terms of employment
		  iii. every seafarer has a right to decent working and living conditions on board ship
		  iv. every seafarer has a right to health protection, medical care, welfare measures and other forms of social protection
		b. The Convention applies to all ships, whether publicly or privately owned, ordinarily engaged in commercial activities, other than ships engaged in fishing or in similar pursuits and ships of traditional build such as dhows and junks. This Convention does not apply to warships or naval auxiliaries
		c.
		  i. Title 1: Minimum requirements for seafarers to work on a ship
		  ii. Title 2: Conditions of employment
		  iii. Title 3: Accommodation, recreational facilities, food and catering
		  iv. Title 4: Health protection, medical care, welfare and social security protection
		  v. Title 5: Compliance and enforcement

90	What type of vessels might still require a Crew Agreement?	MGN 474 details those to whom MLC does not apply, but in which seafarers might still be employed; so: • Fishing vessels • Naval auxiliaries, eg, the RFA • Pleasure vessels not on coastal voyages where >4 crew receive wages • Ships of traditional build
91	a. What do you understand by the term SEA? b. What T&Cs should be in a SEA?	a. Seafarers Employment Agreement – a contract of employment, compliant with MLC provisions, between a seafarer and employer b. • The full name, birthplace and date of birth (or age) of the seafarer • The name and address of the shipowner • The place where the agreement is entered into • The date on which the agreement is entered into • The capacity in which the seafarer is to work • If the agreement has been made for a definite period, the termination date • If the agreement has been made for an indefinite period, the period of notice of termination required and the circumstances in which such notice may be given • If the agreement has been made for a particular voyage, the destination port and the period following arrival after which the agreement terminates • The health and social security benefits provided to the seafarer by the shipowner • The maximum period of service on board following which the seafarer is entitled to repatriation

	Questions	Answers
91		• The seafarer's entitlement to repatriation (including the mode of transport and destination of repatriation) and the circumstances in which the seafarer is required to meet or reimburse the shipowner for the costs of repatriation • The maximum compensation the shipowner will pay the seafarer in respect of any loss of personal property arising from the loss or foundering of the ship • Details of any collective bargaining agreement that is incorporated (in whole or part) into the agreement or is otherwise relevant to it • The wages (either the amount or the formula to be used in determining them) • The manner in which wages must be paid, including payment dates and the circumstances (if any) in which wages may or must be paid in a different currency • The hours of work • The paid leave (either the amount or the formula to be used in determining it) • Any pension benefits to be provided to the seafarer, including any entitlement to participate in a pension scheme • The grievance and disciplinary procedures

COLREGS

	Questions	Answers
92	What do the rules say about keeping a lookout? a. What are those 'all available means'?	Every vessel shall at all times maintain a proper lookout by sight and hearing as well as by all available means appropriate in the prevailing circumstances and conditions so as to make a full appraisal of the situation and of the risk of collision a. Radar, AIS, Echo Sounder, VHF, ECDIS/Plotter, Navtex, Compass, Log and any other item of bridge equipment that may be fitted
93	List six factors to establish a safe speed.	• The state of visibility • The traffic density, including concentrations of fishing vessels or any other vessels • The manoeuvrability of the vessel with special reference to stopping distance and turning ability in the prevailing conditions • At night the presence of background light such as from shore lights or from back scatter of her own lights • The state of wind, sea and current, and the proximity of navigational hazards • The draught in relation to the available depth of water
94	How might radar assist in your determination of a safe speed?	By taking into account: • The characteristics, efficiency and limitations of the radar equipment • Any constraints imposed by the radar range scale in use • The effect on radar detection of the sea state, weather and other sources of interference • The possibility that small vessels, ice and other floating objects may not be detected by radar at an adequate range • The number, location and movement of vessels detected by radar • The more exact assessment of the visibility that may be possible when radar is used to determine the range of vessels or other objects in the vicinity

QUESTIONS AND ANSWERS

	Questions	Answers
95	a. What are the 'characteristics and limitations' of the radar equipment? b. What might be the constraints of the range in use? c. Do you know which vessels are required to carry a radar reflector? d. What does the 'more exact assessment of visibility' mean?	a. X- or S-Band, horizontal beamwidth, height of scanner, blind sectors, deterioration of magnetron, competence of operator b. Operating on short range means one cannot gain the 'bigger picture' or conduct long-range scanning. Should result in a reduction of speed. c. SOLAS *recommend* fitting on vessels <150GT *if practicable*. Small v/l CoPs *require* fitting of radar reflector d. Use the radar to determine the range of visible objects, and thus measure the range of visibility
96	a. How would you determine if risk of collision (RoC) existed? b. Is it acceptable to align a target vessel with part of the ship's structure and observe by eye? c. Why might RoC still exist when an appreciable bearing change is evident?	a. Take a series of compass bearings of an approaching vessel, and/or a systematic plotting of a radar target b. No – this method is taking *relative* bearings, which might appear to change, while the compass bearing may not necessarily do so. c. • If approaching a very large vessel, a tow or when approaching a vessel at close range • May also be because the target vessel has made a series of small alterations, in contravention of R. 8(b)
97	List four vessel-types to which the word 'impede' refers.	• Vessels < 20m length • Sailing v/ls • V/ls engaged in fishing • Any v/l crossing a narrow channel • Any v/l (other than NUC and RAM) w.r.t a v/l CBD • Seaplanes and WIGs
98	a. Define an overtaking vessel. b. What are the characteristics of a masthead light? c. Might it be possible to see masthead, sidelight and sternlight simultaneously? How and why?	a. A vessel approaching another from a direction more than 22.5° abaft her beam, that is, in such a position with reference to the vessel she is overtaking, that at night she would be able to see only the stern light of that vessel but neither of her sidelights. b. A white light on the F and A centreline showing an unbroken light over an arc of the horizon of 225° from right ahead to 112.5° abaft the beam on either side c. Yes, due to the horizontal cut-off sectors allowed for in Annex 19: 'For stern lights, sidelights and for masthead lights at 22.5° abaft the beam, the minimum required intensities shall be maintained over the arc of the horizon up to 5° within the limits of the sectors prescribed in Rule 21. From 5° within the prescribed sectors the intensity may decrease by 50% up to the prescribed limits: it shall decrease steadily to reach practical cut-off at not more than 5° outside the prescribed sectors.'

	Questions	Answers

99	What's the difference between RAM and NUC?
	a. Give examples of each?
	b. Characteristics and visibility of lights?
	c. Fog signal?
		Both are unable to manoeuvre as required by the rules, the NUC due to some 'exceptional circumstance'; the RAM due to the nature of her work
		a. RAM:
		  i. a vessel engaged in laying, servicing or picking up a navigation mark, submarine cable or pipeline
		  ii. a vessel engaged in dredging, surveying or underwater operations
		  iii. a vessel engaged in replenishment or transferring persons, provisions or cargo while underway
		  iv. a vessel engaged in the launching or recovery of aircraft;
		  v. a vessel engaged in mine clearance operations
		  vi. a vessel engaged in a towing operation such as severely restricts the towing vessel and her tow in their ability to deviate from their course
		NUC:
		  i. Breakdown of main propulsion
		  ii. Breakdown of steering gear
		  iii. Sailing vessel becalmed
		b. NUC – Underway: two all-round red lights; and when making way, sidelights and sternlight
		RAM – Underway: three all-round lights, red, white, red; and when making way, masthead, side- and sternlight
		Range of visibility: 2 or 3NM depending upon length
		c. Prolonged followed by two short blasts

100	Why turn off masthead lights when NUC making way?	• So that the NUC vessel cannot be confused for a vessel aground from certain aspects

Index

A
abandoning ship 108
access: means of 43
  safe access 65
accident reporting 58–9
AFS 12
air draft 72
air pollution 89
  EIAPPC certificate 90
  IAPPC certificate 89–90
AIS (Automatic Identification System) 142–4
anchoring 129–31
Anderson turn 110
anti-fouling 88
APEM (Appraise Plan Execute Monitor) 173–4

B
bank effect 123
barometric pressure 156
baseline 10, 11
Beaufort Scale 155
Bernoulli's principle 123
berthing 126–8
bow cushion effects 122, 123
bridge equipment 135–44
AIS 142–4
compass requirements 138–40
small vessels 138
voyage data recorders 141
bulk carriers, certificates 36–7
buoyage, IALA 180–3
buoyancy 69
business and law 9–24
  questions on 214–18
Buys Ballot's law 157, 209

C
cardinals 181
cargo ships: cargo securing code 44
cargo ship certificates 36–7
noxious liquid substances in bulk cargo record books 84–5
certification: cargo ship certificates 36–7
carriage of noxious liquid substances in bulk 84
EIAPPC certificate 90
IAPPC certificate 89–90
IOPP certificate 82
lifting equipment 55
Safety Management System 50
ship certification 34–7
charts 163–71
chart information 167–8
chart projections 163
chart scale 165
chart types 164
electronic charts 165–6
ENC chart usage bands 165
updates 166–7
Chief Mate 42
code flags 151–2
codes of practice 14
Code of Safe Working Practices (COSWP) 47–8
collisions: emergency actions 107
emergency preparedness teams 117
ColRegs 43
distress signals 105–6
questions on 218–20
radar 192–3
commercial vessels, small 29–31
compasses: compass requirements 138–40
gyro compass 140–1
magnetic compass 185–6
mnemonics 185
contiguous zone 10

INDEX

Continuous Synopsis Record (CSR) 63
conventions 15–24
crew lists 23

D
damage control drills 94
dangerous goods (DGs):
  classification of 86
  IMDG Codes 87
dangerous spaces 53–4
deadweight tonnage 73
Deck Officer 42
deck watch in port 150
density 69
Department for Transport (DfT) 11
digital distress alerting 99–101
displacement tonnage 73
distress signals 105–6
dock water allowance (DWA) 69, 76
doors, watertight and weathertight 67–8
draught: draught marks 70
  factors reducing draught 123, 124
drills, emergency 92–3, 98–9
DSM 48, 50

E
ECDIS 190
emergencies 91–118
  abandoning ship 108
  collisions 107, 117
  digital distress alerting 99–101
  distress signals 105–6
  drills 92–4
  emergency actions 106–18
  emergency preparedness teams 117
  emergency stop 132
  engine failure 109
  engine fire 107
  fire 97–9, 106–7, 117
  flooding 107, 117
  grounding 108, 117
  liferafts 103–4
  lifesaving appliances 96
  man overboard (MOB) 110–11, 117
MAYDAY 101, 105
muster lists 95–6
piracy 112–13
pyrotechnics 102
questions on 199–203
search and rescue 114–16
steering failure 109
towage and salvage 117, 118

emergency plans:
  noxious liquid substances 83
  SMPEP – NL 84
  SOPEP 82–3, 93
emergency wreck marking buoy 180
enclosed spaces:
  dangerous (enclosed) spaces 53–4
  drills 93
engines: EIAPPC certificate 90
engine failure emergency actions 109
engine fire emergency actions 107
EPIRB (Emergency Position Indicating Radio Beacon) 99–100
equipment: bridge equipment 135–44
  lifting and work equipment 55–6
Exclusive Economic Zone (EEZ) 10

F
fairway buoys 180
FAL 12
fire 97–9
  emergency actions 106–7
  emergency preparedness teams 117
  fire class and extinguishers 97–8
  fire drills and testing 92–3, 98–9
fishing vessels, Master's responsibilities 43
flag states 11, 13
flags 151–2
flares 102
flooding: emergency actions 107
  emergency preparedness teams 117
fog 159
freeboard marks 70
fresh water allowance (FWA) 69

G
garbage: garbage record book (GRB) 81–2
  garbage requirements and logs 81
GMDSS Sea Areas 101
gnomonic projection 163
GNSS (Global Navigation Satellite Systems) 188–9
gravity 69

gross tonnage (GT) 72, 73
grounding: emergency actions 108, 117
gyro compass 140–1

H
handling characteristics 124–9
handover of a vessel 41
  watchkeeping 148
health & safety policy 47
high-speed craft (HSC) 37–8
hours of work and rest 44, 56–7
hull markings, load lines 70–3
'human element' 57
hydrodynamic effects 125
hydrostatic release units (HRUs) 103

I
IALA buoyage 180–3
ILLC 12, 13
IMDG: Document of Compliance (DoC) 88
  International Maritime Dangerous Goods Code 87
IMO (International Maritime Organization) 12, 13
IMO (MARPOL) special areas 78–9
incidents: emergency actions 106–7
incident reporting 44, 58–9
inland waters: types of inland water vessels 28–9
  UK inland waters 27–8
interaction 122, 123
internal waters 10
International Air Pollution Prevention Certificate (IAPPC) 89–90
International Regulations for Preventing Collisions at Sea see ColRegs
IRPCS 12, 13
ISM 48, 49, 50
  Master's responsibilities 43
isolated danger marks 180
ISPS Code 44

K
keel clearance, factors affecting 123, 124

L
ladders, pilot 66–7

lateral marks, IALA 182
law, business and 9–24
  questions on 214–18
  legislation: questions on 214–18
  shipping 13–14
  vessels and 25–38
length between perpendiculars (LBP/LPP) 69
lifeboat drills 93
lifejackets 103
liferafts 103–4
  liferaft use 104
  stowage of 103–4
lifesaving appliances 96
lifting and work equipment 55–6
lights 176–9
  light characteristics 176–9, 183
  lights and ranges 179
lightship tonnage 73
load lines 70–3
logbooks 60–3
  Continuous Synopsis Record (CSR) 63
  emergency drill records 96
  Official Logbook (OLB) 61–2
LOLER (Lifting Operations Regulations) 55, 65
lookout, responsibilities of 149
low pressure systems 160–1

M
MAIB (Marine Accident Investigation Branch) 58, 59
Master's responsibilities 44
man overboard (MOB) 110–11
  emergency preparedness teams 117
manoeuvring 119–34
  anchoring 129–31
  berthing and wind 126–7
  boat handling notes 127–8
  effects of water pressure 122–4
  emergency stop 132
  external effects on 126
  handling characteristics 124–9
  manoeuvring information
  regulations 133
  propellers and rudders 120–2
  steering 120

221

towing 134
turning 128–9
Marine Evacuation Systems (MES) drills 94
Marine Guidance Notes (MGN) 14
Marine Information Notes (MIN) 14
marine notices (M notices) 13, 14
marine safety information 176
Maritime & Coastguard Agency (MCA) 11
Maritime Labour Convention (MLC) 13, 20–4
maritime law structure 13
MARPOL 12, 13, 19, 24
 certificates, plans and records 82–90
 mnemonics 78
 questions on 203–4
the Master: anchoring procedures 131
 cargo securing code 44
 details sent prior to arrival 40
 first impressions and visual checks 40
 general responsibilities of the 39–44
 handover 41
 hours of work and rest 44
 ISM responsibilities 43
 ISPS Code 44
 MAIB/incident reporting 44
 safe working responsibilities 46–7
 SOLAS responsibilities 42–3
 STCW responsibilities 42
 watchkeeping 146, 147
MAYDAY 101, 105
 cancelling a false alert 101
MCA 58
measurements, useful 197
Mercator projection 163
merchant shipping, Master's responsibilities 43
Merchant Shipping Notice (MSN) 14
metacentre 69
meteorology 153–61
 fog 159
 low pressure systems 160–1
 scales and terminology 154–7

tropical revolving storms (TRS) 158–9
 weather instruments 154
 wind 125, 126–7, 129, 157
MLC (Maritime Labour Convention) 13, 20–4
movement, safe 66
muster lists 95–6

N
nautical publications 163, 169–71
 updates 166–7
navigation 162–97
 charts and nautical publications 163–72
 compass 185–6
 ECDIS 190
 GNSS 188–9
 IALA buoyage 180–3
 lights 176–9
 marine safety information 176
 Navtex 195
 passage planning 173–4
 questions on 208–14
 radar 190–4
 sextants 196–7
 ships' routeing 175
 small vessels' equipment 138
 techniques 187–8
 terminology 184
 useful measurements 197
Navtex 195
near-miss reporting 58–9
net tonnage (NT) 72, 73
noxious liquid substances 83–5
 cargo record book for carrying in bulk 84–5
 categorisation of 83
 certificate for carriage in bulk 84
 emergency plan 83
 SMPEP – NL emergency plan 84

O
Officer 42
oil: IOPP certificate 82
 oil record books 80–1
 SOPEP certificate 82–3

P
Particularly Sensitive Sea Areas (PSSA) 79
passage planning 173–4
passenger ships: certification 35
 Official Logbook 62
 permit to work (PtW) 52

pilot ladder 66–7
piracy 112–13
pollution prevention 77–90
 air pollution 89
 anti-fouling 88
 dangerous goods 86–8
 garbage 81–2
 IMO (MARPOL) special areas 78–9
 MARPOL 19, 78
 MARPOL certificates, plans and records 82–90
 noxious liquid substances 83–5
 oil 80–1
 Particularly Sensitive Sea Areas (PSSA) 79
 useful mnemonics 85
port authorities 13, 58
propellers 120–2
PUWER (Provision and Use of Work Equipment Regulations) 56
pyrotechnics 102

Q
questions 198–220

R
radar 190–4
 radar checks and limitations 193
 radar use 194
radio watch 149
ratings 42
records 60–3
 Continuous Synopsis Record (CSR) 63
 navigational records 168
 Official Logbook (OLB) 61–2
REG (Red Ensign Group) Code 31–2
rescue boat drills 93
rest, hours of 44, 56–7
risk assessment 50–1
rudders 120–2

S
safe access 65
safe movement 66
safe water marks 180
safe working 45–59
 Code of Safe Working Practices (COSWP) 47–8
 dangerous spaces 53–4
 lifting and work equipment 55–6
 permit to work (PtW) 52

responsibilities 46–7
risk assessment 50–1
Safety Management Systems 48–50
safety, questions on 199–203
Safety Committee 47
Safety Management Systems 48–50, 58
Safety Officer 47
SALVAGE 12, 118
 emergency preparedness teams 117
SAR 12
SART (Search and Rescue Transponder) 100–1
sea areas 10, 11, 33
 GMDSS Sea Areas 101
 IMO (MARPOL) special areas 78–9
 Particularly Sensitive Sea Areas (PSSA) 79
sea state 154–5
seafarers: safe working responsibilities 46–7
Seafarer Employment Agreement (SEA) 22–3
search and rescue 114–15
 Search and Rescue Co-operation Plans (SARCo) 116
 search techniques and patterns 114–15
seaworthiness and seamanship 64–76
security drills 94
sextants 196–7
shipboard oil pollution emergency plan (SOPEP) 93
shipboard operations, questions on 204–8
shipowners, safe working responsibilities 46–7
shipping: basic measurement of length 75
 larger shipping 33
 parts of a ship 74
 ship certification 34–5
 ship classification 33–4
 shipping legislation 13–14
ships' routeing 175
small vessels' bridge equipment 138
smoke signals 102
SOLAS 12, 13, 15–16, 24
 bridge equipment 136–7

222

INDEX

Master's responsibilities 42–3
SOLAS V 16–17
sounds 178
special marks 180
squat 122, 123
stability 68–74
load lines 70–3
Stability Information Book (SIB) 74
terms and definitions 69–70
tonnage definitions 72–3
STCW 13, 18, 24
Master's responsibilities 42
steering 120
steering failure emergency action 94, 109
stream effects 125
turning in close quarters 129
SWL (Safe Working Load) 55

T
terminology 184
territorial sea 10
timings, weather 156
tonnage: tonnage definitions 72–3
TONNAGE (International Convention on Tonnage Measure of Ships) 12
tonnes per centimetre (TPC) 69
towing 118, 134
Traffic Separation Schemes (TSS) 175
tropical revolving storms (TRS) 158–9
turning 128–9
in close quarters 129

U
UNCLOS (United Nations Convention on the Law of the Sea) 10–11, 13

V
vessels: basic measurement of length 75
bridge equipment 135–44
cargo ship certificates 36–7
critical measurements 75
general responsibilities of the Master 39–44
guide to UK vessels 26–7
high-speed craft (HSC) 37–8
inland water vessels 28–9
large yacht codes 31–2
larger shipping 33
legislation 25–38
load lines 70–3
parts of a boat 75
parts of a ship 74
safe access and movement 65–8
safe working 45–59
ship certification 34–7
ship classification 33–4
small commercial vessels 29–31
stability 68–74
visibility 156
volume 69
voyage data recorders 141
voyage planning 173–4

W
watchkeeping 145–52
anchor watch 131
bridge induction 147
code flags 151–2
deck watch in port 150
handover and taking over 148
hours of work and rest 57
lookout's responsibilities 149
radio watch 149
watchkeeping and Master's authority 146
watchkeeping responsibilities 147–50
water pressure, effects of 122–4
watertight doors 67–8
weather 153–61
fog 159
low pressure systems 160–1
scales and terminology 154–7
tropical revolving storms (TRS) 158–9
weather instruments 154
wind 125, 126–7, 129, 157
weathertight doors 67–8
Williamson turn 110
wind 157
and berthing 126–7
turning in close quarters 129
wind effects 125
WLL (Working Load Limit) 55
work: hours of 44, 56–7
lifting and work equipment 55–6
safe working 45–59
World Meteorological Organisation (WMO) Sea State Code 154

Y
yachts, large yacht code 31–2

Sources

COSWP: assets.publishing.service.gov.uk/government/uploads/system/uploads/attachment_data/file/1118843/Code_of_safe_working_practices_for_merchant_seafarers__COSWP__amendment_7_2022.pdf

MGN 71 (M): assets.publishing.service.gov.uk/government/uploads/system/uploads/attachment_data/file/282336/mgn071.pdf

MGN 331 (M+F): assets.publishing.service.gov.uk/government/uploads/system/uploads/attachment_data/file/838283/MGN_331__M_F__Amd_1_Provision_and_use_of_work_equipment_regulations_2006.pdf

MGN 332 (M+F): assets.publishing.service.gov.uk/government/uploads/system/uploads/attachment_data/file/878972/MGN_332__M_F__Amd_1_Lifting_operations_and_lifting_equipment__LOLER__regulations_2006.pdf

MGN 474 (M): assets.publishing.service.gov.uk/government/uploads/system/uploads/attachment_data/file/882859/MGN_474_REVISED_CREW_AGG_AH.pdf

MGN 477 (M): gov.uk/government/publications/mgn-477-m-maritime-labour-convention-2006-seafarers-employment-agreements/mgn-477-m-amendment-3-maritime-labour-convention-2006-seafarers-employment-agreements

MGN 533 (M): gov.uk/government/publications/mgn-533-m-amendment-2-means-of-access/mgn-533-m-amendment-2-means-of-access

MGN 545 (M+F): assets.publishing.service.gov.uk/government/uploads/system/uploads/attachment_data/file/760379/MGN_545.pdf

MGN 564 (M+F): assets.publishing.service.gov.uk/government/uploads/system/uploads/attachment_data/file/791968/MGN564-Amendment1.pdf

MGN 591 (M+F): gov.uk/government/publications/mgn-591-mf-amendment-1-provision-of-safe-means-of-access-to-vessels-in-port/mgn-591-mf-amendment-1-provision-of-safe-means-of-access-to-fishing-vessels-and-small-vessels-in-ports

MGN 600 (M): gov.uk/government/publications/mgn-

600-m-maritime-labour-convention-inspection-of-coded-vessels/mgn-600-m-amendment-3-maritime-labour-convention-inspection-of-coded-vessels

MGN 632 (M+F): assets.publishing.service.gov.uk/government/uploads/system/uploads/attachment_data/file/919758/MGN_632_-_Amendment_1.pdf

MGN 636 (M): assets.publishing.service.gov.uk/government/uploads/system/uploads/attachment_data/file/922887/MGN_636_Amendment_1_-_FINAL.pdf

MGN 659 (M+F): assets.publishing.service.gov.uk/government/uploads/system/uploads/attachment_data/file/1072817/MGN_659__M+F__Amendment_1_merchant_shipping_and_fishing_vessels__entry_into_enclosed_spaces__regulations_2022.pdf

MIN 516 (M): assets.publishing.service.gov.uk/government/uploads/system/uploads/attachment_data/file/486226/MIN_516_-_7_DEC_2015.pdf

MSN 1676 (M): assets.publishing.service.gov.uk/government/uploads/system/uploads/attachment_data/file/959628/MSN_1676_Amendment_1.pdf

MSN 1875 (M): assets.publishing.service.gov.uk/government/uploads/system/uploads/attachment_data/file/580291/MSN_1875.pdf

MSN 1877 (M): gov.uk/government/publications/msn-1877-m-maritime-labour-convention-2006-hours-of-work-and-entitlement-to-leave/msn-1877-m-amendment-2-mlc-2006-hours-of-work-and-entitlement-to-leave-application-of-the-hours-of-work-regulations-2018

REG YACHT CODE PART A: redensigngroup.org/media/1094/reg-yacht-code-january-2019-edition-part-a.pdf

The Workboat Code Edition 2: assets.publishing.service.gov.uk/government/uploads/system/uploads/attachment_data/file/827913/The_Workboat_Code_Edition_2_-_Amendment_1.pdf

Endnotes

Excerpts from selected IMO publications are reproduced with the permission of the International Maritime Organization (IMO), which does not accept responsibility for the correctness of the material as reproduced: in case of doubt, IMO's authentic text shall prevail. Readers should check with their national maritime administration for any further amendments or latest advice. International Maritime Organization, 4 Albert Embankment, London, SE1 7SR, United Kingdom

SECTION 3
1. *STCW Convention and STCW Code*, 2017 Edition, page 22
2. *STCW Convention and STCW Code*, 2017 Edition, page 114
3. *STCW Convention and STCW Code*, 2017 Edition, page 274
4. *STCW Convention and STCW Code*, 2017 Edition, page 332
5. *SOLAS Consolidated Edition*, 2020, page 376
6. *ISM Code & Guidelines*, 2018 Edition, page 18
7. *Collision Regulations Convention (COLREGS)*, 2003 Edition, page 5
8. *Guide to Maritime Security and ISPS Code*, 2021 Edition, page 307
9. *Guide to Maritime Security and ISPS Code*, 2021 Edition, page 283
10. IMO Resolution A.714(17) – *Code of Safe Practice for Cargo Stowage and Securing* – (Adopted on 6 November 1991), page 11

SECTION 4
11. IMO Resolution A.1050(27) – *Revised Recommendations For Entering Enclosed Spaces Aboard Ships* – (Adopted on 30 November 2011), page 2

SECTION 6
12. MSC.1/Circular.1380 – *Guidance for Watertight Doors on Passenger Ships Which May be Opened During Navigation* – (10 December 2010), page 5

SECTION 7
13. *IMDG Code*, 2020 Edition, page 28
14. *IMDG Code*, 2020 Edition, page 464

SECTION 8
15. *Collision Regulations Convention (COLREGS)*, 2003 Edition, page 51

SECTION 9
16. *SOLAS Consolidated Edition*, 2020, page 374
17. *SOLAS Consolidated Edition*, 2020, page 371

SECTION 11
18. *STCW Convention and STCW Code*, 2017 Edition, page 275
19. *STCW Convention and STCW Code*, 2017 Edition, page 277
20. *STCW Convention and STCW Code*, 2017 Edition, page 276
21. *STCW Convention and STCW Code*, 2017 Edition, page 276

SECTION 13
22. *SOLAS Consolidated Edition*, 2020, page 371
23. *SOLAS Consolidated Edition*, 2020, page 375
24. *SOLAS Consolidated Edition*, 2020, page 375
25. *SOLAS Consolidated Edition*, 2020, page 379
26. IMO Resolution A.893(21) – *Guidelines for Voyage Planning* – (Adopted on 25 November 1999), page 2
27. *Collision Regulations Convention (COLREGS)*, 2003 Edition, page 8
28. *Collision Regulations Convention (COLREGS)*, 2003 Edition, page 9
29. *Collision Regulations Convention (COLREGS)*, 2003 Edition, page 16